Children of Different Worlds

Children of Different Worlds

The Formation of Social Behavior

Beatrice Blyth Whiting
Carolyn Pope Edwards

In collaboration with

Carol R. Ember   Sara B. Nerlove
Gerald M. Erchak   Susan Seymour
Sara Harkness   Charles M. Super
Robert L. Munroe   Thomas S. Weisner
Ruth H. Munroe   Martha Wenger

Harvard University Press
Cambridge, Massachusetts, and London, England
1988

Library of Congress Cataloging-in-Publication Data

Whiting, Beatrice Blyth.
  Children of different worlds.

  Bibliography: p.
  Includes index.
  1. Socialization—Cross-cultural studies. 2. Social
interaction in children—Cross-cultural studies.
3. Mother and child—Cross-cultural studies.
4. Childhood friendship—Cross-cultural studies.
I. Edwards, Carolyn P. II. Title.
HQ783.W52 1988   303.3′2   87-19742
ISBN 0-674-11616-X (alk. paper)

Contents

Preface

This volume is an extension of the work inaugurated in *Children of Six Cultures: A Psycho-Cultural Analysis* (Whiting and Whiting, 1975). That study, which involved comparison of the naturally occurring behavior of 134 children aged 3 to 10 years who lived in communities in India, Okinawa, the Philippines, Mexico, Kenya, and the United States, documented the powerful influence on children's behavior of their relationship to the people with whom they interacted. The findings raised many questions about how salient characteristics of the social partner (for example, his or her relative age, sex, and kinship relation) influence the behavior of children in communities around the world. This book attempts to answer some of those questions.

Following the Six Culture Project, further observational studies of children's social behavior were conducted in Kenya under the auspices of the Child Development Research Unit (CDRU) at the University of Nairobi. Funded by the Carnegie Corporation and directed by John Whiting and Beatrice Whiting, the CDRU enabled American social scientists and graduate students to train and work with students at the University of Nairobi and to conduct basic child development research in many Kenyan research sites.

As with the Six Culture Project, the charter of the CDRU called for the collection of comparable data in different cultural communities. Accordingly, Beatrice Whiting, Susan Abbott, Carol Ember, Sara Harkness, Charles Super, Thomas Weisner, and Martha Wenger, collaborating with Kenyan secondary and university students, collected and coded behavior observations using a modified version of the methods developed for the Six Culture Project. Carolyn Edwards studied the influence of cultural and educational factors on the development of moral judgment in Kenyan secondary and university students and in community leaders from a variety of ethnic groups. She also worked with Beatrice Whiting to analyze sex differences in children's social behavior using both Six Culture and Kenyan data. In addition, Gerald Erchak (as a member of Michael Cole's project on the relationship of culture and learning) observed and recorded the behavior of children in Kien-taa, a Kpelle community in Liberia. Susan Seymour (as a member of Cora DuBois's project in Bhubaneswar, India) observed the interaction of mothers and children in households from two different parts of the city of Bhubaneswar.

In 1976 this group, financed by the Ford Foundation, met at the Laboratory of Human Development at the Harvard Graduate School of Education to develop a plan for pooling data in order to investigate cultural similarities and differences in the social behavior of girls and boys 2 to 10 years old. Beatrice Whiting and Carolyn Edwards took the primary role in designing the strategies for joint analysis of the data. Ruth Munroe and Robert Munroe, who had analyzed the physical and social dimensions of children's environments in Kenya and organized a cross-cultural study including material from Kenya, Guatemala, Peru, and the United States, joined the project, as did Sara Nerlove, a member of both the CDRU and Munroe research projects. John Whiting, Carol Jacklin, and Amy Koel also participated in the conference and helped to formulate strategies and goals.

The quantity and complexity of the pooled data presented us with both a great opportunity and a great challenge. We have been able to answer many of our original questions, but also, as in all scientific endeavors, we have raised new ones for future comparative research. To that endeavor, this volume is dedicated.

Acknowledgments

This book is the joint effort of many people, and we are grateful to all of them. Our collaborators, listed on the title page, deserve the highest tribute. Scholars from the disciplines of anthropology, psychology, and education, they share with us a concern for discovering the effects of culture, gender, and age (development) on children's social behavior. The ten-year history of our joint project, described in the Preface, would not have been possible had we not shared the profound conviction that scientific understanding of human development can only advance when findings reported in one culture are tested cross-culturally.

The collaboration involved not only the pooling of data but an intense exchange of ideas. Our collaborators commented in detail on each stage of the manuscript and thereby contributed to its clarity, accuracy, and completeness of cultural description as well as to the interpretation of findings. The book has benefited greatly from this multilevel criticism.

The individual research of each collaborator has also contributed to our basic thinking about the issues involved in this book. Carol R. Ember conducted observational research on Luo-speaking children in western Kenya. Her well-known study demonstrated the influence of boys' task experiences on their social behavior. Boys who for reasons of family demography participated in more feminine household work showed a more feminine profile of social behavior (Ember, 1970, 1973, 1981; Bookman and Ember, in press).

Gerald M. Erchak made observations in a Kpelle-speaking community in Liberia, as a member of Michael Cole's project on the relationship between culture and learning. Erchak has shown that Kpelle boys' and girls' behavior differs in both social and nonsocial realms and that these sex differences reflect adult roles—in particular, women's dominance in productive and reproductive domains but their subordination to men in political and religious activities (Erchak, 1974, 1975, 1976a, 1976b, 1977, 1979, 1980, 1985).

Sara Harkness and Charles M. Super have conducted an extensive series of studies in Kipsigis-speaking communities in western Kenya and also in the United States. Harkness's early papers studied the relationship between the language development and the mother-child interaction of young Kipsigis children. Super's research provides the basis for a comprehensive cross-cultural analysis of the physical, cognitive, social, and affective development of infants. Together, the two researchers of this anthropologist-psychologist team have elaborated the concept of the "eco-cultural niche," defined in terms of the child's social and physical environment, culturally regulated customs of child rearing, and the psychology of the caregivers (Harkness, 1975, 1977; Harkness and Super, 1982, 1983, 1985; Harkness, Edwards, and Super, 1981; Super, 1981, 1984; Super and Harkness, 1982, 1986).

Robert H. Munroe and Ruth L. Munroe, another anthropologist-psychologist team, have contributed to the field the method called "spot observation" and used it to discover how salient dimensions of routine experience influence the cognitive and social development of Logoli- and Kikuyu-speaking children in Kenya. Collaborating with colleagues, they have replicated and extended their conclusions, using data collected all over the world. Findings from this important series of studies form the basis of conclusions presented in Chapter 2 of this volume (see Bolton et al., 1976; R. H. Munroe and R. L. Munroe, 1971, 1978, 1980a, 1980b, 1984; R. H. Munroe et al., 1983; R. H. Munroe, R. L. Munroe, and Shimmin, 1984; R. L. Munroe and R. H. Munroe, 1971; Nerlove, Munroe, and Munroe, 1971).

Sara B. Nerlove has applied the spot-observation technique in performing research on children's cognitive competence in Kenya and rural Guatemala. Her work succeeds in documenting "natural indicators" of competence in self-guided aspects of children's work and play activities. Children's competence appears to be part of what adults respond to when assigning them relatively more mature responsibilities (Nerlove et al., 1974; Nerlove and Snipper, 1981).

Susan Seymour's research in Bhubaneswar, India, has identified the complex and pervasive ways in which caste and class constrain mother-child interaction, including maternal nurturance, children's dependence, children's workloads, and even patterns of schooling. Her findings have influenced our analysis and interpretation of the data from North India presented in this volume (see Seymour, 1971, 1974, 1975, 1976a, 1976b, 1980, 1981, 1983, 1985).

Thomas S. Weisner is known for his innovative approach to analyzing the powerful influence of residence on parent and child behavior; he studied Abaluyia-speaking families in Kenya who lived part of each year in urban and rural locations. He is also the coauthor of an influential essay on sibling caretaking. His recent work involves the study of parents' ideals and behavior in California families (Ross and Weisner, 1977; Weisner, 1973a, 1973b, 1976a, 1976b, 1976c, 1976d, 1979; Weisner and Abbott, 1977; Weisner, Bausano, and Kornfein, 1983; Weisner and Gallimore, 1977; Weisner, Gallimore, and Tharp, 1982; Weisner and Martin, 1979).

Martha Wenger observed children in a Giriama-speaking community in eastern Kenya and focused on cross-age interaction, a topic neglected in American research. Earlier she analyzed the data collected by Beatrice Whiting in Ngeca, Kenya, to compare how children of different ages interact with 2-year-olds; these findings are described in several chapters of this volume (Wenger, 1975, 1983).

The ethnographic data, the figures showing the layout of the villages and towns and the floor plans of typical houses in the Six Culture samples, and some of the photographs of children in these communities have appeared in earlier publications (Minturn and Lambert, 1964; B. B. Whiting, 1963; B. B. Whiting and J. W. M. Whiting, 1975). Much of this research was done in the 1950s and does not describe the modern scene. Richard Shweder contributed an idealized house plan of a Brahmin household in Bhubaneswar and a genealogy of the residents. The floor plans for typical Liberian houses in Kpelleland are adapted from Corahann Okorodudu's doctoral dissertation, presented to the Harvard Graduate School of Education, Harvard University, in 1966.

In addition to our collaborators, many other individuals have given generously of their time and assistance. First and foremost, we are grateful to John Whiting, who has supported this project and offered continuing consultation and advice on theoretical and analytical issues since its inception. His contribution cannot be measured.

Robert LeVine has shared with us his research findings and his insights on the effect of culture on human development. The observations that he collected in his original study of Nyansongo, Kenya, are still among the best we have and appear as examples in many of the chapters in this book.

A. Kimball Romney advised us on strategies for analyzing the data and introduced us to Optimal Scaling. Francesca Cancian, Anne Colby, Wendy Goldberg, Artin Goncu, Jean Lave, and James Thompson offered excellent criticisms of the manuscript. Lawrence Baldwin, Carol Trainer, and Martha Wenger helped analyze the data and made countless computer runs as we experimented with different ways of analyzing the data. Bonnie Gray analyzed the settings frequented by children in the Six Culture sample. Eleanor Thuemmel helped with the momentous task of typing the text and tables in each revision. Mary Ellen Geer edited the volume. Richard Edwards, Samuel Edwards, and George Edwards were supportive and patient throughout the many years of work on this project.

The Ford Foundation, the Center for Advanced Study in the Behavioral Sciences, the Spencer Foundation, and Radcliffe College provided the financial support for this project.

Finally, we are grateful to the faithful observers who served as our eyes and ears in the sample communities. Because so many of the central insights of this volume derive from our work and experiences in Kenya, we especially want to thank our student collaborators, who taught us much about their country: Jane Chesiano, Grace Diru, Irene Kamau, Wanjiku Kagia, Rose Maina, Ezra Maritim, Achola Pala, and Sara Sieley.

Children of Different Worlds

Chapter 1

The Initial Question

The genesis of sex differences in behavior has been an issue of active and prominent concern to social scientists since the 1960s. A review of the current research literature suggests that there are three major competing explanatory systems: the biological model, which points to constitutional (usually hormonal) factors as the major cause of sex differences; the cognitive–developmental stage model, which asserts that children's cognitive discovery and construction of knowledge about gender identity and sex roles lead them to choose sex-differentiated patterns of behavior; and the socialization model, which looks to the direct and indirect actions of socializing agents as the primary cause of observed sex differences.

The third model, predominant for a long time in the social sciences, has in the last decade lost ground, especially in developmental psychology. For example, the influential review by Eleanor Maccoby and Carol Jacklin (1974) concludes that sex differences in a few behavioral dimensions (aggressive behavior and verbal, mathematical, and visual-spatial abilities) are most likely a result of biological predispositions, but that evidence for sex differences in many other domains is not clear or consistent. Moreover, further damaging the case for the socialization theory, Maccoby and Jacklin assert that there is not even strong evidence that parents consistently act differently toward boys and girls. Although the findings of Maccoby and Jacklin have been forcefully criticized by other researchers (see, for example, Birns, 1976; Bloch, 1976; Brooks-Gunn and Matthews, 1979), the socialization model is no longer seen as adequate by itself to explain the development of sex differences. In the field of developmental psychology, the other two models have received increasingly greater attention.

Anthropologists, in contrast, have continued to assume, following Margaret Mead (1935, 1949), that human behavior is infinitely malleable and that sex roles are determined by culture and not by hormones or cognitive processes. Anthropologists have thus tended to stress the great cultural variation in the definition of appropriate male and female behavior, using ethnographic data to explore the varied symbolic systems in human societies that define a people's theory of the natural bases for sex differences and justify ideals for masculine and feminine behavior (see, for example, papers in edited volumes by MacCormick and Strathern, 1980; Ortner and White-head, 1981; Reiter, 1975; Rosaldo and Lamphere, 1974). Nancy Chodorow (1974, 1978), a sociologist influenced by both anthro-pological and psychoanalytic theory, has suggested that there are universal tendencies for the attainment of masculinity to be proble-matical, to require denial of attachment and relationship to others, and to involve the devaluation of femininity. She theorizes that these tendencies can best be explained by the fact that in all societies, women rather than men are responsible for all early child care and for the later socialization of at least girl children. Among the anthro-pologists, only the biological anthropologists (who study human ev-olution and primate behavior) have been willing to credit and con-sider evidence for biologically based gender differences in human beings (see Hrdy, 1981; Konner, 1982).

In this intellectual milieu, we and our collaborators—a group com-posed of both anthropologists and psychologists—agreed on the need for a new cross-cultural comparison of the social behavior of chil-dren, based on observations collected in naturally occurring settings of children. Our previous studies had identified sex differences in certain types of social behavior (Edwards and Whiting, 1974, 1980; Whiting and Edwards, 1973; Whiting and Whiting, 1975). Neverthe-less, we believed that the study of socialization of sex differences has remained in its infancy. In particular, we felt that the conceptuali-zation of socialization has been too narrow. A comparative perspec-tive, by offering a more complete analysis of children's learning environments, can enable us to conceptualize socialization in a much broader way than before. Psychological research has tended to focus too exclusively on the modeling, teaching, and reinforcing behaviors of teachers and parents without considering the surrounding complex of social interactions and routine activities that critically support this adult interaction. As John Whiting and his colleagues put it (1966,

p. 83): "Certain aspects of the childrearing process seem to have the effect of, if not creating, at least strengthening values far beyond the conscious intent of the agents of socialization."

Our goal, therefore, was to move toward an improved understanding of socialization by accomplishing two main tasks: clarifying the processes by which the culturally determined environment affects the development of sex-differentiated behavior during the childhood years, and, at the same time, considering how these cultural processes may interact with biological and cognitive-developmental aspects of child behavior. Far from denying biological and cognitive influences on the development of sex differences, we wished to examine the development of children's social behavior in broad cultural perspective and to determine exactly how, when, and where biological and cognitive factors seem to be operative.

Summary of the Project and Preview of Findings

In planning the project, we and our collaborators agreed that the first task was to describe the cross-cultural variation in social experience that typifies the life of children in each of our sample communities. We did not have either fine-grained observations of mother-child behavior or extensive maternal interview data, and our data did not include infants as focal subjects. Therefore, we concentrated on describing the settings frequented by girls and boys between the ages of 2 and 10, the activities in which they engage, the social partners with whom they interact, and the profiles of their social behavior with each category of social partner. Cultural differences were expected to be reflected in the organization of people in space (the composition of households, yard groups, neighborhoods, work groups, and schools) and the rules that prescribed who should be present in these settings and how they should behave.

The observations involved in our analyses were collected as part of more comprehensive studies of family life and child development. Observations of children's social interaction were done in seven sample communities between 1960 and 1980 (four in Kenya under the auspices of the Child Development Research Unit at the University of Nairobi). Observations of social interaction in six other societies were added to broaden this data base. These observations, done in the 1950s by the field researchers of the Six Cultures Project, were reanalyzed in terms of our new research questions. Finally, "spot observations" of children's daily activities, location in space, and social companions were used. These observations were done in six sample communities between 1967 and 1975 under the leadership of Robert L. Munroe and Ruth H. Munroe.

Stated succinctly, our main hypothesis is that patterns of interpersonal behavior are developed in the settings one frequents, and that the most important characteristic of a setting is the cast of characters who occupy the set (as identified by their age, sex, and kinship relation to the actor). The settings one frequents are in turn related to the culturally determined activities that occupy males and females of various ages in the normal course of daily living, activities that are determined by economic pursuits, the division of labor, and the organization of people in space. Our theory holds that knowing the company that children keep (the proportion of time they spend with different categories of individuals) makes it possible to predict salient aspects of their interpersonal behavior. Because the types of companions differ from one society to another, for boys and girls, and for different age groups within each society, children have varied opportunities to interact with different categories of individuals. They learn and practice patterns of behavior that characterize their most routine interpersonal interactions.

There is an identifiable script for the daily life of children of the age groups on whom we have observational data. We have adopted Margaret Mead's classification of age groups, based on her research on childhood in six different societies. Her four age grades are characterized in terms of the "world" of the child at each stage: first comes the *lap child,* then the *knee child,* followed by the *yard child,* and finally the *community* or *school-age child.* These groupings correspond to general age changes in the settings that children frequent and in their social behavior. However, the specific characteristics of changes are not necessarily identical either across the different types of social behavior or across the cultures. In defining these age groups in terms of specific chronological ages, we settled for the best overall fit: the lap child is the infant aged 0–1 year, the knee child is the toddler aged 2–3 years, the yard child is the older preschool-age child of 4–5 years, and the community child is in the middle-childhood period of 6–10 years.

Ecology and the social and economic organization of society determine the daily routines of adults and children, the individuals who frequent the same settings, and the activities that are performed. The scripts for the daily life of each age group are consonant with rules concerning appropriate behavior in each of the settings. These scripts detail the work expected of girls and boys, the nature of their play, and the hours they spend in school; they also detail the people who share the settings.

Our focus is on the shared experience of children who frequent similar types of settings. Since the majority of the social interaction recorded is dyadic interpersonal behavior, the age, sex, and kinship relation of the individuals with whom a child interacts are essential components of the analysis. An important theoretical question is whether there are identifiable patterns of dyadic interaction across cultures that are associated with frequency of interaction with specific categories of individuals. Is there evidence that child actors classify their companions on the basis of common characteristics and interact with them in similar, predictable ways? Is there evidence that the discriminations children make are similar across cultures? If there are similar patterns of dyadic interaction when children of a given age and sex interact with particular types of social partners, is there evidence that children who spend time with specific classes of these companions develop predispositions for interpersonal behavior that generalize to other classes of individuals?

Thus, in searching for the genesis of sex differences, rather than limiting our analysis to asking whether socializers treat girls and boys differently in face-to-face interaction, we ask whether girls and boys are assigned to different settings where they interact with different categories of companions. The characteristics of the settings and the companions of the different age groups of children are the proximate cultural conditions that are the primary focus of our exploration.

It is clear, however, that the questions we ask have a broader theoretical import. If there are identifiable differences in patterns of dyadic interaction, the age changes in children's social behavior may well be associated with changes in their typical setting occupancy and companions. Similarly, individual differences and sibling-order differences in behavior may also be associated with different setting occupancy and frequency of types of dyadic interaction.

In one sense we are standing the theory of socialization on its head. Rather than analyzing the age, sex, and cultural differences in children's activities and companions as simply the *result* of developmental changes of socialization pressure by parents, other caregivers, and teachers, we are analyzing these differences as a *cause* in the process of socialization. We do not discount either the influence of developmental changes or the role of parents and their surrogates in molding the social behavior of young children. However, in trying to understand and account for sex, age, and cultural differences in behavior, we are impressed by the evident, but little discussed, way in which differences in children's behavior are associated with the settings that they frequent, their activities, and especially the companions with whom they spend their time.

In interaction with companions, the child learns to discriminate among behaviors appropriate to different classes of people: those who are the same age, younger, or older, kin or non-kin. We characterize these categories of social partners in dyadic interaction as *elicitors*. Early in the analysis, there appeared to be similarity across cultures in the eliciting power of specific categories of social partners (Whiting and Whiting, 1975, pp. 152–169). We then became faced with the question of what determined these eliciting values. If the eliciting power was similar across all of the communities with their diverse cultures, how could this similarity be explained? Was the eliciting power the result of physical appearance, relative size, typical behavior, or some status factor recognized in all cultures? What were the mechanisms involved?

Although we cannot hope to specify or even speculate about the exact mechanisms involved, the fact that there are such pervasive cross-cultural similarities in children's behavior toward particular categories of social partners suggests that panhuman biological or cognitive-developmental predispositions, or both, may be involved. As we shall discuss in detail in later chapters, the concept of "biological preparedness" provides a way to distinguish between, on the one hand, a few prepared or predisposed behaviors that are learned easily and extinguished only with difficulty, and, on the other hand, many other kinds of behavior with no prepared basis, the learning of which is best described by traditional behavioral (social learning) explanations. We believe that our findings on cultural similarities in children's responsiveness to categories of social partners are best interpreted by assuming, following Seligman (1970), that children bring to their experiences in interpersonal behavior certain preadapted sensory and receptive equipment and associative predispositions with a long evolutionary history.

In our judgment, two probable examples of such predispositions involve children's response to lap children (infants) and to children younger than themselves. As we shall show, in all of our sample communities lap children elicit nurturance, that is, behavior that seeks to meet the needs of the lap child. In interpreting the obvious and distinctive eliciting power of infants, we have found Konrad Lorenz' description (1943) of "releasing features" of the infants' appearance to be persuasive. He noted that the physical characteristics of infants—their proportionately large heads, round and protruding foreheads, small facial features, and short, elastic limbs— trigger or elicit positive responsiveness from adults and children. Furthermore, we have drawn upon the complementary interpretation of John Bowlby (1969) and the attachment theorists, who have used the ethological perspective to claim that species-specific "caretakingbehaviors" (holding, feeding, seeking to soothe and to interact socially) are predictably elicited in the human caregiver by the infant who looks, smiles, follows, quiets, and so on, in the caregiver's presence. Culture modulates this responsiveness: in communities where children gain sufficient practice in infant caregiving but are not overburdened beyond their capacities, children are most consistently nurturant.

In the case of children's behavior to children younger than themselves, the dimension of predisposed behavior that we have noted involves hierarchical dominance, the "pecking order" of childhood by size and strength (Omark and Edelman, 1975; Omark, Strayer, and Freedman, 1980). In all of our sample communities, children respond to children younger and smaller than themselves (but who are not infants) by asserting dominance over them. Again, culture shapes this response: in communities where children are responsible for the welfare of younger children and are assigned a significant role in the household economy, the dominance patterns appear to be transformed from overt egoistic forms (for example, commands to fulfill a desire of the commander) into prosocial forms (for example, commands related to household tasks and socially prescribed behavior).

Cognitive-developmental factors are also surely involved in some of the transcultural similarities in children's social responsiveness. One clear example, we suggest, involves the universal preference of children for same-sex child companions—a preference that develops during middle childhood into an avoidance of opposite-sex peers. These responses to other children are likely elicited by cognitively based predispositions to want to find out about oneself by observing, imitating, and interacting with others judged to be like the self. Cognitive theorists (see Kohlberg, 1966; Lewis and Feiring, 1979; and discussion in Edwards, 1984, 1986c, and Edwards and Lewis, 1979) have long asserted that children have an internally regulated competence motivation to find out about the self and others by constructing knowledge about salient social categories. Adults make order of the social world by classifying people on the basis of household, residence, kin group, occupation, religion, and so forth, but young children must use more concrete and visible cues. Thus, familiarity, age, sex, and race (skin color) may be the first attributes that children employ to form social categories. Distinctions between people based on age and size seem to be noticeable to children as young as infants. Distinctions based on sex appear to be salient from early childhood onward, although acquiring knowledge in the gender domain is complex, multifaceted, and characterized by sequential steps. Research conducted in many Western countries indicates that, between about ages 2 and 7, most children learn to label the self and others by gender, to understand the stability of gender over time, and to understand that the "defining" characteristic of gender is the genitals. During the same years, through analogous steps, children gradually develop culturally appropriate sex-role stereotypes and preferences. It is assumed that these developments are associated with cognitive reorganizations related to the maturation of the brain, as well as supportive social experiences.

Other similarities across cultures in dyadic behavior may be attributed to similar learning experiences. Certain categories of people—mothers and mother surrogates—may satisfy similar needs and desires of children in all communities. Thus mothers, and those persons designated as supplementary caregivers by mothers, are experienced by children as the "keepers of the warehouse," the providers of many physical and emotional resources desired by children. Children learn that mothers, other adults, and older children are the category of people to whom it is most effective to direct dependency behaviors, such as seeking comfort, food, protection, approval, and information.

This learning from experience occurs because human behavior is purposeful. Actors have goals, and they repeat behaviors that are successful. These behaviors tend to become habitual and generalized to similar situations. In coding behavior, we have identified the actors' goals in terms of the resources that the actor is judged to desire. Social behavior is conceived as consisting of interchanges of resources. In planning behavior, a child attempts to gain the desired resources. Behaviors that are successful are repeated in interaction with the same or similar individuals. Assuming that humans have many similar desires regardless of the society into which they are born, we expect a finite number of types of exchanges. We also assume that in all cultures there are some categories of partners who are perceived to control the resources desired by the children of different age groups. Thus, the similarity in the profile of behavior in similar dyads may be the result of similar experiences that reinforce particular patterns of behavior with that class of partners.

There are identifiable changes with age in the settings that children frequent and the social partners with whom they interact. In the earliest years these changes are governed primarily by the changing physical and cognitive capacities of the child and by the degree to which the child must be protected from the physical and social dangers of the environment. Lap and knee children require constant supervision. There are cultural differences, however, in the designated guardians of the children. When these guardians are older siblings, we expect the experience of interacting with lap and knee children to affect the patterns of social behavior practiced by the older children, particularly if we find that these lap and knee children have identifiable eliciting power that shapes the behavior of their guardians. There are also similarities and differences in the settings that yard and school-age children frequent that are related to cultural differences in the arrangement of people in space and differences in the economic pursuits and social structure of the communities.

In sum, in the analyses that follow, where we have identified similarities in the behavioral profile of specific dyads across cultures, we have attempted to assess the relative contribution of three factors: biology (prepared responses); developmental factors (similar physical and cognitive capacities and transculturally shared motives or goals); and similarities in the social environments and partners of children of a given gender and age (similarity in the social behaviors that these social partners elicit, or similarity in the categories of social partners across cultures who control the developing child's desires).

Prior Assumptions and Methodology

Since our approach is eclectic, it is useful to summarize some of the prior assumptions that we have made in recording, coding, and analyzing the social behavior. First, we assume that all theories about human behavior and development can and should be tested cross-culturally. We are interested in the universal principles that govern patterns of interpersonal behavior and the extent to which these patterns are influenced by the experiences programmed by culture. We believe that the answers to these questions can best be discovered by replicating studies in a variety of cultural contexts. We have been able to conduct this study because a group of us have collected parallel data on thirteen samples of children on four continents and have agreed to pool the data and arrange it in such a way that comparable analyses can be made on each sample.

Second, we assume that in spite of individual differences, there are behavior regularities for children of a given age and sex in each cultural community. That is, there are meaningful norms, and this book is about those norms, not about idiosyncratic facets of personality. Much of the description of norms is of an anthropological type. Anthropologists are trained to report shared belief systems, value orientations, technical practices, and norms of ritual and mundane behavior. Our focus is on the last category, the mundane or typical patterns of interaction between frequent social partners. However, our study differs from many anthropological studies in that the norms are not inferred from ethnographic interviews and participant observation but rather from quantitative data recorded with the use of systematic standardized observations. These quantitative data enable the researcher to validate subjective impressions.

Third, in designing a method for observing and coding interpersonal behavior, we assume that most of it is intentional. People have goals that motivate their behavior. We assume that in social interaction individuals can and do judge each others' intentions; if it were not possible to judge intention, sustained interaction would be impossible. We assume that in the early years the ability to judge intention may be limited, but that it increases with maturation and experience. At the same time, a person's goals and strategies for reaching goals also become more complex with age.

Although the content of goals becomes more complex with age and social experience, a general classification of goals across age and cultural groups is possible. There are a limited number of types of effective social behavior, and these types define basic behavior categories. Because all social behavior is motivated by a desire for responsiveness from another individual, the type of response that is desired provides a way to categorize intentions. The desired response may be simple sociability, or it may be behavior from another that helps the actor to accomplish a specific objective.

In coding social interaction (exchanges) we have adopted the concept of *mand,* defined as an attempt on the part of an individual to change the behavior of his or her social partner. It is assumed that the individual who mands has an intention (goal), and that the intention may be classified by the type of response the individual seeks to elicit. It is further assumed that a mand involves an exchange of resources, and that the beneficiary of the exchange may be the *mander* (ego) or the *manded* (social partner), or some other person or group of persons. Thus each mand is classified with respect to both resources and beneficiaries. The resources include instrumental help, comfort, food, material goods, information, attention, privileges, permission, control, physical pain, psychological pain (insult, derogation), friendship, social participation, cooperation, competition, services, and compliance to group norms. The social partner in interaction can comply, ignore, or refuse to comply.

There are six major categories of mands: ego-dependent, ego-dominant, nurturant, prosocial, sociable, and teaching (see Table 1.1). In ego-dependent and ego-dominant mands, the mander seeks resources for himself. Nurturant mands have the intent of offering resources to a social partner for that person's benefit. Prosocial mands have the intent of changing the social partner's behavior to make it fit the mander's perception of behavior that is socially approved, or behavior that serves the needs of the family or a larger social group. Prosocial behavior is considered to have the intent of benefiting others. Sociable mands have the intent of soliciting friendly interaction. Teaching mands are judged to have the intent of transmitting knowledge or skills.

Throughout this book we will seek to identify similarities of age and gender in the social behavior of specific categories of social partners that replicate across cultures, and to explore cultural differences. Comparisons will be based on the proportion of specific categories of mands in types of dyads defined by the age, gender, and kinship of the interacting social partners.

In all the communities sampling was based on census data collected by the field researchers. The age and gender of all members of each household were recorded, which often required many visits because birth records were not available in most of the communities. The collection of detailed life histories was often necessary in order to

Table 1.1. Categories of social behavior

Ego-Dominant Mands
Seeks physical injury; assaults; attempts to assault
Seeks to annoy; seeks to tease (when not for sociability)
Seeks to insult
Seeks submission
Seeks freedom from interaction
Seeks competition

Ego-Dependent Mands
Seeks comfort and support
Seeks physical contact[a]
Seeks help
Seeks information
Seeks approval, praise, attention, or admiration
Seeks material goods
Seeks food
Seeks permission to do something for own pleasure or convenience

Nurturant Mands
Offers comfort and support
Offers instrumental help, etc. (see above)

Prosocial Mands (suggests responsibly in Six Culture code)
Mands economic chore or household chore
Mands child care
Mands hygiene or approved social behavior and etiquette
Reprimands when related to the above mands[b]

Sociable Mands (seeks or offers when observer judges that it is possible to distinguish. If it is not possible, code under sociability)
Verbal teasing
Physical teasing or horseplay[c]
Other friendly response

Sociability
The summary category of sociability includes social play, laughing together, dancing together, when it is not clear who initiated the interaction. Also included is all friendly interaction when it is not possible to judge who initiates the interaction. For some analyses, sociability and social mands are combined.

Teaching Mands
Mander transmits general information and/or abstract knowledge
Mander transmits information about skills necessary for the performance of a chore or other economic activity

Note: Unless otherwise noted, coding categories are similar to those described in *Children of Six Cultures* (Whiting and Whiting, 1975).

a. It is often hard to distinguish between seeking and offering physical contact. Physical contact is coded as ego-dependent behavior in the chapter on the mother-child dyad. In child-child interaction, if it is impossible to distinguish seeking and offering, it is coded as sociability.

b. Reprimanding is criticism after the fact. It is often dominant rather than prosocial.

c. When physical teasing was judged to have the intent of hurting, it was coded as ego-dominant assaulting. When it was judged as having the intent of eliciting a playful response, it was coded as sociable physical teasing.

estimate the birth dates of adults and children. Genealogical data were collected to discover the relationship between families. Because, with the exception of the Bhubaneswar sample, the families chosen for study were judged able to identify each others' children (that is, they were members of a "primary sampling unit" as defined in J. W. M. Whiting, Child, Lambert, et al., 1966), we hoped to be able to identify with little extra research the age and kin relation of the children's social partners. House plans and maps of the homesteads or courtyard groups were drawn up, as well as maps of the area that identified the relations between neighboring families. Some of the households consisted of more than one family. Some of the houses were clustered around shared courtyards, or, as in subsaharan Africa, were part of the homesteads of polygynously married men.

Thus it is possible to derive the proportion scores that constitute the unit of comparison; these scores are based on the frequency of the categories of mand types within a dyad type identified by the age category of the actors (for example, knee, yard, or school-age child) and by the actual or relative age of the social partner. Our data are not dense enough to allow for elaborate statistical analysis. The number of individual dyads that are the basis for computing the proportion scores for a dyad type vary greatly, and the range of scores of the individual dyads that are averaged to compute the norm for a dyad type is often great. We do not attempt in this book to explore the experiences associated with these individual differences; rather, we report and analyze similarities and differences across the communities in the average proportion scores of the categories of social behavior within dyad types. Our interest is in findings that replicate across the communities.

We have debated the usefulness of presenting contingency statistics of probability and decided to omit any standard tests of significance. Since the number of children, the number of minutes of observation, and the frequency of dyad types vary so greatly across the samples, comparisons based on associations that fail to reach levels of significance are misleading. Our focus is on comparisons that show similar directional tendencies across cultures. In some comparisons, we have found it useful to use scaling procedures that contrast profiles of the proportions of clusters of categories of mands (see the discussion of canonical analysis in Kendall and Stuart, 1961, pp. 568–578).*

---

*The researcher may start out with a sample of girls and boys matched by age. In observing in naturally occurring settings, however, there is no way of controlling for

Because a cultural "insider" is best able to judge an actor's intentions, it is necessary to use individuals who are members of the cultural group as assistants in adapting the research plan to a specific community, and in observing and coding the social behavior. The research teams had little difficulty in teaching observers the mand categories, which are obviously transcultural and designed in such a way as to be content-free. Nor did we find the concept of intentionality foreign to the observers' way of thinking about the social behavior of children. In training observers, all of the field researchers found it rewarding for both the observer and the supervisor to explore the local definitions of insults and other forms of aggression. Detailed ethnographic information was needed to identify prosocial dominance as well as the subtleties of egoistic dominance or friendly overtures. We have found that observing and coding behavior with a member of the culture of the children being studied is an extremely useful way in which to learn about the culture of a community. Most of the observers had had experience caring for younger siblings. The Kenyan students were skilled naive psychologists; having watched and taken care of siblings, half-siblings, and cousins, they had a practical knowledge of children's behavior.

The observer followed the eyes of the focal child, identifying, whenever possible, the instigations to the focal child's social behavior and the responses of the partner to the child's social acts. The records were taken in consecutive English sentences. No coding was done during the observations because it was found that judgments of the

---

the number of times these girls and boys will encounter and interact with mothers, infants, or older and younger children. The relative frequency of encounters of an individual child with any one category of partners will depend on the number of observations per child and the settings prescribed by the child's culture, as well as on the number of siblings, housemates, and yard mates who frequent these settings (see Chapter 2). Social partners who were not in the initial sample appear in interactional sequences as actors (initiators of mands), thus increasing the size of the sample. In Appendixes B, C, E, and G we present samples of the frequency of the social behaviors on which our tables and figures are based and examples of the range of individual scores, in order to inform the reader of the characteristics of the data base.

In Chapters 2 and 3 we present phi values for chi-square tables. The proportion scores for the behavior in the mother/child dyads given in these chapters are restricted to the sample of focal children and their mothers. In later chapters we simply note the direction and magnitude of the difference in the proportion scores of the behavior of all the girls and boys of different ages as they were observed interacting with specific categories of social partners.

intentions and goals of the behaviors could only be made when an entire sequence of interacts could be studied. Before an observation was started, a record was made of the date, the time of day, the exact location, the people present in the interactional space, and the activities in progress. The observer kept a running record of the time in the left-hand column of the paper, noting when people left or entered the interactional space. The time was also recorded when the observer judged the focus of interaction to change. With the exception of Bhubaneswar, the observations were limited to the daylight hours and were distributed over four or five periods during the day. In the Six Culture Study the observations were 5 minutes in length; in the other studies they varied between 15 minutes and 1 hour, with the majority 30 minutes in length (see Table 2.2 for the average number of minutes of observation per focal child in each community). The training of observers was roughly the same across the communities. The researcher and the assistants observed together until about 80 percent of their written descriptions of social behavior agreed as to the number of codable units observed. Disagreements that fell within the major mand categories (see Table 1.1) were computed as one-half agreements. Once this level of agreement was reached, the observers in most of the communities were assigned to specific children because it was found that introducing several different observers increased the self-consciousness of the children. For this reason no conventional estimates of reliability are possible. Periodic checks were made of the coding of the written protocols by pairs of coders.* An indirect measure of the reliability of the observations can be found in the amount of repeated similarity between the dyad scores of girls and boys growing up in similar cultures whose behavior was observed and coded by different field teams.

Our fourth assumption is that in order for a child to judge correctly the intention of his social partner, the two must share beliefs, values, and techniques or recipes for practical action. The child must know how to interpret the explicit and implicit cues of gesture, tone, and language by which people express their goals—the shared schemata of a culture. We assume that a child as well as an adult has a desire

---

*For variations in the methods used to observe, record, and code behavior and to check reliability, see the research reports of the various members of the project listed in the References. The observations made in Bhubaneswar differ from those described above in that Seymour focused on the behavior of the mothers. Her data appear in Chapters 3 and 4 only.

for predictability and is motivated to develop schemata of the behavior patterns of these companions that are congruent with their schemata. We assume that children in a culture (or subculture) share much of their knowledge with one another. Thus, in similar settings children share not only goals (desired outcomes) with others in their group, but also scripts and schemata about normative social action.

Finally, we assume that children can and do learn from social experience; the laws of learning suggest key ways in which children can profit from different types of social experience. The response may be modeled after that of an individual who is observed to have reached the desired goal; it may be discovered through trial and error and strengthened as a habit through successful repetition; or it may be the result of someone's direct instruction as to how to reach the goal. Thus several processes play a part in learning: observation and imitation of models, trial and error, and direct instruction.

Models are available at all periods of children's development, but they are obviously different, for example, for children growing up in the traditional polygynous homesteads of subsaharan Africa, the large joint families of North India, or the bilateral hamlet communities of the Philippines. In each case, however, the children attentively monitor the behavior of models when they are encouraged to assume the model's role and when the model's behavior is perceived to be successful in reaching a goal valued by the child. For example, maternal models are clearly important in the learning of nurturant and prosocial behaviors; the children responsible for the care of their lap-child and knee-child siblings find it expedient to model some of their behavior on that of their mothers.

Trial and error is also an important process in social learning: responses that work will be repeated. Most often during the younger ages a child will perceive without being told that she has been successful in reaching her goal. We stress the importance of intrinsic reinforcements in learning. Extrinsic rewards, especially praise, seldom occur in the societies we studied and cannot be the major reinforcement in learning. In many situations, however, by trying out responses, a child can perceive without comment by others that she has succeeded in reaching a desired goal. A child caring for a younger sibling, for example, can perceive without being told that her charge is contented.

Learning through direct instruction, the third category, usually involves demonstration in our observational material. Demonstration is the predominant form of instruction because what is being taught is mostly practical skills and appropriate social behavior. In fact, since much of the training in agricultural societies is in motor skills, particularly in those societies that do not have schools or where universal education has only been available for a generation, demonstration is a favored technique of instruction in many of our samples. In this type of learning situation as well, a child can frequently perceive for himself that he has been successful in learning the skill.

In sum, we do not propose to explain all aspects of children's behavior. We focus on normative aspects, those shared by children of a similar age, sex, and cultural community. The power of culture, we argue, ultimately lies in the way cultural forces interact with parental pressure, behavioral predispositions, and developmental processes to program the daily lives of individuals, to map the settings they frequent, and to provide the rules of behavior governing the actors who share each setting. We are impressed by the fact that there are a finite number of general programs governing the lives of children growing up throughout the world, as well as a finite and transculturally universal grammar of behaviors that children can use in interpersonal interaction. We are also impressed by the consistent way in which similar activities and social partners elicit similar behavior in all of our sample communities. Therefore, insofar as socializing agents assign children to similar settings where they perform similar activities and interact with similar categories of individuals, we will expect similarities in the children's behavior that are evoked by the organization of the activities and elicited by the distinctive characteristics of their social partners. In contrast, insofar as children are assigned to different settings, we will expect differences in their behavior. Because age, gender, and cultural community are the dimensions having the most influence on children's assignment to or choice of settings, activities, and social companions, these dimensions will be of central concern throughout this book.

Chapter 2

Settings and Companions

Overview of the Sample Communities

Our study included 12 communities in which children between the ages of 2 and 10 were observed and their behavior recorded. These communities are listed in Table 2.1, along with information about their national and linguistic affiliation, type of settlement pattern, and estimated population at the time of the study. Five of the communities are located in Kenya, East Africa, and one is in Liberia, West Africa. The other communities are scattered around the world: North India (two communities), Okinawa, the Philippines, Mexico, and the United States. For our analyses we have divided these samples into two groups, the New Samples and the Six Culture Samples, because the observation methods, coding categories, and ages observed were different enough to require separate analyses.* Table 2.2 lists the field researchers who studied each community, the years in which they collected data, and the number of households and focal children in each sample.

Each of the communities can be thought of as the theater in which social interaction takes place. Major transcultural forces shape the drama taking place on the stage—forces that include ecological, historical, economic, political, religious, social structural, and ideological factors. For example, to understand the drama, that is, the recurrent patterns of social interaction, we need to know the household composition, the rules of residence and marriage, and the daily

---

*Data from two additional Kenyan samples are used in Chapters 5 and 6. Carol Ember observed 10 children aged 8 to 12 in Oyugis, a Luo community in the Western Province, and Martha Wenger observed 105 children aged 2 to 11 in Kaloleni in the Coastal Province.

Table 2.1. Communities where children's social interaction was observed

Location	National affiliation	Linguistic affiliation	Type of settlement	Population
New Samples				
Kien-taa	Liberia	Kpelle, Mende	Section of a town	200
Kokwet				
Western Province	Kenya	Kipsigis, Nilo-Hamitic	Farm homesteads	447
Kisa				
Western Province	Kenya	Abaluyia	Farm homesteads	3,000
Kariobangi, Nairobi				
Central Province	Kenya	Abaluyia	Housing estate in city	13,000
Ngeca				
Central Province	Kenya	Kikuyu, Bantu	Village surrounded by farm homesteads	6,000
Bhubaneswar				
Orissa	India	Oriya	City	50,000
Six Culture Samples				
Nyansongo				
Western Province	Kenya	Gusii, Bantu	Farm homesteads	208
Juxtlahuaca				
Oaxaca	Mexico	Mixtecan	Barrio, Indian section of a town	600
Tarong, Luzon	Philippines	Iloco	Scattered hamlets	259
Taira	Okinawa	Hokan and Japanese	Village	700
Khalapur				
Uttar Pradesh	India	Hindu	Town, clustered	5,000
Orchard Town				
New England	U.S.A.	English	Part of a town	5,000

routines of men, women, and children, including both their work and leisure activities. In addition, we need to understand the cultural beliefs pertaining to childhood: ideas about the nature of infants and children, differences between boys and girls, and conceptions of ideal behavior for each sex and age group.

Nine of the communities we studied are primarily agricultural. Although the inhabitants were once purely subsistence farmers and herders, they are now tied into the national economy of their countries and have become dependent on the products of the industrial world. All of the farmers now sell some of their produce to get cash in order to pay taxes and purchase tea, sugar, cooking fat, tools, clothing, and other goods. In three of the Kenyan communities, the families live on farms ranging in size (at the time of the study) from

Table 2.2. Characteristics of the samples

Location	Field researcher	Years of field work	Sample
Kien-taa, Liberia	Gerald Erchak	1970–1971	15 households; 20 children aged 1–6 (360 minutes of observation per child)
Kokwet, Kenya	Sara Harkness Charles Super	1972–1975	64 children aged 3–10 (120 minutes of observation per child)
Kisa and Kariobangi, Kenya	Thomas Weisner	1970–1972	24 urban and rural families matched by age, education, and kinship ties; 68 children aged 2–8 (120 minutes of observation per child)
Ngeca, Kenya	Beatrice Whiting	1968–1970, 1973	42 homesteads; 104 children aged 2–10 (45–300 minutes of observation per child)
Bubaneswar, India (state of Orissa)	Susan Seymour	1965–1967	24 households (8 upper, 8 middle, 8 lower-class); 103 children aged 0–10 (16 hours of observation per household)
Nyansongo, Kenya	Robert Levine Barbara LeVine Lloyd	1955–1956	18 homesteads; 16 children aged 3–10 (75 minutes of observation per child)
Juxtlahuaca, Mexico	A. K. Romney Romaine Romney	1954–1956	22 households; 22 children aged 3–10 (79 minutes of observation per child)
Tarong, Philippines	William Nydegger Corinne Nydegger	1954–1955	24 households; 24 children aged 3–10 (135 minutes of observation per child)
Taira, Okinawa	Thomas Maretzki Hatsumi Maretzki	1954–1955	24 households; 24 children aged 3–10 (74 minutes of observation per child)
Khalapur, India[a]	Leigh Minturn	1954–1955	24 households; 24 children aged 3–10 (95 minutes of observation per child)
Orchard Town, U.S.A.	John Fischer Ann Fischer	1954–1955	24 households; 24 children aged 3–10 (82 minutes of observation per child)

a. Minturn returned to Khalapur in 1974–1975. The data used in this volume do not include the restudy.

2 or 3 to 20 acres. A fourth Kenyan community, Ngeca, includes both farm homesteads and a village with stores and public buildings, with the families living on quarter-acre plots. Figure 2.1 shows the homesteads in Nyansongo, including the houses of co-wives and married sons of the headman. Figure 2.2 presents a section of the land owned by one of the two largest sublineages in Ngeca. The lineage lands have been divided into homesteads that include senior men, their wives, and married sons. Gardens and pastures are behind the dwellings. In the other communities the houses are clustered into hamlets (Tarong, Philippines; Fig. 2.3), villages (Taira, Okinawa, and Kien-taa, Liberia; Figs. 2.4 and 2.5), and sections of towns (Santo Domingo barrio in Juxtlahuaca, Mexico, and Khalapur, India; Figs. 2.6 and 2.7). In all of the clustered settlements, the farmlands surround the settled areas. Khalapur is the largest of these agricultural towns, with a population of about 5,000 when the study was made.

The remaining three sample communities consist of families in urban communities, with the men working as wage earners, entrepreneurs, or professionals. Bhubaneswar is a city incorporating an ancient temple town (Old Town) and the New Capital of the state of Orissa, India (Fig. 2.8). The sample families were drawn from lower-, middle-, and upper-status groups in both sections of the city; for purposes of analysis we have categorized the families into lower-status versus combined middle- and upper-status groups. Kariobangi is a housing estate in Nairobi, the capital city of Kenya (Fig. 2.9), with a population (at the time of study) of 13,000. Orchard Town is a section of a town not far from a large New England city (Fig. 2.10). All of the fathers in this sample are salaried wage earners or self-employed.

In each of the communities a sample of 20 to 50 families was selected for study. An attempt was made to select families who shared cultural beliefs, values, and practices, and who knew each others' children.* Preferably the homes were on contiguous land. In some of the communities there were clusters of related families. In Kenyan rural samples these groups belonged to the same sublineage, tracing descent through the male line from known ancestors. In the village of Kien-taa the families in the area were traditionally related through the male line. In the hamlets of Tarong and the Mixtecan barrio of

---

*See the description of a primary sampling Unit (PSU) in J. W. M. Whiting, Child, Lambert, et al., 1966.

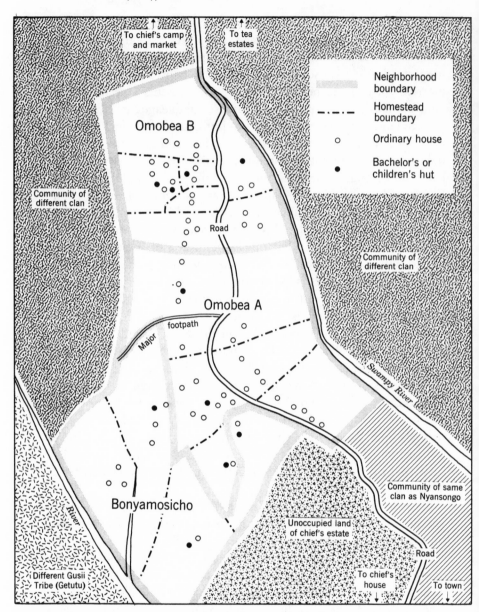

Figure 2.1. Nyansongo community, Kenya, showing three kin-based neighborhoods.

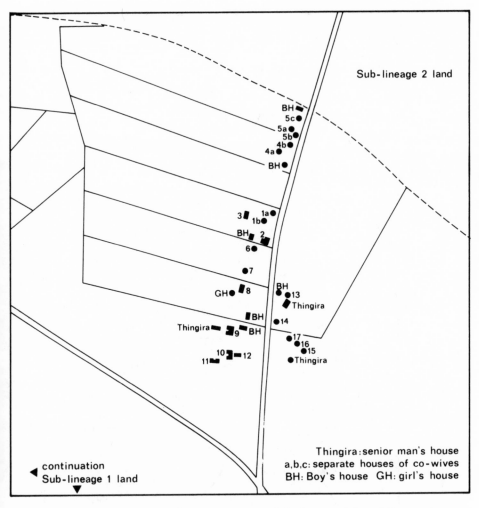

Figure 2.2. Section of land belonging to one of the largest of the sublineages in Ngeca, Kenya.

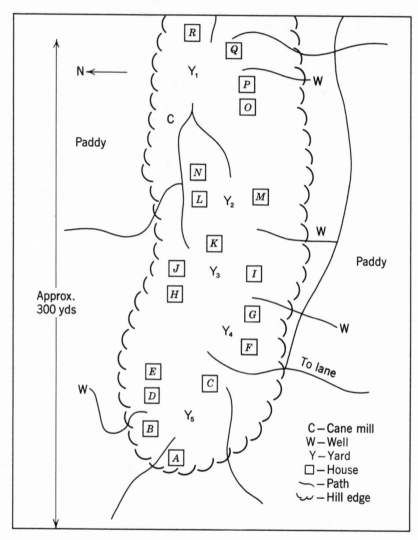

Figure 2.3. Largest of the hamlets in Tarong, Luzon.

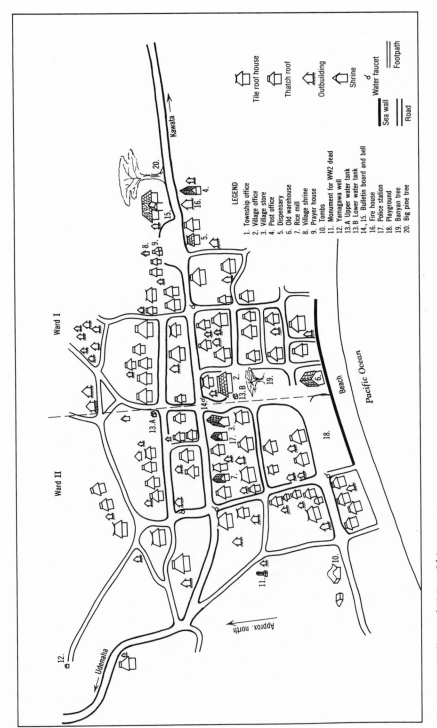

Figure 2.4. Village of Taira, Okinawa.

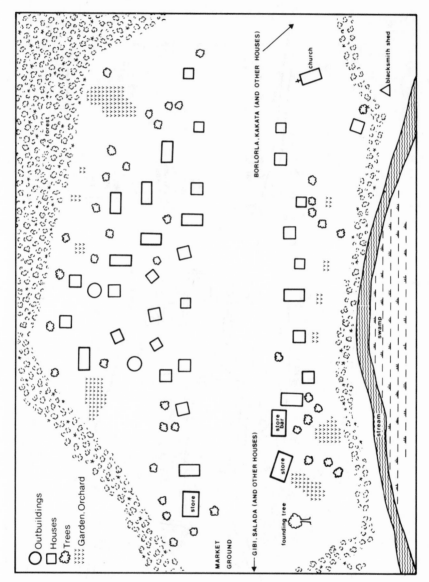

Figure 2.5. Village of Kien-taa, Kpelleland, Liberia.

Juxtlahuaca, the communities included relatives of both the fathers and mothers of the sample children.

Sampling in cities is always difficult. In North India the families in each subsample belonged to the same caste and socioeconomic status. In the housing estate of Kariobangi, Nairobi, sample families were migrants from the Kisa area in the Western Province of Kenya, and most still owned farms there. In Orchard Town, all of the sample families were connected to the same church or associated with people connected to the church.

In some of the communities, the households consisted of more than one nuclear family. In the Indian samples there were households that included patrilineal extended families, that is, families related in the male line, including the grandparental generation or collateral relatives or both (Figs. 2.11 and 2.12). Half of the families in Taira, Okinawa, included members of the grandparental generation (Fig. 2.13). The subsaharan Africa samples were unique in that many of the men had more than one wife. A farm homestead might include a senior man and his wives as well as some of his married sons and their children (for example, Fig. 2.14). Traditionally in Kenya, women who were polygynously married had their own separate houses, and the senior man preferably also had a house of his own. In Kien-taa co-wives generally shared a house (Fig. 2.15).

Many of the families shared patios, yards, and homesteads with collateral or lineal relatives, or both. In the barrio of Santo Domingo, Juxtlahuaca, a man and his married children often share a patio area (Figs. 2.16 and 2.17). In Tarong two to four houses often share a yard (Figs. 2.3 and 2.18). Kenyan homesteads may include as many as eight separate houses (see Fig. 2.1). Many of the families also had kin living on contiguous land. The exceptions were the families in Orchard Town, U.S.A., Taira, Okinawa, the families in the housing estate in Kariobangi, Nairobi, and in the upper- and middle-status residential area of New Capital, Bhubaneswar.

In addition to the communities just discussed, six other samples were studied using a different observational technique focused on the content of children's routine settings, activities, and social companions. These "spot observations" were made of children between the ages of 5 and 7 in communities located in Kenya (three communities), Guatemala, Peru, and the United States (see Table 2.3, p. 43).

All of the communities are described in depth in Appendix A. Further details about each cultural community will also be presented throughout the book as relevant.

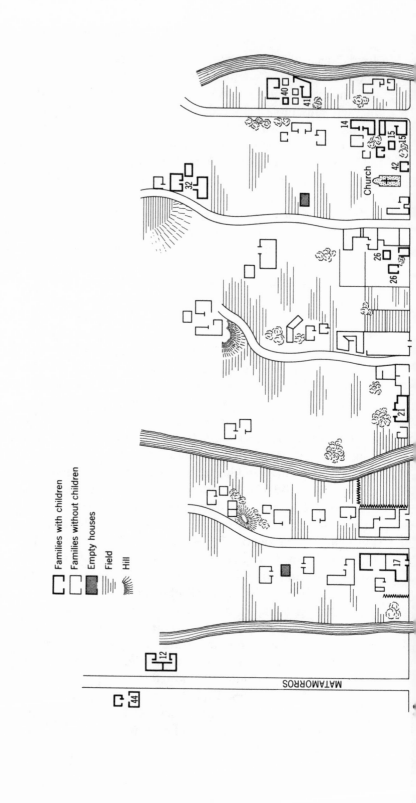

Families with children
Families without children
Empty houses
Field
Hill

Church

MATAMORROS

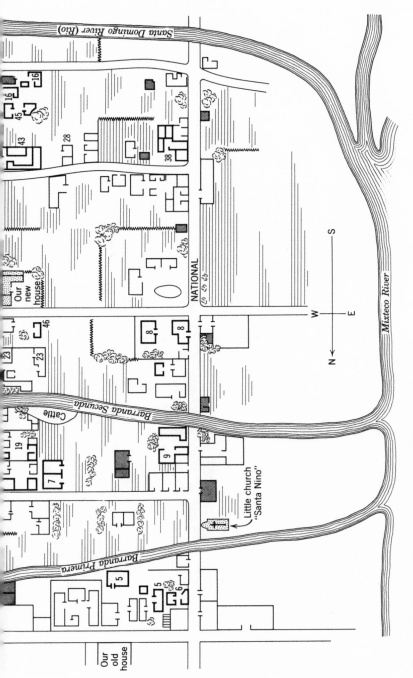

Figure 2.6. Barrio of Santo Domingo, Juxtlahuaca, Mexico.

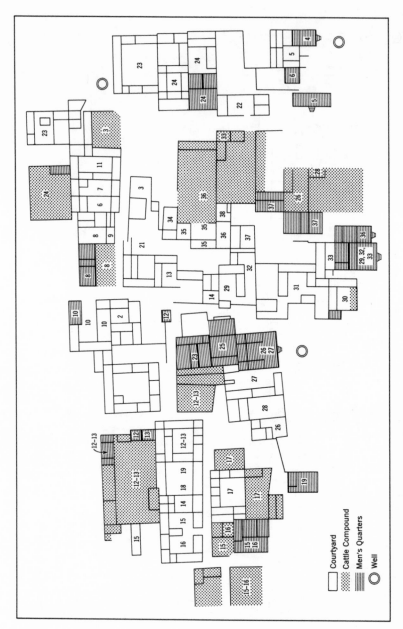

Figure 2.7. Section of the town of Khalapur, India.

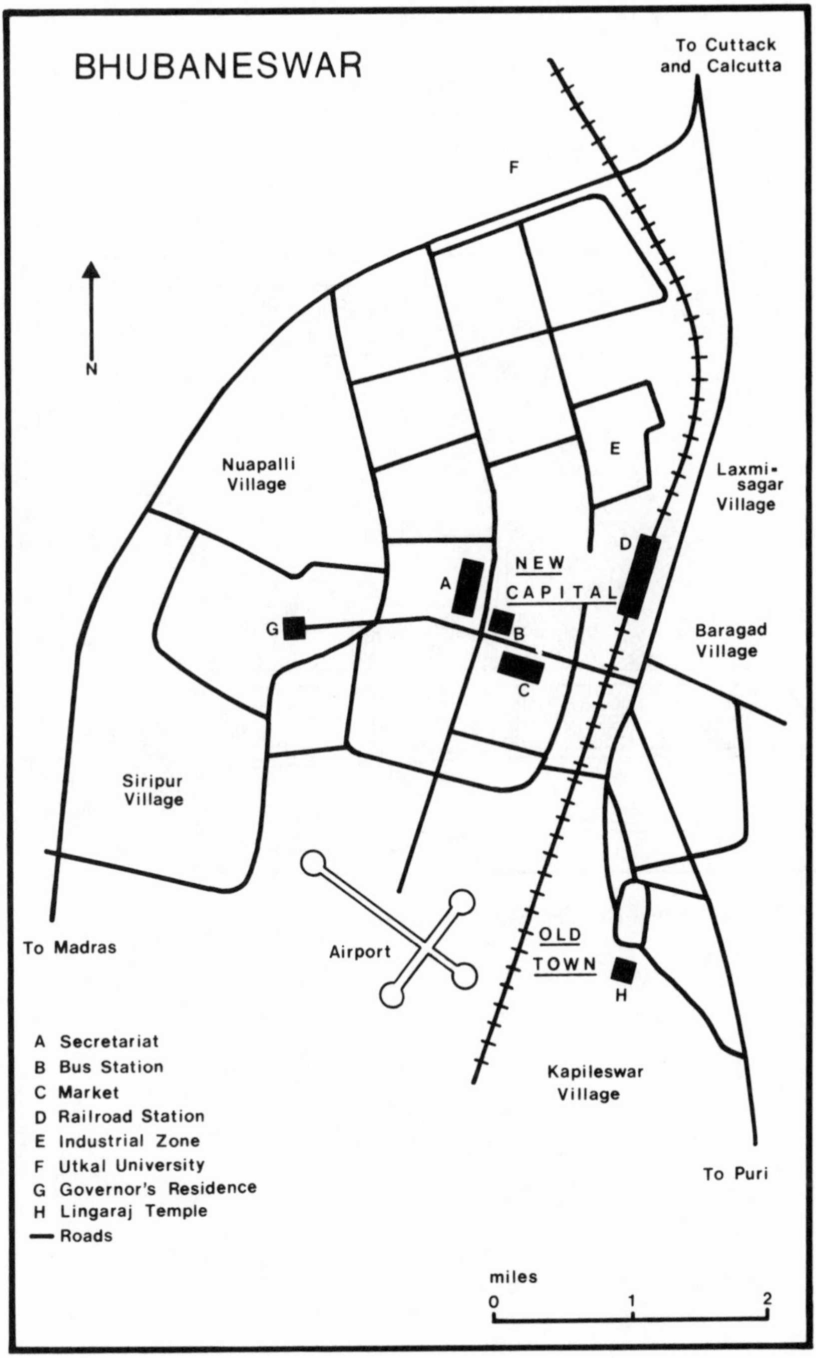
BHUBANESWAR
To Cuttack
and Calcutta
F
N
E
Nuapalli
Village
Laxmi-
sagar
Village
D
NEW
CAPITAL
A
G
B
Baragad
Village
C
Siripur
Village
To Madras
Airport
OLD
TOWN
H
A Secretariat
B Bus Station
C Market
D Railroad Station
E Industrial Zone
F Utkal University
G Governor's Residence
H Lingaraj Temple
Roads
Kapileswar
Village
To Puri
miles
0
1
2

Figure 2.8. New Capital and Old Town, Bhubaneswar, India.

Figure 2.9. Kariobangi Housing Estate in Nairobi.

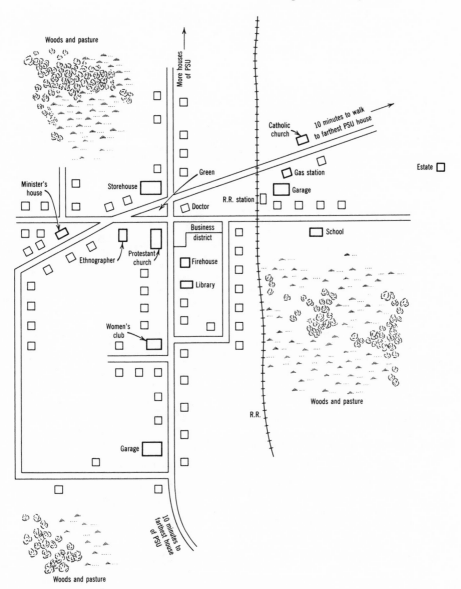

Woods and pasture

More houses of PSU

Catholic church

10 minutes to walk to farthest PSU house

Estate

Green

Gas station

Minister's house

Storehouse

Garage

Doctor

R.R. station

School

Business district

Ethnographer

Protestant church

Firehouse

Library

Women's club

Woods and pasture

R.R.

Garage

10 minutes to farthest house of PSU

Woods and pasture

Figure 2.10. North Village, Orchard Town, U.S.A.

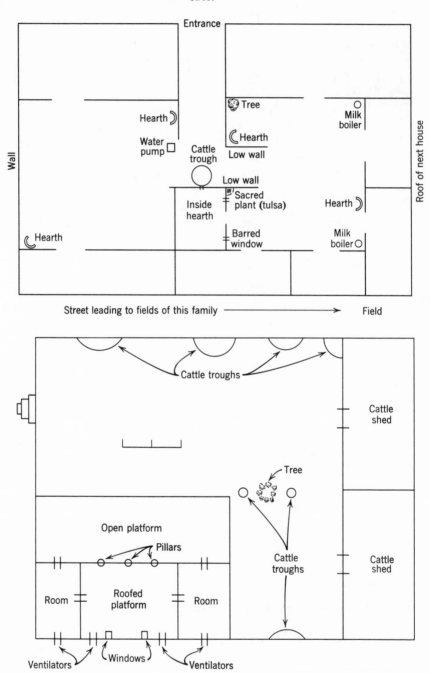

Figure 2.11. Floor plan of women's courtyards (*top*) and men's sleeping platform (*bottom*) in a joint family household in Khalapur, India.

The Importance of Setting

Our theory holds that patterns of social behavior are learned and practiced in interaction with various types of individuals in a variety of settings. In part, the effect of culture on these patterns in childhood is a direct consequence of the settings to which children are assigned and the people who frequent them. Socializing agents orchestrate children's participation in these learning environments by assigning children to some and proscribing others. Our theory holds that the power of parents and socializers to mold social behavior lies primarily in this assignment of boys and girls to different settings where they interact with different categories of individuals. To understand the effect of culture, age, and gender on the development of patterns of social interaction, one must study the characteristics of these settings. What is the nature of these environments where children learn patterns of interpersonal behavior? Who are the individuals who are available as role models? What are the most frequent opportunities for practicing various styles of social interaction?

Parents make the rules that regulate the company their children keep, but these rules are circumscribed by the physical and social characteristics of the community, the norms for social behavior, and the physical and cognitive abilities of their developing children. Customary rules governing forms of marriage, residence patterns, the division of labor, community organizations, and educational institutions, as well as adult values and world view, determine the environment into which children are born and mature. Inasmuch as these differ from one community to another, we will expect to find some group differences in the social behavior of the children. However, because there are similarities in the physical and cognitive abilities

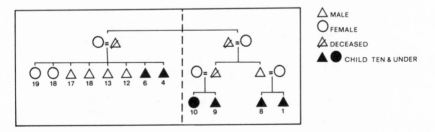

Figure 2.12. Genealogy of the residents of a joint family household in Khalapur.

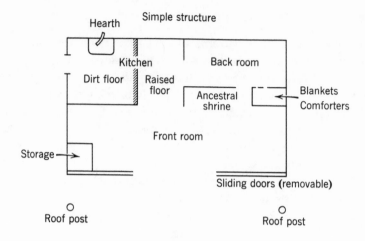

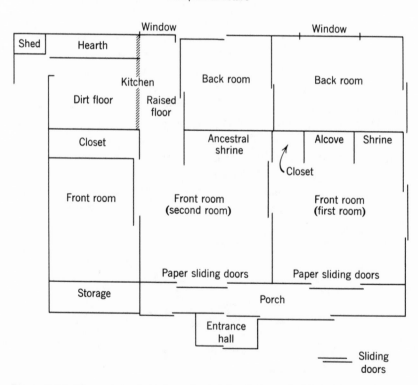

Figure 2.13. Floor plan of single and stem family households in Taira. (Stem family includes the parents of the father of the sample children.)

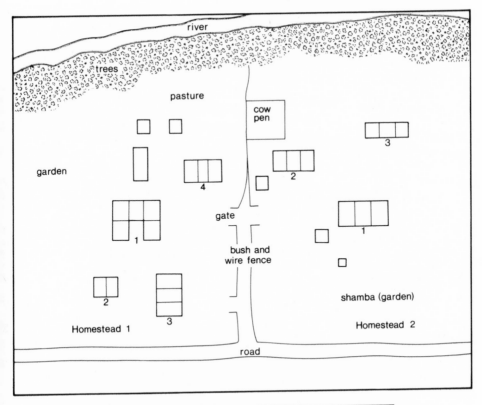

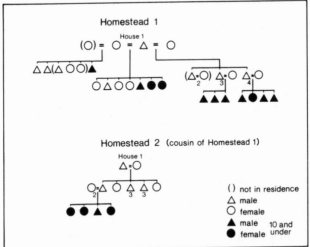

Figure 2.14. Two adjacent homesteads in Ngeca (*top*) with genealogy of residents (*bottom*).

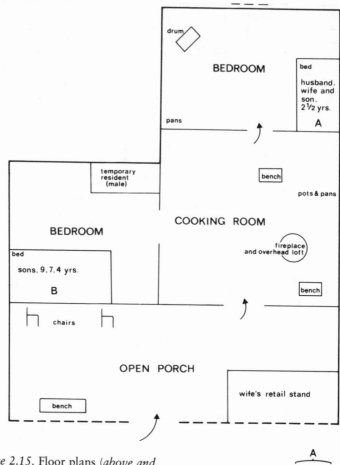

Figure 2.15. Floor plans (*above and opposite*) of typical houses in Kpelleland, showing sleeping arrangements of occupants.

of children of different age grades (regardless of where they grow up), as well as in their needs and desires, we will also expect similarities in behavior.

Indeed, because there are similarities across cultures in the general characteristics of the settings that each age grade frequents, it is possible to define age groups in terms of these settings.*

---

*Because birth records were not kept in many of the sample communities, sample children were assigned to age groups based on estimates of their ages.

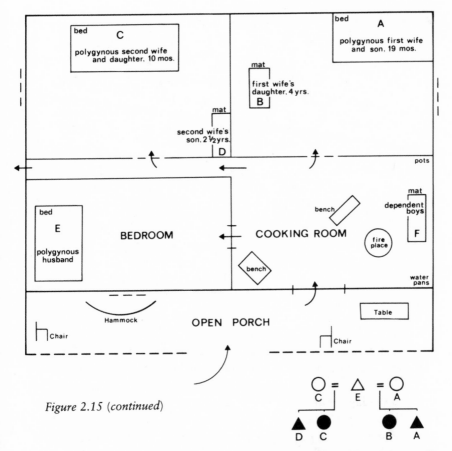

Figure 2.15 (continued)

F: two related boys, temporarily living in the house.

1. *The lap* or *back child* (0–2.5 years). In the earliest years, the infants in all of the sample communities live in a bounded space centered on the emotional and physical presence of the mother and other people who share intimate space with her or take over the caregiving role when she delegates it.
2. *The knee child* (2.6–3.5 years). A major change occurs when the infant becomes ambulatory and graduates from a lap or back to a knee child. As a toddler, the child becomes competent to move into a larger area, though still an area that can be monitored constantly by caretakers.
3. *The yard child* (3.6–5.5 years). By age 4 to 5, the child gains independent access to the entire house and yard or homestead

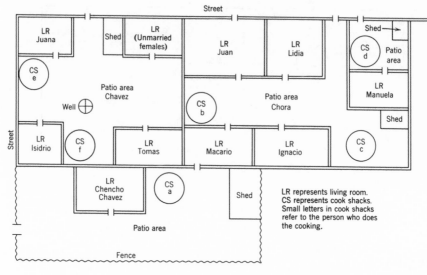

Figure 2.16. Adjacent patios in Santo Domingo, Juxtlahuaca.

area. Cultural differences in the variety of children's settings become more salient. Yard children in most communities may visit families living on adjacent land. In the communities with clustered housing, they may even play in more distant parts of the village that are considered safe, though they remain under the indirect supervision of older siblings and non-family adults who act in lieu of parents if need arises. In the four communities with preschools (Taira, Kisa, Kariobangi, Ngeca), children walk to places where they spend time under the supervision of non-family women (designated as "nursery teachers," though they have little or no formal training).

4. *The community* or *school child* (5.6–10.5 years). By age 6 to 7 the child may wander still further from home to attend school, perform chores, or join groups of peers in play—all activities that take children away from their immediate homestead into the center of town or to fields and pastures that are out of sight and sound of the homestead. In these settings children are less apt to be in the company of adults, and their activities are frequently unsupervised.

How exactly are children affected by the company they keep? The people who frequent the same settings serve not only as role models and teachers of approved social behavior, but also as elicitors of

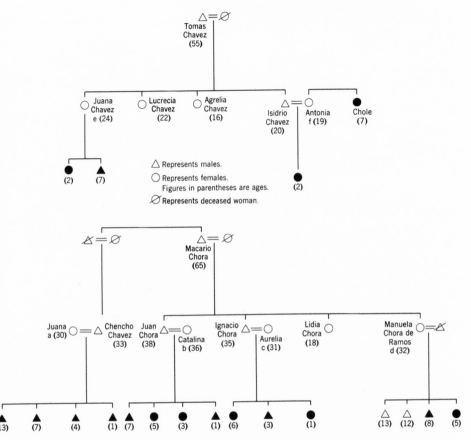

Figure 2.17. Genealogies of residents of the adjacent patios in Figure 2.16.

specific categories of behavior. Children respond to and initiate overtures to their companions depending on their gender, age, and kin relationship. They may seek help or resources from them, try to assist or work with them, play with them, fight with them, or otherwise engage in the events that constitute the drama of a child's life. In interaction with the different categories of individuals in the settings they frequent, children practice the types of behavior that these people most frequently elicit. Thus, the children's social selves are shaped by the reciprocal behavior that characterizes the typical patterns of dyadic interaction. Our theory contends that it is the age, gender, and kin relationship of these partners that best predict the type of interpersonal behavior the child will habitually practice.

Although there are similarities in the settings that the children of

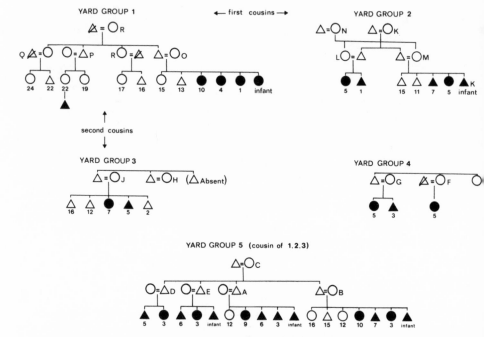

Figure 2.18. Genealogy of residents of the five yard groups in the Tarong hamlet (see Fig. 2.3).

these age groups frequent, there are also cultural differences in the choices of settings and companions offered that are determined by household and neighborhood arrangements, the daily routine of adults, physical and social dangers, and parental goals, including beliefs about appropriate male and female behavior.

Lap and Knee Children: Infants and Toddlers

Our observations begin with the knee child, but our ethnographic data enable us to outline the infant's companions. As we have noted, in the earliest years the child's primary contacts are with the individuals who sleep in the same room and live in the same house.

In the case of the infant, the most time is spent with the individuals who share sleeping areas. Except in Orchard Town, where they sleep in cribs, and a few Ngeca homes with basket cradles, infants in our samples customarily sleep in the same bed with their mothers until they are weaned. In later years they may continue to sleep with the mother or may move into a bed with an older sibling or a grandparent who sleeps in the same house. The mother and child may also share the bed with the father, as in Tarong, Juxtlahuaca, and some Bhubaneswar homes. In Taira all the household members spread their sleeping mats on the floor (see Fig. 2.13); the infant sleeps beside the mother and at weaning moves to the side of the father, grandmother, or grandfather. The infants of Orchard Town are the only ones who are ever routinely put in a separate room, away from their mothers (Fig. 2.19).

The number of individuals who care for or interact with lap and knee children depends on the size of families and households and the composition of yard groups. The number of people present in the household and yard groups varies in our sample communities: the largest households are the extended families of Bhubaneswar (Fig. 2.20) and Khalapur, North India (see Fig. 2.12); the smallest are the nuclear households of Orchard Town.

Across the samples, as many as 24 people may live in a household. In the North Indian samples the household may include as many as four generations related patrilineally, including grandparents and sometimes granduncles and grandaunts of the sample child, aunts,

Table 2.3. Communities where spot observations were collected

Location	Field researcher	Dates	Subject
Nyansongo (Gusii), Western Province, Kenya	Sara Nerlove	1967	10 girls, 12 boys
Vihiga (Logoli), Western Province, Kenya	Ruth Munroe Robert L. Munroe	1967	8 girls, 8 boys
Ngeca (Kikuyu), Central Province, Kenya	Ruth Munroe Robert L. Munroe	1970–1971	12 girls, 9 boys
Conacaste and Santo Domingo, Guatemala	Sara Nerlove	1971	28 girls, 25 boys
Santa Barbara (Canchitos), Peru	Charlene Bolton Ralph Bolton Carol Michelson	1974	5 girls, 6 boys
Claremont, California, U.S.A.	Amy Koel	1975	7 girls, 10 boys

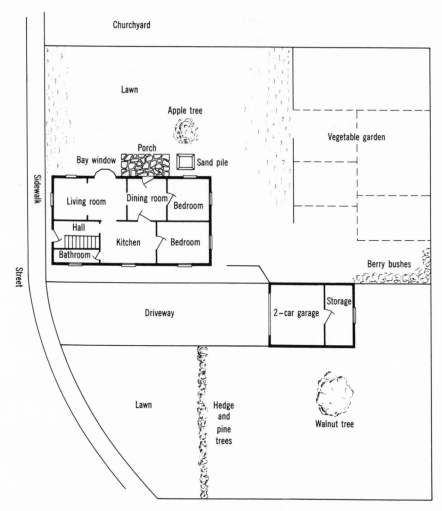

Figure 2.19. Yard and ground floor of house in North Village, Orchard Town, U.S.A. Second floor, not shown, includes additional bedrooms.

uncles, and cousins, as well as siblings. A sample child's married brother's wife may also live in the courtyard. The average number of people in the extended-family households in Khalapur is 11 (3 adult females, 3 adult males, and 5 children). Children growing up in Old Town Bhubaneswar live in households like those in Khalapur, with an average of 3 adult females, 3 adult males, and 7 children. The next largest households are those in Taira, Okinawa. Half of the sample children's households include one or two paternal grand-parents. The Kenyan households are also large because, although they do not include grandparents and may not include the father of the sample child, the number of children is large (see Table 2.4); on an average there are 5 to 7 living children per mother in Ngeca, Kokwet, Kisa, and Kariobangi—almost twice as many as in Orchard Town.

The frequency of children's contact with the father varies across the communities. During the lap child period, it is lowest in subsa-haran Africa and Khalapur, India. In most of the Kenyan commu-nities (where polygyny was traditionally the preferred form of mar-riage), fathers do not handle lap children and on some homesteads do not sleep in the same house as the mother. Sleeping arrangements vary with the number of years that the husband and wife have been married. Young couples may share a bed. With the birth of the first child, the man moves into a bed of his own but may sleep in the same room with his wife and child (Fig. 2.21). With the birth of more children, or when he decides to take a second wife, the father moves into a room or house of his own. Later-born children, then, see less of the father than do firstborns. In Khalapur, India, a few of the young couples sleep together, but most men sleep in separate living quarters, sometimes several blocks from the women's court-yard. In Juxtlahuaca many fathers work and live outside the barrio, some as far away as the United States.

Since in the majority of the communities children are frequently carried during the first two years, they are able to observe, smile at, and make contact with the people around them. Except in Orchard Town, New England (where with two exceptions in our sample, the households are isolated from relatives), in most of our sample com-munities there are many relatives, for example grandparents, aunts or uncles, and cousins, who share yards and interact daily. Further, in the polygynous Kenyan homesteads there are co-wives and half-siblings. In Juxtlahuaca the grandparents may live in a separate house but share a courtyard with their children and grandchildren. In Tar-ong the houses often face on yards shared by relatives.

When the lap child becomes an ambulatory knee child, she begins to explore actively the area and people that have previously been observed from the back, lap, crib, or baby carriage. The carried infant had the opportunity to smile and make eye contact with people and to look at and reach for things, but she could not wander at will or explore and handle objects on the ground. Crawling is not encouraged in households with open cooking fires or yards with animal droppings and other environmental hazards. The ambulatory knee child, in contrast, is able to seek and control more actively her interaction with all the members of the household, and may explore and handle objects within reach in the house and yard.

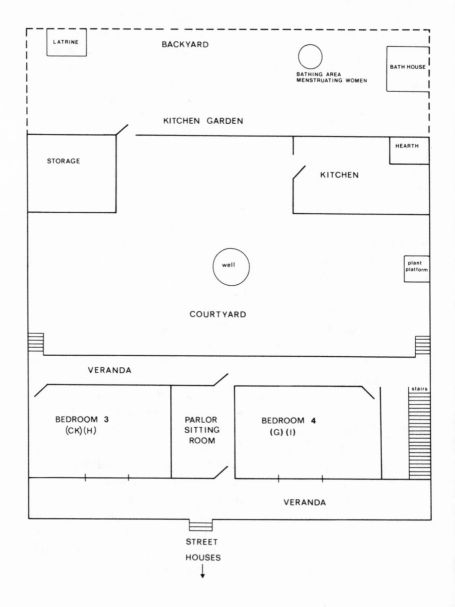

Yard Children: 4- to 5-Year-Olds

The yard child has more autonomy than the knee child. She may now visit unaccompanied the areas that were previously frequented with a caretaker. The child may explore areas considered safe, and, if bold, may venture further from home. The areas designated as safe depend upon the arrangement of households in space and the relationships between their members. In an average of 90 percent of the observations in Nyansongo, Juxtlahuaca, and Orchard Town (see Table 2.5), children aged 4 and 5 years were found at home or close to home.

When the neighboring families are not related and yards are owned by single families who value their privacy, the 4- and 5-year-olds are relatively confined. For example, in Orchard Town neighbors are rarely kin, and furthermore people do not consider themselves responsible for the neighborhood children. The 4- and 5-year-olds usually play in their own yards or the yards of friendly neighbors who also have children. How far from home they may go depends on the location of roads with heavy traffic and other real dangers.

In the hamlets of Tarong, yard children have somewhat more freedom. They play under the houses (Fig. 2.22) and in the shared yards between the house clusters of their own family and close neighbors. As can be seen in Figure 2.18, as many as 12 or more children age 10 and under may be daily companions.

In the town of Khalapur, where the closely built houses line the

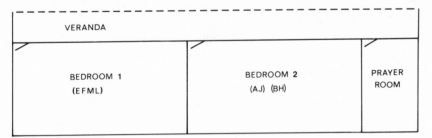

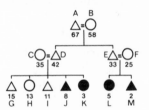

Figure 2.20. Ideal floor plan (*above and opposite*) of Brahmin household in Bhubaneswar, India, with genealogy of families.

Table 2.4. Distribution of families according to number of living children

Community	Numbers of families with the following no. of children:										Mean
	1	2	3	4	5	6	7	8	9	10⁺	
New Samples											
Kien-taa	1	2	4	4	0	3	0	0	1	0	4
Kokwet	0	1	1	1	4	5	5	3	5	4	7
Kisa	1	0	2	1	6	3	2	3	1	0	6
Kariobangi	1	2	3	1	2	1	3	1	1	0	5
Ngeca	3	2	2	5	9	2	8	4	5	2	6
Bhubaneswar											
Lower class	0	2	4	1	4	0	1	0	0	4	5⁺
Middle & upper	0	2	2	1	1	0	0	1	1	0	4
Six Culture Samples											
Nyansongo	1	3	3	3	4	1	0	1	0	0	4
Juxtlahuaca	0	1	6	9	4	0	1	1	0	0	4
Tarong	2	7	5	2	4	1	1	0	2	0	4
Taira	0	3	5	9	6	1	0	0	0	0	4
Khalapur	2	7	3	5	4	1	2	0	0	0	4
Orchard Town	2	8	6	5	2	1	0	0	0	0	3

narrow street (see Fig. 2.7), girls and boys as young as 3 years of age are sent to the store to make purchases for their mothers, who are confined to the courtyards by the custom of *purdah* (seclusion). An average of 20 percent of the observations of the yard children find them away from home (in the houses of other children, on the streets, and along the riverbank).

Children have the most autonomy in the central section of the village of Taira, Okinawa (see Fig. 2.4). This is the only sample in which the yard children are found to be away from home in 50 percent or more of the observations. In this compact village the yards are small, and the houses are open during the day so that conversations can be heard from one household to another. Parents feel responsible for all of the children of the village, and children wander freely in the streets and the public areas of town.

In the New Samples of subsaharan African families, yard children are as the label implies: they spend the majority of their time on the family homestead. Exceptions are the children living in the village of Kien-taa, Liberia (see Fig. 2.5), the housing estate of Kariobangi, Kenya, and the central part of Ngeca, Kenya.

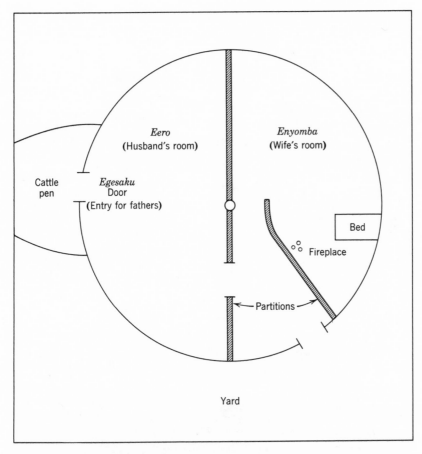

Figure 2.21. Floor plan of ordinary house in Nyansongo.

In all of the settlements with clustered housing and public areas, children have relatively more opportunity to interact with children who are not siblings, half-siblings, cousins, or other relatives. Thus, in Old Town, Bhubaneswar (India), the children play in the streets and the 4- and 5-year-olds may have playmates who are not kin. In Kariobangi, the housing estate in Naroibi, children also have some opportunity to play with non-relatives. Mothers tend to restrict their young children's freedom of movement, however. There is frequent turnover of the residents in the estate, and the families come from many different parts of Kenya and frequently speak a different language. The mothers, who are afraid that the children will fight and hurt each other, prefer to have their children stay in the front yard,

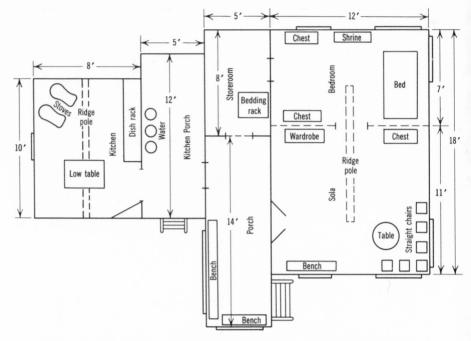

Figure 2.22. Floor plan of typical Tarong house (elevated 5 to 6 feet above the ground).

Boys playing with bottle-powered noisemaker, Tarong (1955)

a small area bordering on a drainage ditch and a road that has considerable automobile traffic. The policy of trying to keep the children in the house and a small yard may also be a carry-over from the country, where, as in the rest of the Kenyan samples, parents prefer to keep the children on family land. There is mistrust between non-relatives, and parents want young children to interact with children who are siblings, half-siblings, or cousins. They believe that if there is conflict between families, there is danger of "poisoning" by witchcraft.

Children playing house, Taira (1955)

Community Children: 6- to 10-Year-Olds

Children aged 6 and above can be termed "school" or "community" children to identify their expanding social horizons. Two types of activities are responsible for increasing the number of settings the children frequent: the assignment of work and attendance at school. In any community the introduction of schools provides the opportunity for children to interact with other children who are not kin. In many of the sample communities primary school represents the first such opportunity. While schools have existed in some of these communities for a long time, in others they are very new (see Chapter 7 for details).

The assignment of errands and tasks offers another opportunity for older children to gain access to their community. Although some of the sample children as young as 3 years are sent on errands to neighboring homesteads or to a neighboring store, it is usually not until somewhere between the ages of 5 and 7 that children are sent on errands that take them unaccompanied into the shopping area of town, to the wells, and to the rivers to get water. Even though the performance of tasks and errands may take young children relatively far from home, most of their travel is along routine paths that do not vary much from occasion to occasion. Parents do not encourage wandering by children sent on tasks and errands; they expect them to do the job requested and come right back. Wandering far from home concerns parents not only because they are aware of the physical dangers of the environment, such as cars, cliffs, and rivers, but also because of their fear of social dangers, such as the "poisoning" mentioned earlier or the more generally shared fear across the communities that children will be influenced by "bad" companions.

Comparative Study of Children's Activities and Companions

The ethnographic description of a child's life at each age grade suggests dramatic changes in children's whereabouts, activities, and social partners as they get older. Because these changes are so important in shaping children's typical profiles of social interaction, as we will show, we would like to examine them in a more precise way and compare our findings to other studies of children's everyday environments.

Access to the Wider Community

Table 2.5 shows how children's access to the wider community increases with age for the Six Culture groups. (We were not able to perform this analysis for the New Samples because most of those observations were restricted to the home area.) The table indicates the percentages of time that younger versus older children are observed to be different distances from home: at home (in the house, yard, or homestead); in the immediate neighborhood of home; and outside the immediate neighborhood. Data are presented separately for girls and boys, and the sex differences are noted at each age (4–5 versus 6–10 years).

The change in access to the wider community between the younger and older children is most dramatic for Orchard Town, New England, where once children are of school age, they may walk to and from school, visit friends along their way, and attend club meetings or other activities scheduled by their parents. In contrast, the change is least dramatic for the children of Nyansongo, who even in the older age group still primarily frequent the homesteads and adjacent gardens and pastures. Only one Nyansongo child attended school at the time of the study.

The table shows that boys are found more frequently than girls beyond the immediate neighborhood. The exceptions are Taira and Tarong. In Taira (Okinawa), both boys and girls are allowed at an early age to roam freely throughout the community. In Tarong, older girls are found more often than boys beyond the immediate neighborhood, but this gender reversal may reflect a sampling problem: the older group of Tarong girls is actually chronologically older than the group of boys.

The Six Culture findings thus suggest that overall, across cultures, older children and boys have more access to the wider community than do younger children and girls. Other data collected by our collaborators confirm this suggestion.

Spot observation is a method ideally designed for gathering systematic data on children's typical whereabouts, activities, and social companions. This method is a technique with extremely high interobserver reliability that permits the observer to obtain standard information on a focal child with minimal disruption of the activities and interaction in progress (R. H. Munroe and R. L. Munroe, 1971;

Table 2.5. Age and sex differences in percentage of observations in which children are found closer to or farther from home

Community (Six Cultures)	MOST CLOSE In house, yard, or homestead area			In immediate neighborhood			MOST DISTANT Farther than immediate neighborhood			Total no. of observations	
	Girls (%)	Boys (%)	Diff.	Girls (%)	Boys (%)	Diff.	Girls (%)	Boys (%)	Diff.	Girls	Boys
Nyansongo											
4–5 years	96	86	+10	4	10	−6	0	5	−5	47	42
6–10 years	84	82	+2	12	2	+10	4	16	−12	57	58
Juxtlahuaca											
4–5 years	98	93	+5	0	4	−4	3	4	−1	38	27
6–10 years	72	59	+13	0	2	−2	28	39	−11	70	51
Tarong											
4–5 years	87	68	+19	11	6	+5	2	26	−24	88	70
6–10 years	42	58	−16	2	10	−8	56	32	+24	156	161
Taira											
4–5 years	38	28	+10	10	16	−6	53	55	−2	41	49
6–10 years	20	13	+7	6	16	−10	72	71	+1	77	83
Khalapur											
4–5 years	81	77	+4	0	0	0	18	23	−5	38	31
6–10 years	75	36	+39	3	4	−1	22	60	−38	115	100
Orchard Town											
4–5 years	91	86	+5	2	7	−5	7	7	0	87	90
6–10 years	26	8	+18	0	2	−2	74	90	−16	72	52

Note: Throughout the tables, in the Diff. column, a plus sign before the number indicates that the percentage for girls is greater than that for boys; a minus sign indicates that the percentage for boys is greater than that for girls.

R. H. Munroe, R. L. Munroe, Michelson, et al., 1983; Rogoff, 1978). The observer locates each child in order (following a prearranged, randomized list). He first records the scene mentally and then writes information on the specific activity of the child, his whereabouts, the age and gender of individuals who are near the child, interacting with the child, or engaged in the same activity as the child, what kind of objects the child is holding or using, and so forth. Then the observer approaches more closely to greet people and gain any additional information desired (for example, information on the mother's activity if she is not present, and on whether the child's activity is being directed or supervised by any person present).

Table 2.6, which is based on spot observations of children in six communities, contains several interesting findings. First, children's average distances from home are nowhere really large: the greatest mean distances are in the communities in Guatemala and Peru where children do agricultural and animal-care chores that may take them about one-tenth of a mile from home. Second, cultural differences in children's distances from home are striking. The Claremont, California, children are found to be much closer to home than the children from the Kenyan, Guatemalan, and Peruvian communities. The Claremont observations were done after school and on weekends and thus do not reflect children's access to the wider community through school. The Claremont data on 5- to 7-year olds look much like the Orchard Town data on 4- to 5-year-olds and suggest that young American children in both of our samples experience relatively restricted environments except in situations where school provides them access to settings beyond the home.

Table 2.6 also suggests that "directed" activities (tasks and errands) provide children aged 5–7 with the opportunity to go farther from home than do "undirected" activities (free play and idle sociability). By 6 years of age, in fact, children in most of our samples are expected to help with chores that involve a degree of responsibility and that may take them away from home, depending upon where the major tasks take place. For example, the Peruvian boys and girls go to pastures fairly far from home to herd llamas. Nyansongo children of the same age also herd animals (cattle), but the pastures are adjacent to their homesteads. Vihiga children engage in gardening and animal husbandry, but as a result of population pressure, family plots are small and generally close to home.

The cognitive changes involved in the transition to middle child-

Table 2.6. Sex differences in children's mean distance from home

Community (Spot Observations)	No. of girls in sample	No. of boys in sample	Mean distance from home (in feet) during "directed" activities[a]			Mean distance from home (in feet) in "undirected" activities[a]			Proportion of "directed" observation		
			Girls	Boys	Diff.	Girls	Boys	Diff.	Girls (%)	Boys (%)	Diff.
Nyansongo, Kenya	10	12	190	254	−64	33	58	−25	58	54	+4
Vihiga, Kenya	8	8	131	146	−15	29	78	−49	52	32	+20
Ngeca, Kenya	12	9	263	252	+11	25	44	−19	57	44	+13
Conacoste/ Santo Domingo	28	25	338	406	−68	78	128	−50	25	19	+6
Santa Barbara, Peru	5	6	477	563	−86	2	24	−22	78	46	+32
Claremont, California, U.S.A.	7	10	48	39	+9	44	29	+15	18	19	−1

a. "Directed" activities are defined as activities that the child was assigned to do, typically tasks and errands. "Undirected" activities are activities selected by the child, typically play and idle sociability.

hood lie behind these observed changes in children's access to the wider community through work and chores. In fact, Rogoff and colleagues (1975) have analyzed ethnographic reports on 50 cultures from the Human Relations Area files and found the age period centering on 5–7 years to be a time of transition: parents in many cultures dramatically increase children's responsibilities at that time or heighten expectations for mature social and moral behavior. Further corroboration of our observational data comes from the maternal interview results in another cross-cultural study. Harkness and Super (1983) present data from Kokwet (Kenya) and Boston (Massachusetts) to show that the transition to middle childhood is accompanied by a shift in maternal expectations: mothers generally consider children aged 6 and older to be mature enough to take messages to other households and to go unaccompanied to shop for small purchases.

Finally, Table 2.6 indicates an interesting gender difference. During directed activity, boys are found farther from home than are girls in four of the six communities. During undirected activity, the differences are stronger (five of six communities). In fact, t-tests of the differences between means are not significant for the directed scores but are significant at the $p < .05$ level for Vihiga, Ngeca, Conacaste/Santo Domingo, and Santa Barbara.

The significance of these findings is amplified by the fact that boys spend more time than girls do in undirected activity (that is, free play and idle time), as shown in Table 2.6; boys thus spend more time than girls in the very kind of activity that accentuates male/female differences in self-directed access to the wider community. Robert Munroe and Ruth Munroe (1971), who first discovered the gender difference in distance from home during undirected activity, hesitate between hormonal and social learning explanations but speculate that the difference is important. They suggest that access to the wider community during free play actually results in the greatest learning about that environment because during task performance, children are instructed to follow a set, unvarying route of travel (for example, to the water hole and back) and are told not to wander or "fool around" on their way. Carrying wood and water, marketing, and running errands may take children far from home, but they involve little opportunity to follow one's own impulses or to explore just out of curiosity.

Children's Daily Companions

Gender and age differences are seen not only in children's physical whereabouts within the community but also in their social environment, that is, the company they keep. Culture, age, and gender differences are striking in the categories of people who are available to children and with whom they spend their time. These are the people whom children watch, imitate, respond to, receive help and instruction from, fight with, receive commands from, and who otherwise serve as the co-actors in the play of events that constitutes the drama of each child's life. The child's social self is necessarily shaped by the types of individuals with whom she most often has face-to-face relations. Culture has force because it so strongly determines children's daily companions through such macro features as community layout, living arrangements, and the work schedules of adults and children.

Mothers and Fathers as Companions. In all of our samples, children are observed to be with their mothers more frequently than their fathers and to be with adult females more frequently than adult males. Contact with the mother tends to decrease with age, especially after age 6 for children who attend school. Contact with the father may increase with children's age, particularly in those communities where older boys help their fathers with work.

Table 2.7 presents the percentage of observations in the Six Culture Sample in which girls and boys 4–5 and 6–10 years of age are in a setting with their mother or father. The table shows that children are seen with their mothers two to four times more frequently than with their fathers. Although there is evidence that the fathers in some of our samples left when the observer arrived (or stayed and engaged the observer in conversation, making recording impossible), the information on the daily routines of the families indicates that there are substantial differences in all of the cultures in the amount of time that children are with their mothers versus their fathers.

Both girls and boys spend more time with mothers than with fathers, but they do not do so equally. Table 2.7 also shows that in all but two of the twelve comparisons, girls outscore boys in amount of observations present with mothers, while boys outscore girls in amount of observations present with fathers. The cultural patterns are suggestive. The gender differences in relation to the presence of the mother and father (for the older girls and boys) are least in

Table 2.7. Children's contact with mothers and fathers

Community (Six Cultures)	Percentage of observations in which the mother is present					
	Age 4–5 years			Age 6–10 years		
	Girls (%)	Boys (%)	Diff.	Girls (%)	Boys (%)	Diff.
Nyansongo	34	24	+10	37	31	+6
Juxtlahuaca	52	41	+11	47	23	+24
Tarong	53	42	+11	26	28	−2
Taira[a]	19	4	+15	7	8	−1
Khalapur	71	21	+50	36	23	+13
Orchard Town	80	63	+17	20	10	+10

Community (Six Cultures)	Percentage of observations in which the father is present for girls and boys aged 3–10[b]		
	Girls (%)	Boys (%)	Diff.
Nyansongo	7	14	−7
Juxtlahuaca	8	12	−4
Tarong	17	17	0
Taira[a]	4	4	0
Khalapur	3	4	−1
Orchard Town	10	10	0

a. Honoring the cultural feeling about privacy, the Maretzkis and their Okinawan assistant undersampled observations in the houses and yards.

b. It is probable that the percentages for all fathers are underestimated because both researchers and fathers often appeared constrained in the observations, and fathers avoided entering the settings if an observation was in progress. The frequencies were so low that the age groups were pooled.

Tarong and Taira, which are the two communities judged to have the most egalitarian relations between husband and wife. In contrast, the gender differences are greatest (for the older age group) in Juxtlahuaca and Khalapur, two of the communities that stress gender differences beginning in early childhood.

Table 2.8 presents Spot Observation data on the percentage of adults present who are female, the percentage of observations in which the nearest adult is female (when the nearest person is an adult), and the percentage of observations in which the child is observed interacting or engaged in the same activities as adult females and males. These measures are not identical to those discussed earlier

Table 2.8. Contact of 5- to 7-year-old children with male versus female adults

Community (Spot Observations)	Percentage of adults present who are female			When nearest person is an adult, percentage who are female			Percentage of observations of adult females interacting or engaged in same activity as the child			Percentage of observations of adult males interacting or engaged in same activity as the child		
	Girls	Boys	Diff.	Girls	Boys	Diff.	Girls	Boys	Diff.	Girls	Boys	Diff.
Nyansongo	87	77	+10	92	73	+19	18	12	+6	0	3	-3
Vihiga	76	83	-7	74	88	-14	19	13	+6	4	4	0
Ngeca	88	83	+5	88	79	+9	24	22	+2	2	6	-4
Conacoste/Santo Domingo	85	76	+9	91	81	+10	36	29	+7	7	11	-4
Santa Barbara	80	49	+31	100	63	+37	24	14	+10	0	5	-5
Claremont	69	54	+15	78	55	+23	29	21	+8	15	21	-6

for the Six Cultures because the "adult males and females" counted in the Spot Observations are not necessarily the parents of the sample child. However, because the 5- to 7-year-olds are usually close to home when not performing chores, it is probable that the adult females are mothers or mother surrogates and the males are fathers, grandfathers, or uncles. In any case, the comparisons lead to a similar conclusion: both girls and boys have more contact with adult females than with adult males (though girls have relatively more contact with adult females than boys do, while boys have relatively more contact with adult males than girls do). Similarly, adult females are more likely than adult males to be interacting or engaged in the same activity as children (although girls are with adult women more frequently than are boys, and boys are with adult males more frequently than are girls).

Rogoff's findings (1981a) from the rural highlands community of San Pedro, Guatemala, corroborate our conclusions. Rogoff observed 100 Mayan Indian children aged 6 months to 14 years. Her observations took place an equal number of times on each of six days of the week over a two- to three-month period. For all ages of children, the adults available (present) are far more likely to be women than men. Furthermore, except during the lap and knee child periods, girls have relatively more contact with women than do boys, while boys have more contact with men than do girls.

Similarly, Morelli (1986) has presented extensive observational data on 1- to 3-year-olds from two ethnic groups, the Efe (Pygmy) and Lese (Bantu), who live side by side in the tropical rain forest of Zaire. She found that for both groups, mothers are present in a much higher percentage of observations than are fathers (about 80 percent versus 50 percent for both groups). However, the 50 percent figure for fathers seems higher than is typical for other subsaharan African communities. Fathers seem to be relatively available in both groups— not so surprising perhaps for the Efe, since the group is still partially a hunting and gathering society; Efe men are mostly occupied with hunting, tool preparation, and related pursuits (see Katz and Conner, 1981, for a discussion of the relatively high contact between hunter-gatherer fathers and young children).

Edwards, Logue, Loehr, and Roth (1986, 1987) have obtained spot-observation data for American children aged 2–30 months living in a small Massachusetts city. Half of the children attended center-based day care, while the other half were taken care of by parents or other caretakers exclusively in home settings. Children were studied by means of telephone spot observations in morning, afternoon, and evening time periods, seven days a week, over eight months. Averaging across groups and time periods, mothers are found to be in the immediate vicinity of the child (in the same room, or "in view") in 73 percent of observations, compared to 44 percent for fathers, during children's at-home time. Mothers are found to be the "closest adult" for 64 percent of these at-home observations, compared to 33 percent for fathers. The day-care children experience more adult male contact than the home-care children because the center staff included male teachers and because their fathers were slightly more involved in their care. However, there are no differences between girl and boy children in contact with adult males versus females (Edwards et al., unpublished results).

What explains this consistent pattern of greater contact with mothers than fathers? The norms and rules pertaining to intimacy between husband and wife and their division of labor influences young children's contact with parents. In all our samples mothers have the primary responsibility for infant care, but the amount of paternal responsibility varies widely. For example, in the Six Culture communities, participation of fathers in child care is lowest in Khalapur (India) and Nyansongo (Kenya); many of these fathers actually sleep in different buildings from their wives and young children. Fathers are most involved with lap and knee children in Tarong (Philippines) and Juxtlahuaca (Mexico), societies where fathers share a bed with their wives and children, and in Taira (Okinawa), where all the members of the household sleep side by side wrapped in their quilts. The Tarong fathers actually take charge of the older children during the 11 to 30 days of the postpartum period in households where the wife lacks a close relative (mother, sister, adolescent daughter) who can take over for her (Nydegger and Nydegger, 1963). In Taira fathers differ in the amount of care they give to lap and knee children; in households where there are no grandmothers, Taira fathers sleep with the knee children who are being weaned. In all communities, however, even the most involved fathers do not take the everyday responsibility for the routine care of lap and knee children.

We asked the ethnographers of the New Sample and Spot Observation communities to make an estimate of the fathers' participation in the care of lap and knee children (Table 2.9). The Kenyan fathers were judged to be the least involved in the care of lap children. The cultures in these Kenyan communities favor polygynous marriages, and there is a high proportion of mother-child sleeping arrangements, with the fathers frequently having a house or a room of their own. Furthermore, there is often a required postpartum period when sexual relations between the husband and wife are prohibited. In comparison to cultures with monogamous marriages and nuclear households, husbands and wives have an aloof relationship (J. W. M. Whiting and B. B. Whiting, 1975). As reported by the ethnographers, the fathers never care for lap children even in the mothers' absence and rarely hold the child even at home. The Kien-taa (Liberia) fathers who share a house with their wives play with lap children more often and hold them frequently, although they never care for or take charge of them in the absence of the mother. All of the African fathers are more involved with knee children than with lap children but still do not care for, carry, teach, or take charge of the knee children more than occasionally. Their most frequent interaction is judged to be that of disciplining. It seems a safe conclusion that across the Six Cultures, New Sample, and Spot Observation samples, the African fathers have the least contact with lap and knee children, while the Tarong and Claremont fathers have the most.

Fathers' involvement with young children is directly affected by the amount of time spent by the former in the home setting. As we have seen, knee and yard children spend most of their time close to home. Unless the fathers are working around the house, which is rare in our samples, children are with their father only when he returns to the house to eat, relax, or sleep. The general pattern of aloofness or intimacy between husband and wife also influences the amount of leisure time that the husband spends in the company of his wife and children. Intimacy is lowest in the Kenyan and Khalapur families* and greatest in Tarong, Orchard Town, and Claremont.

Besides the amount of time spent by the father at home, the occupation of the father has the most direct influence on the amount of contact between fathers and children, especially sons. The care of large animals is considered "men's work" and is the most important economic activity that leads to early contact between fathers and sons. In the communities with farms that include large animals, boys, beginning as young as age 4, may be trained by their fathers to help in the care of livestock. Table 2.10 presents the levels of involvement

*In Bhubaneswar men slept in the house with their wives rather than in a separate men's sleeping platform, as in many Khalapur families.

Table 2.9. Fathers' participation in care of lap and knee children

Community	LAP-CHILD CARE TASKS				
	Play, entertain	Hold	Carry, outside house	Care for (dress, feed, bathe)	Take charge in mother's absence
New Samples					
Kien-taa, Liberia	2	4	1	0	0
Kokwet, Kenya	1	1	0	0	0
Kisa, Kenya	0	1	1	0	0
Kariobangi, Kenya	1	1	1	0	0
Bhubaneswar, India	2	2	2	1	2
Spot Observation Samples					
Nyansongo, Kenya	0	1	0	0	0
Vihiga, Kenya	1	1	0	1	1
Conacoste/Santo Domingo, Guatemala	1	2	1	0	1
Santa Barbara, Peru	2	2	1	0	2
Claremont, U.S.A.	4	4	3	2	1

Table 2.9 (continued)

Community	KNEE-CHILD CARE TASKS								
	Play, entertain	Hold	Carry, outside house	Care for (dress, feed, bathe)	Teach chores	Teach symbolic material	Physically discipline	Verbally discipline	Take charge in mother's absence
New Samples									
Kien-taa, Liberia	0–1	0–1	0	0	0–1	0	0	1	0
Kokwet, Kenya	2	2	1	1	2	0	0	4	1
Kisa, Kenya	2	2	2	0	1	1	1	2	1
Kariobangi, Kenya	2	2	2	1	2	0	1	3	1
Bhubaneswar, India	2	2	2	1	1	1	0	2	2
Spot Observation Samples									
Nyansongo, Kenya	1	1	0	0	NA[a]	0	NA	NA	0
Vihiga, Kenya	1	1	1	1	0	0	2	2	2
Conacoste/Santo Domingo, Guatemala	2	4	2	1	1	0	NA	2	1
Santa Barbara, Peru	2	2	1	1	1	0	1	2	2
Claremont, U.S.A.	4	4	3	2	1	1	2	4	1

Scale: 0 = never performs; 1 = rarely performs, 2 = occasionally performs; 3 = performs weekly; 4 = performs daily. Each ethnographer rated independently, using objective data in his/her files supplemented by personal impressions.
a. NA = nonascertainable.

Table 2.10. Percentage of girls and boys observed or reported to take care of large animals

Community (Six Cultures)	Age 4–10 years		
	Girls (%)	Boys (%)	Diff.
Nyansongo	24	88	−64
Juxtlahuaca	0	10	−10
Tarong	0	100	−100
Taira	0	9	−9
Khalapur	11	64	−53
Orchard Town	0	0	0

Community (Spot Observations)	Age 5–7 years		
	Girls (%)	Boys (%)	Diff.
Nyansongo	1	14	−13
Vihiga	2	2	0
Ngeca	3	8	−5
Conacoste/Santo Domingo	20	80	−60
Santa Barbara	9	7	+2
Claremont	0	0	0

of Six Culture and Spot Observation boys and girls in the care of large animals. It can be seen that with the exception of Santa Barbara, Peru (where both girls and boys herd llamas), boys are more involved in animal care than are girls. Boys from Nyansongo and Khalapur are observed to care for livestock the most frequently of all children in our samples.

Participation of children in work with adult males comes later in agricultural work than in animal husbandry. This is especially true where the farm equipment includes plows and the gardens are distant from the homestead. For example, in Juxtlahuaca men do the farming and often have plots that are as distant as several miles from their residences. None of the boys in this community were observed to work in the fields with the men. In Khalapur, however, where agricultural work is done by the men, boys aged 6 and over do go out to the fields with the men and carry back fodder for the cattle. Even in communities such as Taira, where both men and women do agricultural work, there is usually a division of labor into tasks for men and tasks for women, and children usually help the women. In the

Kenyan communities women are the primary agriculturalists; people primarily practice hoe agriculture. Women teach both girls and boys as young as 4 or 5 to help break the soil, plant, and weed.

Thus, for all household and economic tasks except those connected to the care of large animals, women rather than men are the adults who assign and teach the performance of chores to young children. During the years when children spend the majority of their time in the house and yard, women are usually the adults present. These mothers are busily engaged in child care, household chores, agricultural work (if there are gardens adjacent to the house), and the care of any animals that are in the yard. They train their children to help with chores that are considered to be women's work.

Perhaps because mothers are the adults most often assigning and training children, or perhaps because the work that mothers assign is considered to be "female work," girls are recruited to help relatively more often than boys of the same age. This can be seen clearly in Table 2.11, which presents a comparison of the percentage of observations in which girls and boys are observed working.

For the Six Culture samples, this score excludes child care from all other household and economic tasks. The top half of Table 2.11 shows that where there are sex differences, girls are observed working more frequently than boys, with the exception of Nyansongo, where boys herd cattle. At ages 4–5, an average of 12 percent of girls' observations versus 8 percent of boys' involves work. At ages 6–10, an average of 21 percent of girls' versus 17 percent of boys' observations involves work. (For further discussion of girls' and boys' task involvement in the Six Culture samples, see Minturn and Lambert, 1964; Whiting and Edwards, 1973; and Whiting and Whiting, 1975.)

In the Spot Observation samples, the measure of working includes child care. Girls are observed working more than boys in four of the six communities. Boys from Nyansongo are again the exception. (For further discussion of the work of children in the Spot Observation samples, see Munroe, Munroe, and Shimmin, 1984.) Girls' greater involvement in responsible work is thus a strong finding, and it is corroborated by numerous other studies conducted in many parts of the world, including those communities that constitute our New Samples.

Barry, Bacon, and Child (1957) found evidence of transcultural differences in the assignment of chores. The ratings by these researchers include a measure of "responsibility and dutifulness training"

Table 2.11. Percentage of observations in which children are observed performing chores

Community (Six Cultures)[a]	Age 4–5 years			Age 6–10 years		
	Girls (%)	Boys (%)	Diff.	Girls (%)	Boys (%)	Diff.
Nyansongo	36	29	+7	43	51	−8
Juxtlahuaca	4	0	+4	19	7	+12
Tarong	19	14	+5	24	7	+17
Taira	5	4	+1	16	14	+2
Khalapur	8	3	+5	16	16	0
Orchard Town	0	0	0	8	4	+4

Community (Spot Observations)[b]	Age 5–7 years		
	Girls (%)	Boys (%)	Diff.
Nyansongo	18	36	−18
Vihiga	40	21	+19
Ngeca	50	30	+20
Conacoste/ Santo Domingo	20	17	+3
Santa Barbara	46	30	+16
Claremont	3	6	−3

a. Child care excluded in the Six Culture Sample.
b. Child care included in the Spot Observation Sample.

that was judged mainly by ethnographic statements about children's training in the performance of chores in the productive and domestic economy. Barry, Bacon, and Child found that pressure toward assuming responsibility is greater for girls than for boys in 61 percent of the 85 societies in which there were sufficient ethnographic data to make a judgment.

Rogoff in her study of Guatemalan children (1981b) interviewed parents about children's participation in chores. At age 4, both boys and girls begin to run errands, sweep, and shell corn, and tasks are not differentiated by sex. By age 5 or 6, however, children become aware of gender roles through the teasing of older children, and as they grow older and undertake increasingly complex tasks, their work becomes more sex-typed. For example, girls more often run errands, carry water, take corn to the mill to be ground, and do cleaning chores, while boys more often gather firewood and fodder from the

Ngeca girl carrying water (Frances M. Cox, 1975)

woods and feed animals. Overall, at age 9, girls are found performing chores (excluding child care) in 41 percent of spot observations, boys in 33 percent.

Detailed spot-observation data on children's chores are also available for the large sample of Kipsigis children observed by Sieley

(1975) in Western Kenya. The children were aged 6–7 and 10–11 years. Girls are observed more often than boys doing the following chores: looking after the house, collecting firewood, collecting vegetables, shelling maize, making the fire, boiling milk and making tea, serving food, washing dishes and clothes, sweeping the house, and renewing the house walls by smearing mud. Boys are observed more often than girls doing such chores as herding cattle, sheep, and goats, separating and holding calves, driving oxen, and dipping cattle and milking them. However, sex differences are not clear-cut in activities related to gardening and farming, except for clearing fields (a masculine task).

Seymour (1981, 1985) has presented information on the kinds and number of chores performed by children in Bhubaneswar, India. Lower-status children are observed to perform many more chores than middle- and upper-status ones, and the types of chores emphasized differ by status group, in a way reflective of their mothers' workloads. The age of children is also important: the 6- to 10-year period is the age at which the major increase in chores occurs. Finally, at each age and for each status group, girls perform chores at a rate two to three times greater than boys.

Erchak (1976a) has analyzed observations from Kien-taa, Liberia, in terms of "responsibility" behavior and has found that girls act more responsibly than boys. Kpelle girls begin to care for infants, sweep the house, and fetch water at about age 5 or 6, while boys perform few chores before age 10 or 11. Women play the dominant role in subsistence activity and the cash spheres of the economy. As in the other subsaharan African communities, girls are prepared earlier than boys for their adult economic roles.

Morelli (1986), in her study of Efe and Lese children in Zaire, has found sex differences in subsistence-related activity to appear first at age 3. At that age, girls spend more time than boys "monitoring" (watching others perform subsistence-related activity), "paralleling" (modeling others' activity), and actually performing subsistence tasks. Summing across all three categories, Efe girls are observed in subsistence-related activity in 35 percent of observations, but boys in only 18 percent. For Lese girls and boys, the comparable scores are 35 percent and 17 percent.

Finally, Bloch and Walsh (1985) have used the spot-observation method to study American middle-class children living in Madison, Wisconsin. At ages 5–6, but not before, they find girls to perform

Nyansongo girls shelling maize (1956)

Six-year-old and two-year-old cutting vegetables, Bhubaneswar (Susan Seymour, 1966)

significantly more housework than boys (13 percent of girls' observations versus 3 percent of boys').

On the basis of these converging studies, we conclude that girls are generally more involved in economic and domestic work than are boys of the same age. The extent of the gender difference observed in a particular cultural community is affected by the types of chores into which children can be recruited and the adult division of labor into male and female tasks. At what age the gender difference begins to be observed is also affected by mothers' workloads: in communities where women carry heavy subsistence responsibilities, as in much of subsaharan Africa, the difference may appear by ages 3–4, but where women's domestic workload is lighter, as in the North American communities, the difference may not appear until after age 6 or 7.

Lap and Knee Children as Companions. Lap children are in the company of girls more than that of boys. They are also under girls' care and responsibility relatively more. These conclusions emerge strongly from both our study and all previous reports.

In the Six Culture Study, 40 percent of the sample mothers had lap babies. Most of the children aged 5 and over were judged to be in charge of the lap baby during at least one of the observations. Table 2.12 shows the percentage of observations in which girls and boys aged 5–10 who had a sibling under 18 months old were judged to be in charge of them. To compute these scores we summed the number of observations that girls and boys in each sample were in charge and divided by the total number of observations made of that group. It can be seen that on average girls are observed taking care of a lap baby twice as frequently as boys (15 versus 7 percent). Tarong girls are the only exception; both girls and boys are observed caring for lap baby siblings in 9 percent of the observations. Again we note that the Kenyan children are more frequently responsible than the children in the other samples: both the girls and the boys are in charge at least twice as frequently as the children in the other samples.

Table 2.12 also presents the percentage of the Spot Observations in which boys and girls (all children in the samples, not just children who had siblings of the appropriate age) are seen holding or carrying a lap child. In those samples where any children are observed holding or carrying lap children, girls are observed to do so at least twice as frequently as boys (significant for the pooled sample).

Table 2.12. Children's involvement in child care

	Percentage of observations in which children aged 5 and over (who have a sibling 0–3 years old) are responsible for a lap child or a knee child					
	Responsible for lap child[a]			Responsible for knee child[b]		
Community (Six Cultures)	Girls (%)	Boys (%)	Diff.	Girls (%)	Boys (%)	Diff.
Nyansongo	32 (5)	22 (4)	+10	11 (3)	31 (3)	−20
Juxtlahuaca	13 (7)	6 (8)	+7	17 (5)	9 (6)	+8
Tarong	9 (3)	9 (3)	0	13 (3)	13 (3)	0
Taira	15 (7)	6 (3)	+9	27 (5)	19 (3)	+8
Khalapur	9 (7)	1 (4)	+8	0 (3)	0 (1)	0
Orchard Town	10 (1)	0 (1)	+10	0 (1)	0 (21)	0

	Percentage of observations in which children aged 5–7 are holding a lap child or engaged in child care (for child of any age)					
	Holding a lap child			Engaged in child care		
Community (Spot Observations)	Girls (%)	Boys (%)	Diff.	Girls (%)	Boys (%)	Diff.
Nyansongo	14	7	+7	21	8	+13
Vihiga	10	1	+9	14	4	+10
Ngeca	7	3	+4	6	3	+3
Conacoste/ Santo Domingo	3	1	+2	9	6	+3
Santa Barbara	6	0	+6	10	0	+10
Claremont	0	0	0	2	0	+2

a. The number of children with a sibling aged 0–18 months are given in parentheses.
b. The number of children with a sibling aged 18–30 months are given in parentheses.

Another section of Table 2.12 shows the percentage of observations in the Six Culture Sample where children are judged to be in charge of a knee child (18–30 months). In this case the judgment was based on the fact that there were no adults present and the sample child was the oldest child in the setting. The ethnographic data indicate that the oldest child in Nyansongo, Tarong, Juxtlahuaca, and Taira would be held responsible if anything happened to the knee child that could have been prevented with proper supervision. It can be seen that the gender differences are less consistent than those reported for the care of lap babies. For example, Nyan-

Ngeca girl nurse (Frances M. Cox, 1975)

songo knee children are supervised as often by older boys as by older
girls. These knee children liked to join the boys who were herding
cattle in the pastures, which undoubtedly explains the high frequency
with which boys are found to be the oldest child in settings with
knee children. In some cultural communities knee children are almost

never supervised by older children; for example, the few knee children in the Khalapur and Orchard Town families were never observed alone with older siblings.

Finally, Table 2.12 presents the percentage of the Spot Observations in which a girl or boy of 5–7 years is observed doing child care. This includes the care of both lap and knee children, and care is defined here as active caretaking or entertaining, not just being in the vicinity of or talking to a young child. The girls' scores are higher in each of the six samples (and significantly higher for the pooled sample).

Recent research reports on the New Sample and other communities indicate similar findings. Seymour's discussion of her findings for Bhubaneswar (1985) is particularly interesting because it demonstrates the interaction of mother's workload, child's gender, and family status in determining the amount of child care and other responsible tasks assigned to children 6–10 years of age. In lower-status families where the mothers work outside the home, girls take care of younger children six times more frequently than do middle- and upper-status girls. Lower-status boys perform child care twice as frequently as middle-status boys, while upper-status boys are never observed caring for younger children. In all three status groups girls perform child care more frequently than boys, the difference being three times greater in the lower-status families.

Rogoff (1981b) presents findings based on the spot observations of 9-year-old children in San Pedro, Guatemala. The girls are observed caring for a younger sibling three times more frequently than boys (17 percent versus 6 percent, respectively).

The spot observations made in Kokwet by Harkness (1975) of children's companions and activities randomized over three periods of the day corroborate the gender differences indicated by the ethnographic and social-interaction data for this community. Kokwet girls aged 2–6 are observed tending babies in 9 percent of the observations, versus 1 percent for boys. Similarly, girls aged 7–14 are observed tending babies in 8 percent of observations, versus 3 percent for boys.

Sieley (1975) also made spot observations in the adjacent Kipsigis community, where she observed 58 children aged 6–7 years and 47 children aged 10–11. One task she described was "baby care," which included comforting or entertaining a baby, keeping it away from the open cooking fire, and protecting it from overexposure to the sun, eating dirt, and being hurt by other children. In the 6–7 age group, 48 percent of the girls and 34 percent of the boys were observed caring for babies. In the 10–11 age group the differences are greater, with the girls observed caring for babies more than twice as often as boys (56 versus 25 percent).

Wenger's study (1983) in the large polygynous homesteads in Kaloleni, Giriamaland, Kenya, involved spot observations of who was nearest to the focal child, who occupied his social interactional space, and who was within the compound. She found that infants (under 18 months) are more often present in the interactional space of 2- to 11-year-old girls than of boys, especially at ages 8–11, when boys' contact with infants drops dramatically while that of girls rises. Girls are also involved in doing child care more often than boys (15 versus 8 percent).

Cross-cultural studies of larger samples of societies have involved ratings of ethnographic data (Barry, Bacon, and Child 1957, 1967; Barry and Paxton, 1971). These studies furnish final supportive evidence of transcultural gender differences in the assignment of infant and child care. The Barry, Bacon, and Child ratings were of "pressure toward nurturance" and were judged in large part by ethnographic statements about the assignment of child care. These researchers found pressure toward nurturance to be greater for girls than for boys in 82 percent of the 33 societies in which they found sufficient ethnographic data to make a judgment.

On the basis of all these converging sets of findings, we conclude that girls throughout the world are in the presence of lap children more frequently than are boys, and that the former care for lap and knee children more frequently. The data do not, however, suggest *why* girls are the more frequent companions of very young children. There are several possible explanations, with some evidence to support each one. First, girls may be assigned to the care of young children more often than boys because mothers want to train girls for their future mothering roles. Some evidence for this explanation will be given in Chapter 3. Second, the difference may result from children's own responses to mothers' commands. Perhaps mothers request the help of both boys and girls, but girls are more likely to cooperate or comply with maternal responses. Chapter 4 presents data showing girls to be more cooperative and compliant with mothers' commands. Third, girls may be more attracted to and interested in lap and knee children than are boys of the same age. A large number of studies of U.S. samples have found females of various ages, including preschoolers, to display more interest than males in babies (see the data and reviews in Berman, 1986; Berman, Monda, and Myerscough, 1977; Edwards and Lewis, 1979; Edwards and Whiting, 1980; Feldman and Nash, 1979; Feldman, Nash, and Cutrona, 1977; Fogel, Melson, and Mistry, 1986; Frodi and Lamb, 1978). This interest may be a prepared response that leads girls to initiate more contact and interaction with lap and knee children, or the interest may be motivated by girls' identification with their mothers and desire to imitate maternal behavior. Because the three explanations are not incompatible (all could be true simultaneously), we believe that more research is needed into this striking and cross-culturally general phenomenon.

Children as Companions. Children are another major category of companions of the 2- to 10-year-olds in all the communities studied. In later chapters (especially Chapters 6 and 7) we will examine the amount and content of child–child social interaction and discuss the important developmental implications of this kind of interaction. Here we examine two features of children's companionship: first, the gender dimension (how often children are found in same-sex versus mixed-sex groupings), and second, the kinship dimension (how much contact they have with children who are relatives versus non-relatives). Of course, the organization of people in space and the social structure of households and neighborhoods govern the availability of child companions. As long as children are confined to the immediate environs of the home, their main companions are their siblings, half-siblings, and courtyard cousins. In places where children have more autonomy to explore the neighborhood, or where communal play areas or schools bring together large groups of children, children have more contact with non-relatives and more opportunity to divide themselves into sex- and age-segregated playgroups.

The tendency of children to prefer and associate more frequently with other children of the same sex is a well-known phenomenon in American psychology (see the review in Hartup, 1983). As reported in the literature, sometime after their second birthday both girls and boys begin to be attracted to same-sex peers and to direct more affiliative bids toward them. This same-sex preference develops earlier in some children than in others but is not correlated with degree of sex-typed behavior along other dimensions (for example, their toy preferences). By middle childhood, almost all children prefer same-sex playmates (at least for most activities), and children in groups segregate themselves by gender when given the opportunity, for example, in school work groups, the cafeteria, the playground, and after school. Exclusion and avoidance of the opposite sex become common features of group behavior. Of course, for gender segregation to occur, there must be a sufficient number of potential partners available. Usually what is needed is a pool of children who are close enough in age to be interested in one another's ideas and activities.

Table 2.13 presents findings on percentages of sex-segregated groups observed in the Six Culture and Spot Observation samples. The Six Culture estimates are the percentage of observations in which yard children (aged 4–5) and community children (aged 6–10) are found in settings with children of their own sex only. A setting was defined as the space in which the observer could monitor behavior and hear conversations. Averaging across samples, the Six Culture children are found in sex-segregated groups about a third of the time. Rather surprisingly, the scores for older children are not consistently higher than for the younger ones, and the small cultural differences show no interpretable patterns. As expected, girls and boys are about equally involved in sex-segregated groups (the sex differences balance out).

The Spot Observation findings provide a more detailed picture of 5- to 7-year-old children's preferences. The table shows that no children in any of the communities spend a great deal of time in settings with same-sex children only (no adults present). The scores range from 5 to 30 percent. However, when the closest person is a child, that child is likely to be of the focal child's sex. The percentages range from 42 to 72 percent, and most are over 50 percent. Furthermore, when children are observed interacting or engaged in the same activity with other children only (no adults present), then groups are frequently sex-segregated, especially in Nyansongo, Ngeca, and Claremont. Even more strikingly, when only *same-age* children are present in these interacting groups, then sex-segregated groups predominate. The scores range from 29 to 100 percent, and all but one (the 29 percent score of Ngeca girls) are over 50 percent.

Morelli (1986) has observed the social behavior of very young children, 3 years and under, in the rain forests of Zaire. Her observations indicate that, beginning at age 3, children in both Efe and Lese groups are more likely to play with same-sex individuals. The most frequent interactants or models for 3-year-old boys' sociability and play are boys aged 5–7; for girls, they are girls aged 1–5. That

Table 2.13. Percentage of observations in which children are in settings with children of the same sex only

Community (Six Cultures)	Age 4—5 years Girls (%)	Boys (%)	Diff.	Age 6–10 years Girls (%)	Boys (%)	Diff.
Nyansongo	31	28	+3	35	34	+1
Juxtlahuaca	40	21	+19	27	21	+6
Tarong	23	50	−27	32	23	+9
Taira	36	40	−4	23	35	−12
Khalapur	22	43	−21	23	60	−37
Orchard Town	49	22	+27	39	29	+10

Community (Spot Observations)	The child is present with same-sex children only (no adults are present)			Nearest child is the same sex (when nearest person is a child)			The group is sex-segregated (when children are interacting or engaged in the same activity with children only)			The group is sex-segregated (of children interacting or engaged in the same activity) when only same-age children are in the group		
	Age 5–7 years			Age 5–7 years			Age 5—7 years			Age 5–7 years		
	Girls (%)	Boys (%)	Diff.	Girls (%)	Boys (%)	Diff.	Girls (%)	Boys (%)	Diff.	Girls (%)	Boys (%)	Diff.
Nyansongo	14	22	−8	64	66	−2	60	67	−7	67	60	+7
Vihiga	10	5	+5	50	42	+8	36	32	+4	74	(no same-age groups)	
Ngeca	12	25	−13	42	69	−27	47	78	−31	29	78	−49
Conacoste/Santo Domingo	17	19	−2	61	55	+6	37	47	−10	62	59	+3
Santa Barbara	11	16	−5	58	57	+1	52	41	+11	100	100	0
Claremont	30	17	+13	72	54	+18	59	44	+15	84	75	+9

is, both boys and girls appear attracted to children of the same sex, and boys seem to prefer boys a few years older than themselves.

Wenger's study (1983) in Kaloleni, Kenya, suggests a dramatic increase between ages 2–3 and ages 8–11 in the frequency of observation of exclusively same-sex companions in children's interactional space (when adults are absent). At ages 2–3, girls' scores are 32 percent, boys' 22 percent, while at ages 8–11, the girls' scores are 45 percent, boys' 70 percent (a sex difference likely due to older girls' heavy involvement in infant care). Older children, of course, have much more opportunity than younger ones to go beyond their immediate family in search of companions.

Harkness and Super (1985) have analyzed their Kokwet, Kenya, 30-minute observations of children aged 18 months to 9 years in terms of the composition of children's groups. The children were observed at home in their compounds, where the number of people present usually varied from five to eight, including members of the immediate family, half-siblings, and neighbors. Harkness and Super do not report on the frequency of single-sex groups but instead present findings on the percentage of males present in the peer group, where the peer group refers to children of the same age level (0 to 2.9, 3 to 5.9, and 6 to 8.9 years). The proportion of males present in the peer group is very similar for boys and girls under age 6 but diverges sharply at ages 6–9, when the gender composition of boys' groups is 67 percent male and that of the girls is 76 percent female. Thus, the older children spend more time in sex-segregated than in mixed peer groups.

Finally, Ellis, Rogoff, and Cromer (1981) have used the spot-observation method to evaluate the degree of age- and sex-segregated companionship among U.S. children, aged 1–12, observed on summer afternoons at home and outdoors in a middle-income neighborhood of Salt Lake City, Utah. The groups were typically small, averaging about three children. The findings show that sex-segregated groups increase significantly with children's age; sex-segregated companionship is not more common than mixed-sex companionship until ages 7–8. Interestingly, children in same-sex groups are more likely to be with near-age than cross-age companions, while the reverse is true of children in mixed-sex groups, who are more likely to be with mixed-age than same-age companions. Sex segregation seems to be a feature of same-age, not mixed-age, social interaction.

In sum, our findings taken together with those from the other studies suggest that the emergence of same-sex preferences in childhood is a cross-culturally universal and robust phenomenon. Moreover, there are some suggestions that sex segregation emerges especially in peer groups rather than in mixed-age groupings. In Chapter 7 we will discuss in more detail older children's seeming avoidance of the opposite sex. There our analyses will go beyond the topic of who is merely present in children's interactional space to the actual content of that interaction.

Another important dimension of children's companionship is their kin relationship. Our theory holds that kinship as well as age and gender relationships affect the choreography of children's interaction. Table 2.14 presents findings from the Six Culture study for the percentage of observations in which children are found with relatives only. (We do not have comparable data from the Spot Observation samples.) Lap and knee children, of course, spend most of their time with relatives. It can be seen that the percentages are highest in Nyansongo, where, as we have noted, the children spend the majority of their time on family-owned land (an average of 76 percent for 4- to 5-year-olds, 68 percent for 6- to 10-year-olds). The percentages are lowest in Taira, where yard children, accompanied by their knee-child siblings, roam the public areas of the compact village (11 percent for 4- to 5-year-olds, 7 percent for 6- to 10-year-olds). In Orchard Town there is a dramatic change between ages 4–5 and ages 6–10, when children enter school: the percentage of observations with only kin present drops from an average of 60 percent to an average of 3 percent. Gender differences are not consistent across samples.

The literature of related studies, unfortunately, offers few studies with which we can compare these findings. Ellis, Rogoff, and Cromer (1981), in their summertime Salt Lake City study, do report that children are more often found in groups containing at least one related child (usually a sibling) than in groups composed solely of unrelated children (40 percent versus 20 percent of the observations, respectively). The likelihood of being solely with unrelated children increases with children's age.

In Chapter 6 we will return to the topic of interaction between children who are kin versus non-kin and discuss the implications of the two types of experience.

Table 2.14. Percentage of observations in which children are with relatives only

	Age 4—5 years			Age 6–10 years		
Community	Girls (%)	Boys (%)	Diff.	Girls (%)	Boys (%)	Diff.
Nyansongo	81	71	+10	67	68	−1
Juxtlahuaca	44	71	−27	57	41	+16
Tarong	58	60	−2	38	55	−17
Taira	8	14	−6	6	8	−2
Khalapur	50	56	−6	48	36	+12
Orchard Town	65	55	+10	4	2	+2

Conclusions

The best predictors of the companions available to young children are the composition of households (including the arrangements for sleeping and eating), the division of labor between the mother and father that regulates the routine of family life, and the settlement pattern that organizes the location of houses and work areas in space. The workload of the mother is an important determinant of the amount of work that is expected of children under the age of 10. The location of gardens, pastures, wells and other sources of water, stands of trees used for firewood, and markets determines how far from home children go when performing chores. The degree to which families know and trust one another and the safety of the environment are predictors of the amount of autonomy granted to young children to leave the home setting. In all of the samples, autonomy increases with age. The autonomy of girls is most restricted in those societies that emphasize gender differences from early childhood onward.

There is more similarity in the daily companions of lap and knee children than in those of yard and community children. Culture assumes a more powerful influence as children enter the world beyond the confines of the family and neighborhood group. In the early years, children's companions in all the sample communities are those individuals who sleep and eat together and share the house and yard. Even at the yard and community age, children still spend most of their time with siblings, half-siblings, and close patrilineal relatives in the communities of Kenya. In contrast, older children have more opportunity to leave the family compound in communities with clustered housing where neighbors trust one another and supervise one another's children, as in Taira.

The spot observations demonstrate that children are found further from home when they are assigned chores than when they are engaged in undirected activity. Overall, boys are found farther from home than girls, especially during undirected time. Three of the communities especially restrict the physical autonomy of older girls: in Khalapur and Juxtlahuaca and in upper- and middle-status homes in Bhubaneswar, girls are granted less autonomy than boys. These are societies in which the differential status of men and women is most overt (in terms of women's deference to men), and this is easily observed by young children.

Girls are assigned more work for the family than boys in all the communities, with the exception of the samples in the United States, where none of the children are expected to do many chores, and the Kenyan communities, where boys pasture cattle. With the exception of work with large animals, most of the chores assigned to both girls and boys are in the domain of adult women's work. Although boys may be required to act as child nurses, girls are observed caring for lap babies more frequently.

Girls more often than boys are observed in settings with their mothers and with younger children, while boys are found more often than girls in settings with adult males. Boys especially have more contact with their fathers in those societies having large animals that are the responsibility of the men. Boys also have relatively greater opportunity to be with their fathers in the societies where men and women work together, as in Tarong and Taira.

Both girls and boys are more likely to be in sex-segregated groups of child companions after the onset of middle childhood. Sex-segregated groups are more prominent in peer than in mixed-age groupings. In all of the communities except Taira (where children are free to wander), lap, knee, and yard children have contact mostly with children who are their relatives. After children begin school, they then gain opportunity to interact with non-relatives.

These, then, are the social settings that the children in our samples frequent and the individuals who are their potential social partners. To understand further the importance of children's daily companions in the development of patterns of social behavior, we need to examine the profiles of behavior in different types of dyadic interaction. The following chapters will show how these profiles vary between types of dyads in systematic ways, across all of the cultural communities. We will consider the developmental implication of these profiles for the most prominent and frequently occurring types of dyadic interaction.

Chapter 3

Parents as Teachers and Models of Social Behavior

In America it is assumed by most psychologists and laymen that parents play the major role in the development of their children's social behavior. For this reason our exploration of the genesis of patterns of social behavior begins with the analysis of parental behavior, in particular, maternal behavior, since in all our samples mothers are responsible for the care of infants and preschool-age children. Fathers appear rarely in the observations, which were limited to the daylight hours. However, we do not dismiss the role of fathers in shaping social behavior. Indeed, their very absence may be an important influence.

It would be interesting to determine how much of maternal behavior is shaped primarily by biologically prepared responses associated with reproductive functions and how much is shaped by environmental and cultural influences. Unfortunately our data cannot speak directly to this issue. If maternal behavior as observed and recorded in our diverse sample communities is similar, this may be the result of biologically prepared responses or it may mean that raising infants and young children to maturity requires similar behaviors in any cultural context and there is little leeway for variation.

There are striking similarities in maternal behavior as we have observed it in the sample societies, and these similiarities are surely related to requirements for rearing children who will live to reproduce themselves. There are also differences that are clearly a result of the experience of living in different ecological and sociocultural niches. For example, temperature influences styles of clothing and the amount of time a mother spends dressing children and teaching them self-help skills; the topography of the terrain and the flora and fauna dictate the amount of supervision required for protecting children from physical harm and determine the parental rules that restrict or grant autonomy to the growing child; basic economic factors constrain the occupations of men and women and the daily subsistence and maintenance activities that demand the attention of the mothers; settlement patterns and household arrangements determine how much help or adult company women have during the years when they are caring for young children; maternal beliefs about the nature of the child (for example, about innate, unchangeable qualities versus capacities to learn and be taught) dictate the style of interaction between mother and child.

The analysis of the interaction of mothers with sons and daughters reveals both the similarities across the sample societies that are determined by sex and age and the differences that are determined by culture. As we have seen, mothers in most of the sample communities train girls earlier than boys, and they believe in the faster development of girls. They assign girls more tasks and expect more help from them in caring for younger siblings and performing household chores. The differential treatment of girls and boys is greatest in those societies where there is a clear dichotomy in the daily lives and habits of men and women.

Because mothers are the figures who most frequently set their children's daily schedules, they have the power to shape gender differences by assigning sons and daughters to different settings. In these settings, boys and girls are exposed to different role models, practice different social behaviors, learn different skills, and acquire different cognitive maps of the world in which they live. The power of mothers to assign girls and boys to different settings may be the single most important factor in shaping gender-specific behaviors in childhood.

Universal Dimensions of Maternal Behavior: Tasks of the Socializer in the Early Childhood Years

Mothers and other caregivers have a similar task all over the world in caring for, socializing, and transmitting culture to their children. In broad outline, the maternal role requires five main types of behavior. First, the caretaker must see to the physical well-being of her children by paying attention to their nutritional and other health needs and by protecting them from physical discomfort and harm. Second, the caretaker must relieve the child from anxiety and fear by offering emotional comfort, often in the form of physical contact.

Third, she must see that the child learns sphincter control and proper hygiene. Fourth, she must help the child to learn the culturally approved forms of etiquette and the norms of social behavior. Finally, she must teach the child the skills expected for the early years. Since many of these behaviors and skills are prerequisites for acceptance and survival as viable members of society, the behavior of caretakers the world over is similar.

The details of these five types of behavior may vary, but they share the universal goals just outlined. In some societies the task of keeping a lap or knee child alive is more difficult than in others. Infant mortality was high in subsaharan Africa and India in the 1950s, when the Six Culture study was in progress. In the subsaharan African communities, mothers kept lap children off the ground most of the time; because there were no cradles, cribs, or baby carriages, mothers carried babies on their backs until they were able to walk, thus protecting them from the parasites that infested the ground shared by animals and humans. In Khalapur, North India, the animals were kept out of the family courtyard, and mothers and servants frequently swept the floor to keep it clean. The mothers, who were home all day, could put the babies to sleep on cots or could hold them while performing household chores. In Orchard Town (U.S.A.), Tarong (Philippines), and Taira (Okinawa), keeping a child alive was less difficult than in Africa or India because of the more temperate climates.

Styles of comforting young children vary. In those societies in which lap and knee children are frequently carried, caretakers use physical contact to offer solace and rely less on verbal communication. The age varies at which these caretakers expect children to give up being suckled and carried, yet remains within boundaries set by universal environmental and physiological pressures. In agricultural societies that lack contraceptives, babies are born on an average of every two years, and thus a child must be weaned by age 2 so that the following child can nurse. In some societies the weanling may be allowed occasional comfort and regression by returning to the breast, but in most cases it is expected to relinquish all nursing. Furthermore, in many societies this is expected as soon as the mother is sure that she is pregnant because of a belief that the milk of a pregnant mother will poison the child, or that a nursing child will harm the fetus by depriving it of the nourishment it needs. Weaning from the back does not necessarily coincide with weaning from the breast; the weight of the child and the work demands of the mother set the age at which the child is customarily weaned from the mother's back. The Six Culture studies suggest that weaning from the back (and the physical contact that carrying provides) may be more difficult and stressful for the infant than is weaning from the breast.

Sphincter control is easier to teach in societies with warm climates where young children spend the majority of the time out of doors and wear few clothes. There is less concern for accidents in houses where there are no rugs, upholstered furniture, or polished floors.

The effect of cultural values is obvious in the training for appropriate social behavior. Perhaps the greatest variation is in the behavior expected of a child in interaction with parents and elders: some societies encourage a great deal of adult-child interaction, while others discourage it. When close relatives live in the same or adjacent households and there is frequent interaction between adults, customary rules protect adult sociability from the interruptions that occur frequently in more child-centered households. The emphasis on proper greeting behavior also varies; it is taught earlier in those societies that rely on kin for support. In the traditional societies of subsaharan Africa and in societies with large extended families, children are usually discouraged from initiating interaction with adults. As in earlier periods of American family life, children are taught to speak when spoken to; respect and obedience to elders are valued.

Socializers must also train for self-reliance and adult-like behavior, but their expectations vary for children of various stages of development. In preindustrial agricultural societies where mothers are involved in the production of food, socializers may consider it essential for children to care for their own hunger and thirst at an early age and to learn skills for participating in family work, but they place little value on learning to sleep, play, or work alone. This pattern is still characteristic of the Kenyan samples. In situations where a mother's workload is less demanding, in contrast, she does not need to encourage self-reliance. For example, the Khalapur mothers of North India, who are home all day in households with their mother-in-law and sisters-in-law, continued to bathe children as old as 11 years of age and to hand-feed children of 4 and 5.

During the childhood period, rudimentary skills necessary for adult life are transmitted to the child. The skills taught vary with the ecology of the community and with associated patterns of the adult division of labor (see LeVine, 1974, 1980). Both gender and cultural differences can be seen in the skill training of children. It is probably here that we can identify the most salient gender differences: boys and girls often have different experiences in the amount and timing of pressure they receive to help with the family work. Furthermore, simple and complex societies differ in the degree to which the skills required for survival and success in adulthood involve manipulation of the physical world or the manipulation of symbols. In societies in which subsistence agriculture is the occupation of the majority of adults, there are many important skills that can be taught and mastered in early childhood. In societies with more complex forms of economy, especially those with highly developed occupational specialization, literacy may be the most important skill. The learning of symbolic systems may begin early and continue for many years before the child can master the skills required of adults. Specialized schooling or apprentice training may also be needed to prepare the child for an adult occupational role, but this training occurs beyond the first 10 to 12 years of life. In the preschool and school years, children must first master the cognitive habits and literacy skills necessary for success in complex industrial societies.

In postindustrial societies with occupational specialization and advanced technology, mothers may value the ability of children to do things for themselves, especially if they do not share living space with other adults or have help in child care. Yet they may delay or delegate the teaching of adult skills and even discourage their practice until required by the actual assumption of adult roles (Sears, Maccoby, and Levin, 1957; Whiting and Whiting, 1975). The Orchard Town mothers, home all day but usually alone with the preschool children, teach them early to feed themselves and to be self-reliant in play and cleanliness habits, but they postpone teaching many adult skills. For example, Orchard Town girls may receive no training in the care of lap and knee children and may embark on motherhood with no practice in the prerequisite skills. This inexperience is never the case in preindustrial societies, where most children serve as child nurses.

Thus, although the caretakers of young children do have goals that are universal, there are societal differences in the behaviors of caretakers that are related to the community's ecology, basic economy, social organization, and value systems.

The amount of help a mother receives from others is an important determinant of her style of interacting with her children. In our sample of societies the mother has the major responsibility for the care and training of children of the ages we are considering, but there is great variation in the help that she receives from other adults. If the usual household includes unmarried siblings of the mother, grandparents, or co-wives, she may have helpers who are available around the clock. If she lives in an isolated homestead, however, she has only her husband to help her.

The role of fathers in the care of young children varies (for review, see Katz and Konner, 1981). In some societies, such as those of traditional subsaharan Africa, fathers customarily have little or no contact with infants and only rare contact with toddlers. Fathers do not begin to interact frequently with children until they are about 5 years old and have mastered the rudiments of socially approved behavior. In general, the father's role in child care is in large part determined by the more general aspects of the division of labor between husband and wife, the degree of marital aloofness or intimacy, and the associated arrangement of living space. Where husband and wife sleep and eat apart, the father's contact with his child is delayed, and he typically interacts more frequently with sons than with daughters. In contrast, where husband and wife share a bedroom and there are no other adults in the house, the father inevitably becomes involved in child care.

In analyzing the cultural differences in maternal behavior, two variables appear to be particularly important: the mother's workload and her beliefs about the nature of the child and what factors determine the course of development. In assessing women's workloads we have considered the following variables: the number of people responsible for the care and training of the child; the average number of children a mother bears; the work she does both inside and outside the home; and the types of skills that the community believes a child should learn during early childhood to ensure success in the adult world. Mothers who must carry water from wells, streams, or town taps, who must gather fuel for rudimentary hearth cooking, and who must grind their own flour on stones have the heaviest workloads in terms of household tasks. Women who are responsible for preparing the soil and for planting, weeding, and harvesting the food for their families have the heaviest workloads outside the house.

Maternal behavior is influenced by the culturally shared value placed on children. In societies where children are valued both for their present help with work and their future support in times of conflict and old age, and where infant mortality is high, mothers do not attempt to prevent pregnancy and are honored for giving birth to many children (LeVine, 1983).

Maternal behavior is also influenced by beliefs about the nature of a child and the parents' ability and responsibility for shaping the child's character. What are the shared beliefs about the capabilities of a child? Which characteristics are believed to be inherited or "God-given," and which are believed to be responsive to teaching, thus requiring proper socialization? At one extreme are the Indian mothers of Khalapur and Bhubaneswar, and at the other are the American mothers of Orchard Town (Fischer and Fischer, 1963; Minturn and Hitchcock, 1963; Seymour, 1975, 1980). In accordance with the caste system of traditional India, the former believed that a child's character was preordained—his fate written on his brow—and there was little that could be done to shape a child's personality or behavior. Parents saw their roles as physical caretakers, with the major responsibility of ensuring that the child survived to live out his preordained life course. In contrast, mothers in a community such as Orchard Town, New England, believed that their infant was a bundle of potentialities and that it was the task of the mother to assess these potentialities and to direct the training of the child so as to maximize them. Advice and counsel books, newspaper columns, the advice of pediatricians, test scores—every possible piece of information was scanned to help the mother direct her efforts and channel the child's behavior to ensure achievement in the type of life valued by the parents and society (Whiting and Whiting, 1960).

Ecological Constraints on Mothers: Three Profiles of Maternal Behavior

How do these sociocultural conditions influence the behavior of mothers as we have observed them interacting with their children? To assess the influence of culture, we have contrasted the profiles of the mothers in the 12 societies for which we have comparable data.

There is striking similarity across our samples of mothers in the relative frequency of the 23 social behaviors observed and coded. Twelve of the 23 behaviors occur with sufficient frequency to warrant analysis and can be combined into four categories. First, mothers may nurture children. We have combined routine caregiving and the offering of help, attention, and support into a category of *nurturance*. Second, they may seek to teach their children appropriate skills, social behavior, and hygiene, and they may restrain their children from activities and behavior that are dangerous or considered socially undesirable. We have combined the assigning of chores or child care and the teaching of etiquette into a category of *training*. Third, they may seek to control their children when they are annoying by correcting, reprimanding, threatening, or punishing them. They may also command or dominate their children in order to fulfill their own needs—not for a prosocial purpose or to train their children. We have combined reprimanding, punishing, and seeking to dominate into a category of *control*. (Control seems distinct from training because the emphasis is on restraint and submission rather than on suggestions as to what constitutes acceptable and responsible behavior.) Fourth, mothers may interact with their children in a positive and friendly way: they may exchange information, tease their children, talk or laugh with them, express sociability by coming close or touching them, or use other gestures expressing positive feelings. We have combined all of these friendly behaviors into a category of *sociability*.

In addition to investigating behavior that mothers initiate or direct to their children, we have also assessed their compliance to their children's initiations. A "nurturant" mother would seem to be one who not only gives help and resources to her children, but also responds positively when her child seeks help, comfort, food, support, or information. Accordingly, a fifth category of maternal behavior was created, *responsiveness*, estimated by the percentage of time a mother fulfilled, rather than refusing or ignoring, the dependent requests of her child.

The four summary categories of initiated behavior together account for an average of 95 percent of the social acts of mothers toward children. Comparison of the rank order of the relative proportion of the four main categories of maternal behavior across the samples reveals three distinct maternal styles, which can be called the "training mother," the "controlling mother," and the "sociable mother." The training mother is found in all of our samples from subsaharan Africa (see Table 3.1). The controlling mother is found in Tarong, Philippines; Juxtlahuaca, Mexico; and the two North Indian communities, Khalapur and Bubaneswar. Finally, the sociable mother is found in Orchard Town, New England.

Table 3.1. Rank order of four summary categories in mothers' initiated behavior to children (averaging across all sex/age groups within each sample)

Samples	Training	Control	Sociability	Nurturance
African				
Kien-taa, Liberia	1	2	4	3
Kokwet, Kenya	1	2	3	4
Kisa, Kenya	1	2	3	4
Kariobangi, Kenya	1	2	4	3
Ngeca, Kenya	1	2	4	3
Nyansongo, Kenya	1	2	3	4
Non-African				
Bhubaneswar, India, lower class	3	1	4	2
Bhubaneswar, India, middle and upper classes	2	1	4	3
Khalapur, India	2	1	3	4
Tarong, Philippines	2	1	3	4
Juxtlahuaca, Mexico	2	1	4	3
Orchard Town, U.S.A.	3	1	2	4

The Training Mother

When the four summary categories of initiated behavior are rank-ordered for each of the 12 communities, training always ranks first in the subsaharan communities, accounting for a mean of 40 percent of a mother's observed initiated behavior to her child (averaging across the six samples and the three age groups). Controlling ranks second in these communities, accounting for an average of 25 percent, and an additional 29 percent is accounted for by initiated nurturance and sociability. (The remainder is miscellaneous.)

This profile of the training mother can be illustrated through a concrete example from Nyansongo, Kenya. The observation involves a mother working at home with her 5-year-old son. In a good-humored way, she monitors his behavior and keeps him on task weeding the banana grove. She allows him to interrupt his work only when she sends him in to get her a drink of water. All of her interaction with him involves behaviors in the summary categories of training and control.

Mother tells Joseph (boy, 5) to hoe in the banana grove (where maize will be planted) very near the house. Joseph hoes for a while. He wanders off into the grove, then returns to hoe again, pulling away the weeds with his hands.

Joseph returns to the yard where his mother is. As he comes past her, she tells him to bring her water for drinking. Joseph tries to go into the house to get it but his father and another man are repairing the doorway, chopping at wood with knives. The man tells Joseph to be careful and get out of the way while they're doing that. It is obvious to Joseph (and his mother who is sitting not far away) that he cannot get in to get her water. Joseph runs back to the banana grove and resumes hoeing.

Joseph makes a little squeaking sound while hoeing. His mother looks up at him and says, "Be careful in hoeing; you might hit yourself." Joseph does not answer.

After a bit, Joseph gives up hoeing, walks around mother.

Mother (laughing): "Are you with the devil, walking like that in circles? Go back to digging so that maize can be planted."

Joseph does not answer but returns to his hoeing. (LeVine and LeVine, field observations, 1956)

The data from Nyansongo actually involve only four initiated nurturant acts (2 percent) in mother-to-child behavior. Although this is an unusually low score, the average proportion of nurturance across the 12 communities is only 13 percent. Such generally low amounts of initiated nurturance may not be congruent with the common stereotype of the maternal role as focused on nurturing, but our data suggest that the stereotype should be revised. The picture of nurturance that emerges for the training mother is that of a compliantly nurturant mother, responsive to the dependency of her child when it is culturally defined as appropriate.

In the following example, a Nyansongo mother responds to her 4-year-old daughter's fear and need for nurturance when strangers (the ethnographer and his assistant) arrive:

Agnes runs into the house and comes out following her mother. As her mother greets us and chats with us, Agnes holds on to mother's skirt and her mother puts her arm around Agnes' head. Agnes snuggles against her mother's side. Mother goes into house and Agnes follows, staying inside with other children even when her mother comes out again.   (LeVine and LeVine, field observations, 1956)

The training mothers in subsaharan Africa believe that responsibility and obedience can and should be taught to young children. They begin teaching household, gardening, and animal husbandry skills at a comparatively early age. The Ngeca mothers we interviewed are typical: they believe that they should train a child to be a competent farmer, herdsman, and child nurse and that a child from age 2 on should be assigned chores that increase in complexity and arduousness with age. They punish their children for failure to perform these tasks responsibly or for stubbornly refusing to do what their elders request of them. They allow much of their children's learning to occur through observation and imitation; only occasionally do they instruct them explicitly. Moreover, mothers seldom praise their children lest they become proud, a trait that is unacceptable. They allow the major rewards for task performance to be intrinsic.

The Kien-taa mothers of Liberia follow a similar pattern. They begin training their children at an early age to perform economic tasks, to respect household property, not to waste food, and to follow health, safety, and hygiene rules (Erchak, 1980). In general, the "polite command" is the most common style used by parents with young children; bribing and praise are seldom seen. Parents may embed teaching in their commanding, however, by stating the reason why the act needs to be performed, as in the following example:

> P (Oldman Kpiti, boy, age 2½) is hungry.
> P begins to cry. Mother: "If you want to cry, go out so you don't make the baby cry." . . .
> P walks near fire and sits over firewood.
> Mother: "Move from the firewood before the rice wastes [spills]."
> P moves . . .   (Erchak, 1977, p. 122)

Our observations confirm that these strategies work. Young children see that work is required and expected of their older siblings. In the observations, they appear to try hard to imitate the competent behaviors of their older siblings. What Robert White (1959) has called "effectance" or "competence motivation" seems evident. For example, there are observations of children as young as 2 years trying to weed with a heavy, 24-inch *panga* knife. The Ngeca mothers do not discourage such attempts; they note the developing skills of their various children and assign tasks that are congruent with their capacities. In Nyansongo, girls as young as 3 are given their own hoes and work in the gardens with their mothers and older sisters without being asked. The 4- to 6-year-old girls voluntarily join the older girls and compete to see who can hoe a row fastest.

In the following observation a Nyansongo mother works in the garden with her 6-year-old son. She keeps him involved in the task of hoeing and praises him for his performance. Challenging fellow workers to competition is typical of Nyansongo adult work groups, and thus, by engaging her son in friendly competition, the mother treats him like an older individual (that is, a circumcised boy).

> Aloyse, hoeing a field beside his mother, stops working.
> Mother: "Finish that part quickly."
> Aloyse: "I am looking for some nails that I lost here."
> Mother: "Are you after nails, or digging?"
> Aloyse resumes hoeing. He comments, "Why is the soil so tough? Uh! Uh!"
> Mother: "You fool, why do you leave some places not properly dug?"
> Aloyse: "No. I do it properly. I want to work hard, finish this portion, then go into the shade."
> Mother: "Here or at home?"
> Aloyse (indicating nearby trees): "Here . . . You've gotten so close to me here, I must work hard."
> Mother: "I'm not so close. You're defeating me by digging so quickly."
> Aloyse (resting): "Oh, you're almost overtaking me, I must work hard."
> Mother: "Who dug here so crudely? You, Aloyse?"
> Aloyse: "No . . . I'm afraid you are overtaking me."
> Mother: "No, you are an *omomura* [circumcised boy, or young man—not really true of Aloyse, of course]. I'm just a woman—I can't overtake you."
> Aloyse: "I'm almost reaching the end! You're going to pass me again, and finish before me. It's because I dig properly."
> Mother laughs.
> Aloyse: "Oh, I see that you've passed me now."
> Mother: "No, you dig."
> Aloyse: "I'm strong, you can't surpass me."
> Mother: "Are you really strong? All right, then let's complete this."
> Aloyse works hard to finish. (LeVine and LeVine, field observations, 1956)

Why do the subsaharan mothers score so high in training and control? Our goal in analyzing cultural differences in maternal behavior has been to specify the sociocultural conditions that are associated with the different profiles. We cannot, of course, assess if there are constitutional or temperamental differences between groups of mothers and children. Similarly, our data do not permit us to explore in depth the cultural differences in beliefs, values, or other symbolic aspects of culture. Rather, our focus is on the insights we can get by looking at the daily lives of the mothers, the activities they perform, and the cast of characters with whom they share intimate space and interact on a daily basis. These factors capture our attention because they seem so directly and strongly related to differences in mother-child interaction worldwide.

As already noted, one of the most salient cross-cultural differences involves women's workloads, in particular, the amount of work they do above and beyond housework and child care (since housework and child care are primarily women's responsibility in all cultural communities; see D'Andrade, 1966; Friedl, 1975; Sanday, 1973, 1974; White, Burton, and Brudner, 1977; White and Dow, 1981). The training mothers are the major producers of food for the family. In general, women whose workload goes beyond housework and child care expect more help from their children and are observed to have a higher proportion of training mands in their interaction with their children. This is true even in American families, as found in many studies of employed mothers (Hoffman, 1974, 1977; Longfellow, Zelkowitz, and Saunders, 1982; Nye and Hoffman, 1963).

In Kien-taa, Liberia, and in all of the Kenyan samples, women are involved in subsistence agriculture and are responsible for the production of food for their children. In these subsaharan societies, the traditional division of labor requires that men be responsible for clearing and fencing the agricultural land and helping to prepare the soil, while women do the major planting, weeding, and harvesting of the subsistence crops. Men help their wives most in Kien-taa, Liberia, where the tropical rain forest must be cut back each year or two. Work groups of men do the majority of the clearing; the women follow, working the soil with simple short-handled hoes, and later doing the weeding. The farms are distant from the village, and women may walk 8 to 19 miles a day to care for their crops. Men help the women next most frequently in the Kipsigis community of Kokwet (Sieley, 1975). When oxen and plows were introduced to prepare the soil, the men (as in Europe and other parts of the world) took over the plowing, and the women were relieved from breaking the soil with hoes. In most of the Kenyan samples, women not only plant and weed but also prepare the soil. The amount of help they receive from their husbands in soil preparation depends on their husbands' other activities. In Ngeca, for example, the majority of young men have wage-earning or salaried jobs, and unless they hire help, their wives are left with all of the agricultural work. When men are employed in cities and cannot commute to their homes daily, women carry the entire responsibility for the day-to-day farm work. Hired labor and tractors remain a luxury. The Kisa wives whose husbands work in Nairobi and live in Kariobangi are responsible for the entire food production for their children. Some husbands return to their homesteads only once or twice a year (Weisner, 1976b, 1976c).

Cooperative work groups lighten the agricultural work in many of the sample African communities. In Kien-taa, work groups traditionally consisted of about 5 to 25 people who prepared the rice farms— a work group of men cutting and clearing the land, work groups of women planting and weeding, and men and women harvesting together (Erchak, 1977). Nyansongo and Ngeca women took part in agricultural work groups that might include co-wives, sisters-in-law, or lineage mates. On Ngeca farms where the household head has allocated garden plots to his adult daughters as well as sons, women's work groups might also consist of mothers and daughters.

In Kenya, cattle were the main form of traditional wealth. Marriages were sealed by the payment of bridewealth, with the family of the bride receiving an agreed-upon number of cattle or other type of payment. The care of livestock (cattle, sheep, and goats) was the province of men and ideally still continues to be so among the families who still have sufficient land for pastures. Women have always helped in the milking. In most of the Kenyan communities we have studied, grade cattle have replaced the native herds of precolonial days and milk has become a cash crop. Both Kokwet and Ngeca had dairies, cooperatively owned and operated, at the time of the study.

In those areas where population pressure has drastically reduced the acreage of farms, women may also be responsible for getting fodder and water for the cows that are kept in the small fenced area adjacent to the house. The major burden of animal husbandry also tends to fall on women whose husbands have wage jobs.

In addition to their farming and livestock tasks, the subsaharan women have household chores that are time-consuming and require physical exertion. The women are responsible for providing water for the households and, with the exception of Kien-taa, for supplying their households with fuel. At the time of the field studies, none of the communities had houses with piped-in water and few had water taps in the yard. The task of bringing water from the nearest stream or the town water supply was an arduous one—the hours of work a day dependent on the distance. A similar situation prevailed with the collection of fuel. Because of cost and cooking preferences, only a few of the families in our subsaharan samples had charcoal or paraffin burners used on a regular basis. The families in Nairobi and some of the wealthier rural families cooked over charcoal *jikos*, but in the majority of households families still cooked with firewood, using a simple hearth with three large stones on which the cooking pots rested. Wealthy families might buy their wood, and some fortunate families had wood on their land. In Ngeca, however, most families had small farms and no stand of wattle, the main source of firewood; many women had to walk six miles to a large farm owned by a wealthy man and work in return for being allowed to take home as much wood as they could carry. The women of Kien-taa did not have to collect firewood, since this is a man's task, nor care for cattle, because the disease-bearing tsetse flies make the keeping of dairy cows impractical.

The processing of grains can be an arduous and time-consuming task. With the exception of Kien-taa, however, all the women in the sample communities were able to get their grains processed at a mill and thus were spared the hours of labor traditionally spent grinding maize, millet, or sorghum flour on a grinding stone.

The daily life of the rural women in our subsaharan samples is thus in broad outline very similar. A portrait of the routine of the Ngeca women can serve as the example for all of the sample communities in rural Kenya. In Ngeca women are the first to rise in the morning; they get up at dawn to light the fire and prepare whatever breakfast is customary, sometimes gruel, frequently just tea. Women depart for their gardens around 10:00 A.M. If there are adults or older children at home to supervise the knee child and feed the younger children their midday meal, the women may stay until 3:00 P.M. An infant accompanies the mother to the field until it is able to space its feedings three to four hours apart. Before this time a child nurse may accompany the mother to the field and carry and entertain the baby at the edge of the garden until it is ready to nurse. If a woman has no one at home to tend to the midday meal, she may return home about noon and resume gardening in the late afternoon. The evening meal of maize and beans, the daily fare of most Kenyan rural farmers, is often put on to cook in the early morning or at noon, and the fire must be tended for three or four hours, a task assigned to children as young as 5 years old.

Early in the morning or in the late afternoon, or perhaps at both times, the Ngeca mother makes at least one trip to the stream or town water supply to get a five-gallon container of water. She may also milk the cows in the late afternoon. At least once a week she collects firewood, carrying heavy loads to the house with a tump line.

As in other Kenyan groups, the Ngeca woman does not expect her husband to stay and help around the home. He is free to set his schedule as he wishes—seeing to fences, monitoring his cash crops, tending to the family land or that of a neighbor, visiting his age mates, or going to the community center to gossip and drink tea or beer with his male friends.

A Ngeca woman's workload includes producing and caring for children. Kenyans value a large number of children, and up until very recently women have not attempted to limit the size of their families. The amount of assistance a woman receives in caring for her children depends on the number of other women in her homestead and their willingness to cooperate. Many of the mothers in our study did live on homesteads with other adult women. An average of about one-third of the women had co-wives, and many also had sisters-in-law living on their homesteads. The largest homesteads included men married to more than one woman and some of their married sons with their families.

It is generally characteristic of the subsaharan women that they associate frequently with other women: they may work in cooperative groups, travel together to market, and visit their neighbors and female kin. Their own sisters and their nieces and nephews are often to be found staying with them, and they like to travel to see others on a fairly regular basis. Even the urban Kariobangi women, more isolated in their small apartments, know where all of their natal kin and friendly in-laws live in Nairobi, and the chief social activity of the women is to visit together around the city.

Nevertheless, the actual cooperation that exists between co-resident women varies somewhat from group to group. Co-wives in Kien-taa, Liberia, are expected to share work—the eldest wife assigning work to her younger co-wife. However, the polygynous households often run less than smoothly as a result of jealousy among co-wives (Erchak, 1977). In the Kenyan groups it is up to the women to share or not share, although the male head of the homestead attempts to maintain peaceful and cooperative relationships among the women. In some homesteads the co-wives and sisters-in-law are friendly and willing to help each other, while in others there are hostility, jealousy, and tensions among the women. Grandmothers on the large homesteads find it difficult to divide their favors among the families of their married sons and often remain aloof. The occasional maternal grandmother living with a married daughter was the most likely to give substantial help with child care and housework.

Given this picture of their workload, it is not surprising that the Ngeca women look to their children for help in their busy routine. From an early age, mothers train children by assigning work that they are capable of doing. Girls as young as 2 years of age are expected to begin helping. A mother returning from the fields will greet her 2-year-old who has been cared for during her absence by a child nurse. Soon, as the mother goes about preparing the evening meal, she will ask the knee child to carry out the potato peels or fetch a pan or spoon. Older girls will be sent to get water, and their younger sisters will often request that they too be allowed to go to the stream. Boys who have been pasturing the cattle may be old enough to milk the cows and carry it to the cooperative dairy. Children may be sent to the store to buy sugar, tea, or cooking oil. Mothers assign the chores and set up the routines for their children of different ages. If they have no daughters of the appropriate age, they expect boys to be child nurses and carry water. If they have no sons, the girls may pasture and water cattle.

The daily routines and workloads of the women in our other Kenyan samples do not differ greatly from the Ngeca pattern. All the mothers spend time training their children to do work for the family. By the time the children are 6–8 years of age, an average of 30 percent of the mothers' initiated interaction in the Kenyan samples involves task assignment: running errands, cleaning the house, preparing food, carrying wood and water, caring for animals, performing agricultural work. An additional 10 percent of mothers' initiations are focused on older children's care of younger siblings.

There are, certainly, predictable variations in mothers' daily schedules, both within and across the samples. The greatest cause of variation is related to the changes associated with modernization, that is, a community's increased involvement in the economy of the industrial world, leading to increased dependence on its products. Some aspects of modernization lead to a decrease in women's daily labor. For example, families with wage incomes or income from the sale of cash crops can buy goods such as processed flour; they can also hire trucks to carry food and water for their livestock. With the introduction of metal roofs and rainbarrels or of a town water supply and pipes to people's yards, hours are cut from the women's workload. Even more time is saved when women use store-bought charcoal or kerosene. On the other hand, some aspects of modernization can increase the workload of women. If the husband works for wages away from the rural community, his wife is left to do all or most of the farm work unless there are hired laborers. Most revolutionary of all, when schools arrive, particularly tuition-free government schools, mothers lose their child helpers; the school-aged children disappear during the day and cannot help their mothers as before.

The Controlling Mother

The profile of the training mother is characteristic of the agriculturalists of subsaharan Africa, but what of the other subsistence farmers in our cross-cultural sample? Tarong (Philippines), Juxtlahuaca (Mexico), and Khalapur (North India) were also communities of primarily subsistence farmers in the 1950s when the observations were made (Minturn and Hitchcock, 1963; Nydegger and Nydegger, 1963; Romney and Romney, 1963). However, the profile of maternal behavior in these cultural communities is different from that in the subsaharan African groups because controlling ranks first, training second. The same is true for both lower-class and middle- and upper-class groups in Bhubaneswar, India (see Table 3.1). These groups illustrate the controlling mother profile.

An example of this profile is seen in an observation from Khalapur, India, focused on Sriipal, age 4. The child annoys his mother by fighting over and playing carelessly with a necklace, which she wants him to keep inside. He eventually obeys, but only after an extended delay. All of her interaction with him involves reprimands, threats, and commands.

> Sriipal has a rather large chain around his neck. Viikram (boy, age 4) is near him. Some women are working nearby.
> Viikram wants the chain, and Sriipal says, "No, it is mine."
> Viikram comes back to the observer. His mother says to Sriipal,

concerning the chain, "Put this inside. Otherwise I will break your face. Put it inside." He goes to the corner and puts it by the milk *chuulaa*. He stands there and then stands by the cooking hearth for a while.

Mother says, "Go and put that [chain] inside."

Sriipal says, "I'm not going to lose it. I will play, and then I will put it in." He takes the chain and says, "I don't know where to open it." He tries to unhook it, and then he goes inside.   (Minturn, field observations, 1955)

An example of a controlling mother is seen in an observation of a Tarong mother with her children:

The mother is sitting with her infant in her lap, idly chatting with a woman friend while her two young daughters, ages 5 and 2, orbit around her. She interrupts her talk with her friend to deliver two mild reprimands to the 2-year-old, Luzilda. When the girl grinds candy between her teeth, the mother says, "You are eating like that again? Your teeth!" When the child fusses to be held, the mother gently pushes her off, saying, "Oh, you are not ashamed!" Similarly, to her older girl, Zosima, she delivers several reprimands. When the girl bothers her, she says, "You behave, I say, huh?" When Zosima disturbs the sleeping baby, she slaps her lightly on the bottom and says, "Do not do that." When Zosima tries to remove the baby's spare diaper pin attached to the mother's skirt, she says, "Don't get that, huh? That is the baby's pin."   (Nydegger and Nydegger, field observations, 1955)

Note that in both observations the children are idle, not working at tasks. The mothers in both examples act as if they would like to ignore their children and work or socialize, but the children will not stay quietly out of the way.

Two sociocultural factors seem important in predicting the controlling mother profile. The first is social density. The extended-family households of North India are the largest in our study; as many as 24 people may live in these households, including children of several sisters-in-law. One way in which the mothers seem to respond to the noise and confusion of the large household is through a relatively dominant style of dealing with children. A second factor is maternal workload. High maternal workload was the factor leading to the large amount of training behavior in the subsaharan samples; accordingly, the mothers with more controlling (less training) behavior should carry less of a burden. Such an expectation is indeed met by our data. The controlling mothers of Tarong and Juxtlahuaca have many responsibilities, but they share the workload more evenly with their husbands and with other women. The North Indian mothers of Khalapur and Bhubaneswar, also high in controlling behaviors, have lighter workloads because, with the exception of the lower-status families in Bhubaneswar, they do not work outside the home.

The Work Contributed by Husbands. The men in Tarong, Philippines, do a larger share of the agricultural work than their African peers: they plow with carabao, build and mend dykes for the rice paddies, and manage the irrigation. The women plant and transplant the rice seedlings, but this is done in work groups and does not require more than one or two days of hard labor. Women plant the upland rice that takes little daily care. Although their husbands might work away seasonally, they are home during the period that requires their contribution of labor. Men also help the women with the task of bringing wood down from the surrounding hills. Women do carry water but do not face distances comparable to those required of the majority of Kenyan women (Nydegger and Nydegger, 1963).

The contribution of men to agricultural work is also greater in Taira, Okinawa, than in subsaharan Africa. Here also men do the plowing and manage the irrigation of the rice paddies; they share in the planting and transplanting as well. Similarly, both men and women cut and carry wood that is sold for cash, some of which is used to buy paraffin and charcoal for the household stove. Men and older children bring water to the houses using shoulder poles and buckets. None of the men work away (Maretzki and Maretzki, 1963).

In the preindustrial societies of the New World, most of the agricultural work is done by men (Sanday, 1973, 1974). In Juxtlahuaca, Mexico, only some families own land, while others work the land of absentee owners. Most cornfields are three or more miles from the barrio. The men go the fields early in the morning and return for the noon meal only if the fields are close. Women have small garden plots and fruit trees adjacent to their courtyards. Some sell cooked food in the town marketplace, others make blouses for sale. They spend the day at home, in the marketplace, or at neighbors' houses. Women carry their own water, but the distances are not great (Romney and Romney, 1963).

In Khalapur and in the upper- and middle-status families in Bhubaneswar, North India, only men work in the fields or do other kinds of work outside the home. The women are confined to their courtyards by the custom of *purdah* (seclusion) and are required by tradition not to expose themselves to the outside world except on religious holidays or for important ceremonies. Servants bring water to the houses; sweepers clean the drains and bring dung cakes for cooking fuel. The men make use of the older boys, who water and wash the cattle at the river and help carry fodder and the harvest in from the fields on the outskirts of the village (Minturn and Lambert, 1963; Seymour, 1975, 1980).

Help from Adult Women. In assessing the total workload of the women, it is also necessary to consider how much help and support mothers get from other women. This analysis is more difficult to make. Although the number of adult women residents in a household or compound (Table 3.2) is an indication of the potential for help, the amount of experience the adult women have with one another before marriage and their individual personalities are among the most important determinants of cooperation. The Kenyan women often reside together with co-wives, sisters-in-law, and mothers-in-law, but because these women are seldom relatives, the amount of help they provide one another depends on their interpersonal feelings.

In both Tarong and Taira women receive a great deal of help from other adult females. In Taira half of the families have resident grand-

Table 3.2. Percentage of sample mothers who have other women living in daily face-to-face contact with them

Cultural community	Percentage
New Samples	
Kien-taa, Liberia	66
Kokwet, Kenya	11
Kisa, Kenya	6
Kariobangi, Kenya	0
Ngeca, Kenya	48
Bhubaneswar, India, lower class	88
Bhubaneswar, India, middle and upper classes	
Old Town	63
New Capital	16
Six Culture Samples	
Nyansongo, Kenya	60
Juxtlahuaca, Mexico	86
Tarong, Philippines	96
Taira, Okinawa	67
Khalapur, India	63
Orchard Town, U.S.A.	4

mothers who (unlike many of the grandmothers in polygynous home-steads in Kenya) share in the child care and in the household and gardening chores. The grandmothers are often in the village when the mothers are working in the gardens or off in the mountains getting lumber.

In Tarong, a bilateral society, young married couples take up residence in a cluster of houses that includes relatives of either the husband, the wife, or both. In our sample, 50 percent of the mothers lived in households or yard groups that included their own mothers or adult sisters. Because these female kin have a long history of getting along with one another, mothers receive a great deal of support. Tarong women who share a central communal area are likely to plant their gardens, pound rice, and prepare handiwork for sale together. They supervise one another's children and, when necessary, breastfeed one another's babies. Grandmothers, whether from the maternal or paternal side, also provide help. They have their own households, but in 75 percent of the families they live within the yard group and can be counted on to help their married sons and daughters.

In Juxtlahuaca, young women often bring their new husbands into their parents' home for at least the early childbearing years. As in Tarong, the relationship between women co-residents is based on a long history of cooperation and close interaction. In our sample, 32 percent of the mothers lived in households that included their mother, sisters, or both. Even women who lived with their husbands' parents received support from relatives. Fifteen of the 22 households lived in extended courtyards that included other adult women, and in 13 households there were maternal or paternal grandparents. Every child has godparents who are concerned with the welfare of both the child and her parents. The women visit each other frequently in the after-noons, taking their work with them, and they sit together in the markets.

In Khalapur, India, there were at least two women in two-thirds of the families. Most mothers, therefore, have another woman on hand to help in emergencies. However, because this is a patrilocal society, women co-residents have not grown up together and their ability to get along depends on personality factors. The senior woman, wife of the eldest male, is the woman with greatest formal authority in the extended family. As mother-in-law, she may or may not be helpful to her daughters-in-law. The sisters-in-law may be either cooperative or rivalrous with one another.

A similar situation prevails in Old Town, Bhubaneswar. In the New Capital, families live in a nuclear arrangement, each with its own house. In the majority of upper- and middle-status homes in the New Capital, however, women receive at least some help from other women, who may be household servants or visiting relatives.

The Contribution of Children. How does the number of children relate to women's workload? Since mothers can assign work to children, it is difficult to determine whether a large family increases or decreases the woman's workload.

In Kenya a mother must produce more food if she has a large family; she also needs more cash to buy the products of the industrial world. A large family requires more cash for school clothes, books, and school-related fees (in the past, tuition fees; now, school-building and maintenance fees only). A father with a large family needs to have either a good cash crop or a wage-earning job if he wishes to send all of his children to school. Offsetting these costs, however, is the fact that where farms are still large, the labor of children is undoubtedly an asset, especially if farming is done without plows or if cattle pastures are unfenced. The Nyansongo mothers keep all their children busy. In Kisa and Ngeca, however, where the acreage is small, the mothers have less need for child labor, although they are able to take advantage of the help available. In fact, in Kariobangi (the urban locale for Kisa migrants) children over age 8 are underrepresented because they are left in Kisa for farm work and schooling and because tight living quarters in the city make co-sleeping with older children awkward.

Children also make a major contribution to subsistence in Tarong and Juxtlahuaca. In the Six Culture Study, the children of Tarong rank second after Nyansongo in average number of chores (including child care), while the children of Juxtlahuaca rank third (Whiting and Whiting, 1975, p. 101).

In all agricultural societies there are times, which may be seasonal, when child labor is an asset. In the Six Culture Study, the children of Taira rank fourth in average number of chores. They do little work except during the busy season when the dykes are prepared for rice planting, and again later when the seedlings are transplanted. At those times the men, women, and children are busy. The following

Five- and seven-year-old boys harvesting rice, Tarong (1955)

Tairan brother and sister transplanting rice (1955)

observation portrays the pace of life at the busy season. Children make a real contribution and practice skills required for adult life.

During March, the villagers are busy with transplanting rice, and the children are out of school on vacation. Many parents depend on their children for help with the evening chores—fetching water, cleaning the yard, starting the fires, feeding the horses. The boys being observed have been asked to do chores by their father, who has been out in the paddies with the mother, transplanting rice. Akibo (boy, age 12) is in the kitchen busily getting the fire started to cook food for the pigs, then washing the rice. Terimitsu (brother, age 8) is cleaning the yard and horse stall. Two friends, Atsushi and Fukutaro (boys, age 6), are helping. They have just brought a bucket of water from the tank. Fukutake, cousin of Fukutaro, is helping to clear the little drainage

Children catching small fish, Taira (1955)

ditch just below the sink outside the kitchen door. Terumitsu rakes the dried grass from the horse stall into a neat pile and goes off to get a can of water. Fukutaro joins Fukutake in hoeing sand and laying it in the drainage ditch, adjusting the pipe and boards. (Maretzki and Maretzki, field observations, 1955)

It is much less clear that children contribute to the household economies in the societies of North India. In Khalapur, mothers in *purdah* use their children to carry messages to other courtyards and to make purchases at stores. However, there are few other types of work outside the house that mothers can assign. In the Six Culture Study, the children of Khalapur rank fifth in the average number of chores; they exceed only Orchard Town (Whiting and Whiting, 1975).

The Khalapur mothers make a clear distinction in the chores that they assign to sons and daughters; they consider housework to be women's work. They ask their daughters to help but assign comparatively little work. They know that their daughters will do much household work when they become married (as arranged by their parents) and go to live in a new village. As daughters-in-law, the new wives will cook and keep house under the supervision of their mothers-in-law. Parents, therefore, feel that as children, girls should be treated as "visitors." This is obviously a cultural ideal—in fact, the girls do some child care and housework and run errands, but comparatively speaking, they have more free time for undirected activities.

Similarly, in Old Town, Bhubaneswar, in the large, extended families of the middle- and upper-status households, children's workloads are relatively light. When the children become adults, they may earn salaries or wages that they share with the extended family, but while they are still children, only the older girls contribute appreciable help to the daily workload. The following observation illustrates family life in the courtyard:

> The people present include three of the four adult brothers who share the courtyard, their four wives, and twelve children of the house who range in age from 5 to 14. The time is 11:10 A.M.
>
> Pramod (boy, 11) greets the observer and brings her a stool, so she can sit and watch the women cook. He stands nearby for a while. All of the other children are just back from school and running through the house together. The fourth wife comments, "First they play, then they bathe!"
>
> The women are busy cooking. Jorana (girl, age 14) helps the third

Mother serving breakfast, Bhubaneswar (Susan Seymour, 1966)

wife wash the rice and cook the vegetables. Some of the older girls prepare pita. Sopna (girl, age 11) grinds rice that has been soaked in water. She also grinds the accompanying spices, directed by the third wife. Kalpana (girl, age 13) works with the fourth wife separating the flower of a banana tree. When the banana flower has been separated, the second wife grinds it with some water. Her daughter, Kalpana, comes over and watches her. She argues with her mother as to how it should be done, and after a while takes over and finishes the grinding. Pramila (girl, age 14) is last to arrive home from school. She sets down her things and joins the women.

Dichendra (boy, age 5) wanders in and out of the cooking area. He pulls and pokes at the working women and girls. His mother, the third wife, shouts at him, but he just returns a cocky smile. Sopna (girl, age 11) calls him "very naughty." Several times the third wife leaves her cooking to run after and hit him. He just smiles saucily and runs off.

Later his mother stops cooking to apply oil to Dichendra's body before he bathes. She starts to remove his pants, but Dichendra resists, probably because he is in view of the observer. He tells his mother not to and she doesn't. After being oiled he runs off and disappears. A bit later he reappears freshly dressed, obviously bathed without the help of his mother.

Bina (girl, age 7) also bathes without her mother's help. She bathes in the front courtyard, while the boys bathe out in back. She runs naked around the house for a while.

Dichendra and one of the other boys tease the pet dog. They corner him in a hallway and try to hit him with a heavy piece of wire. Dichendra flings the wire at the dog. His mother hears the dog growl and runs over, looking angry. She lets the dog out into the back yard, but says nothing to the boys.

Prakasa (boy, age 6) pours water for Prapila (boy, age 8) to wash his hands after defecating. Later he bathes himself and comes in wearing clean pants. His eyes are red from crying. He clings to his mother, but she moves away. She pushes him away angrily when he takes a bit of coconut from her. Dichendra and Bina also grab bites of coconut as it is cut up. The third wife notices and yells but does not stop them. The second wife comes over to investigate. Kalpana explains that it is just the end of the coconut that they are eating. The second wife does not do anything more.

The fourth husband watches as Sachikanta (boy, age 7) bathes and oils himself. His father shouts at him several times.

A milkman arrives, and the younger children surround him. They hold out hands or cups and demand milk. (Seymour, field observations, 1967)

In sum, the Kenyan mothers have the heaviest workload and score highest in training mands. The mothers in Tarong and Juxtlahuaca have somewhat lighter workloads and score higher on control than training mands. The Tairan mothers cannot be compared because there are too few observations. The North Indian and the Orchard Town mothers have the lightest workloads and score higher on control than training mands. Clearly, in places where mothers bear a heavy workload, they put the most emphasis on training their children; where they have less to do, they initiate more interactions whose goal appears to be control of the child. The relative proportion of control is highest in North Indian and U.S. samples.

Why does control move to first place when training drops down as a percentage of maternal behavior? There seem to be two main explanations for the ascendancy of control. In the first place, when there are few tasks to assign, the content of what is to be taught to children of various ages is less clear. The mothers still feel responsible for socializing their children during early childhood, but are less specific about what is to be taught. As a result, they frequently reprimand after the fact rather than advising their children what to do beforehand. In the second place, when children do not have specific jobs to perform, they are apt to be underfoot and playing in areas where adults are trying to work or talk to one another. In this case, mothers may command their children to desist from play without advising them to do some constructive or useful activity. They often ask the children to stop interfering with the mother's own activities. To the observer and the child it is not always clear why the mother objects to the child's behavior other than that he causes her personal displeasure. Subsaharan mothers use the assignment of work to put a stop to behavior that annoys them or to stop wrangling between siblings; we often heard the Ngeca mothers dispatch children on various errands when they found them too exuberant or too unhappy. In fact, subsaharan children have learned through experience that it is best to play away from adults lest they be assigned some new chore or reminded of work that they are supposed to be doing.

The Sociable Mother

The third maternal style is represented by our U.S. sample. The Orchard Town mothers are similar to the groups of controlling mothers in that control ranks first in their behavior to children, but different from not only controlling but also training mothers in their unusually high proportion of sociable interaction. Sociability ranks second in their behavior profile, and for this reason we label their pattern the "sociable mother."

These mothers are by far the most residentially isolated, spending their days mostly in the company of their young children. With few exceptions, they do not work outside the home and, when their husbands are gone, they have no other adults to whom to turn for help or sociability (Fischer and Fischer, 1963).

There are few chores assigned to children in the average Orchard Town family. Of course there are always household chores to be done, but the mothers assign only a few. They expect their children to help set and clear the dinner table and to wash dishes; they expect older children, both boys and girls, to keep their bedrooms neat and help with housecleaning on weekends. The Orchard Town mothers rely on their children for sociable interaction more than for help with work. People everywhere seem to share a universal desire for human companionship and interaction, and the Orchard Town mothers, in the absence of adult company, turn to their children. Their interaction with them is characterized by relatively high levels of information exchange and other kinds of reciprocal, friendly interaction.

The following scene from Orchard Town illustrates this pattern. A mother and her 4-year-old daughter, Dottie, are watching television late one morning. The mother engages her little girl in a bout of horseplay, which they both evidently enjoy. When Dottie's kicking gets too rough, her mother attempts to teach her to modulate her force; she tries to teach Dottie to learn the difference between "playing" (acceptable) and "hurting" (not acceptable).

> Dottie lies with legs crossed. Her mother comes back. "What are you sucking your thumb for?" Dottie kicks her legs at her.
> Mother: "What are you doing that for? Come on, pest. I'll get you. I'll get you." She throws the blanket on Dottie's face. Mother sits on couch, and Dotties kicks her, laughing.
> Mother: "Dottie Louise!" (grabs her feet). "I think you're a pest." (She repeats this three times.) Dottie laughs.
> Mother: "Come on, now. I'm not bothering your pillow, am I? [To observer] She's a little pest, Ann." (Repeats three more times and hugs Dottie.)
> Dottie: "I'll do it some more." Mother grabs her, and Dottie giggles.
> Dottie: "I'll get you." She bangs her head against her mother's breast several times.
> Mother: "Ooh! Take it easy. Would you like this pesty daughter at your house, Ann [observer]? (to Dottie) I think I'll have you go down and visit her for a while. She'd like somebody to pester her."
> Dottie: "No."
> Mother: "Now don't kick Mommy. That hurts. Now that isn't nice." Dottie stops. She sucks her thumb and looks at television. She starts kicking again.
> Mother: "No kicking. That hurts now. That's not nice."
> Dottie: "I like to play."
> Mother: "Well, you're kicking and I don't like that."
> Dottie: "I like to play."
> Mother: "Well, you can play but not hurt. You're kicking and that hurts."
> Dottie finally stops. She laughs, and sucks her thumb. (Fischer and Fischer, field observations, 1955)

Here appropriate playful behavior is being taught in the context of play between an adult and a child. In the other sample communities this type of interaction is rare; children learn appropriate play behavior in interaction with older siblings, half-siblings, or cousins. Adult/child play may help prepare American children for entry into school settings where children are rewarded for success in interacting with adults.

Sisters, ages 4½ and 3½, painting at kitchen table, Orchard Town

We have found that the exchange of information, one of the types of behavior included in the category of friendly interaction, increases as parents emphasize the value of schooling and symbolic learning. Mothers encourage their children to play with "educational" toys. Although the mothers do not have many tasks to assign, they provide countless toys and materials (pencils, paper, crayons and paints, blocks, and so forth) to engage the children in the kind of play that is considered precursory to skills rewarded in school. Mothers take time to ask questions about their children's constructions and art-work; they praise their children's drawings and encourage them to show their "work" to others. Mothers also take advantage of children's exploration of household materials to talk with them about the tasks the mothers are doing and how the various types of equipment work. The constant stream of verbal exchanges encourages the development of verbal skills that are important for interacting with teachers in school and for future life in a complex, literate society.

The following is a short excerpt from a much longer sequence occurring one afternoon in Orchard Town in the living room of Deanie (boy, age 4). Deanie's mother has been working on a braided rug and now Deanie is playing with the braid holder, a tool used to hold the braid tight while she works. It has a screw clamp for fastening it to the table or other fixed surface. In the observation, Deanie's mother encourages him to explain to the observer what he is doing, and she praises his intelligence. She obviously sees his play and conversation about it as situations for fostering his cognitive development.

> Deanie asks his mother to unscrew the braid holder from the coffee table, and she does. He takes it to the window sill and tries to screw it on.
> Mother: "Tell Mrs. Fischer what you're doing."
> Deanie: "I'm hitching this."
> Mother: "What are you going to do when it's all hitched?"
> Deanie: "It's so fast you didn't even know it was hitched on" (laughs). He shows the observer a picture of a beagle in the Sunday paper. Then he unhitches the braid holder and takes it into the kitchen. "Mommy, I can unhitch this."
> Mother: "You're a smart man, aren't you?"
> Deanie: "In one minute I did, in one minute."
> Mother: "In one minute, huh?" Deanie nods. He goes back to the living room, screws it onto the coffee table, and tells his mother. She acknowledges his act and says: "I'll undo it for you."   (Fischer and Fischer, field observations, 1955)

Orchard Town mothers treat their children, at times, as if they were their status equals. Such treatment would be inconceivable in the other sample communities, where people's relative ages are associated with their authority and right to dominate. In the following observation Dougie's mother encourages not only his participation but also his self-assertiveness.

> Dougie (boy, age 4) and his mother are in the kitchen making a pie. Dougie, standing on a chair, holds his own small rolling pin. His mother begins to make the crust.
> Mother: "Okay, you gonna help me, Dougie?" Dougie says, "Yep," and his mother exclaims to the observer, "Dougie's the best roller-upper in Orchard Town!"
> Dougie (using his rolling pin): "Oh, it's not enough flour." His mother adds a little flour, asking him, "Okay?" Dougie rolls, says, "Yes."
> His mother finishes her own rolling. She asks Dougie, "Okay, you want to help me more? Smooth it out a little bit." Dougie rolls a little and declares, "That's big enough." His mother asks, "Now what kind of a 'fence' do you want me to put around it?" Dougie answers, and the mother comments to the observer, "Usually they want me to put a

Benson's Wild Animal Farm fence." A few moments later, she asks, "Shall we make strips the way Davie [brother] likes?"

The conversation continues in this vein for some time. (Fischer and Fischer, field observations, 1955)

The Eliciting Power of Children

We have seen that ecological constraints powerfully influence mothers' behavior to children. Transcultural forces, especially mothers' workloads and sources of network support, operate in similar ways across cultural boundaries. Mothers' responses to these universal forces are not idiosyncratic to each cultural setting but rather are broadly similar.

This is not to say, however, that all mothers within a cultural community behave in exactly the same way, or that mothers treat all of their children in one uniform way. Naturally there is variation both within communities and between children in a family in how mothers interact with their children. In order to understand the predictable features of this variation, we must examine how factors related to differences between children—especially their age and sex—affect maternal styles. Children's age and sex have a strong influence in determining the kinds of behaviors that children elicit from their mothers, and we refer to this phenomenon as the "eliciting power of children."

Mothers everywhere seem to operate on theories—and there is a transcultural dimension to these theories—about differences between children. They consciously vary their behavior according to the sex and age of their children, and to a certain extent, they do this in ways that are similar cross-culturally. Young children versus older children, or boys versus girls, tend to elicit certain behaviors rather than others. The ethnographic data indicate that at least some of the mothers are themselves aware of these things; they believe firmly that age affects children's capabilities, maturity, and competence to learn and perform.

Exactly how different is the behavior of mothers to older versus younger children, and to boys versus girls? We have attempted to answer this question by dividing the boys and girls in the New Samples into three age grades (2–3, 4–5, and 6–8 years). The boys and girls in the Six Culture samples can be divided into only two age grades (3–6 and 7–10 years). Age and sex differences in mothers' behavior can then be described in terms of the proportions of nurturance, responsiveness, training, control, and sociability that occur for each sex/age group. The proportions are in each case calculated as a percentage of mothers' total social acts to children (see Appendix B). The sex differences appear in terms of two patterns of results. First, they appear in terms of *consistencies* across cultural communities in whether girls versus boys are favored by mothers for the behavior in question (for this, we count the number of groups for which girls versus boys receive the higher percentage of the behavior). Second, they appear in terms of *statistical tests* (phi tests) of the differences between girls and boys of a given age and culture in the proportion of the behavior.

Maternal Nurturance and Responsiveness

Children's age is a powerful predictor of maternal nurturance. Table 3.3 presents the findings on mothers' proportion of "initiated nurturance," and Table 3.4 gives the proportions of mothers' "responsive nurturance" (compliance).

Table 3.3 shows that mothers' nurturance declines with children's age in both the New Samples and the Six Culture samples. Averaging across the seven New Samples, about 31 percent of mothers' initiations are nurturant for children aged 2–3 years. This proportion is cut in half by age 4–5 (to about 16 percent), and in half again by age 6–8 (to about 9 percent). Similarly, averaging across the five Six Culture samples for which sufficient data on mothers exist, initiated nurturance drops from about 6 percent for younger children to 2 percent for older ones. If one examines each cultural sample separately, it can be seen that the declines with age are found in every sample but one (Nyansongo). Thus, although substantial intracultural variation is seen in maternal nurturance, a transcultural generality involves the power of young children to draw or elicit more nurturance from mothers than do older children.

The overall trends for maternal responsiveness (Table 3.4) are also clear-cut. The seven New Samples show a decline in maternal responsiveness with increasing age of the child: from 66 percent for children aged 2–3, to 60 percent for children aged 4–5, to 46 percent for children aged 6–8 years. Decreases are seen in every cultural group for mothers' responsiveness to children aged 2–3 versus 6–8 years. (Comparable data are not available for the Six Culture samples.)

Children's sex is not a consistent predictor of maternal nurturance: mothers are about equally nurturant to sons as to daughters. The means (averaging across cultures; see Table 3.3) are quite similar for boys and girls of the same age. Furthermore, an examination of Table 3.3 shows that of the 28 son/daughter comparisons that can be made within cultural samples, mothers favor sons in 11 and favor daughters in 14 (with 3 ties). The only tendency for a sex difference occurs at the youngest age group: mothers are more nurturant to their 2- to 3-year-old sons in five of the seven New Samples, significantly so in three communities—Kien-taa, Kariobangi, and Bhubaneswar.

The sex difference in Kariobangi probably results from the situation of urban living, because in the rural area of Kisa, the same Abaluhya mothers are only slightly more nurturant to sons than to daughters. In Kariobangi mothers and children spend much time together in small apartments, and even fathers are around more often than is the case in the rural villages. As a result, in Kariobangi the mothers seem to give much nurturance to their young boys. (Their older boys they tend to leave at home in the villages because there is little constructive activity for older boys in Kariobangi, and their boundless energy becomes disruptive in the crowded apartments.)

One cultural group in which mothers show consistently more nurturance to sons than to daughters of all age grades is the middle- and upper-status families of Bhubaneswar, India. The sex difference is statistically significant at two ages, 2–3 and 4–5 years. Interestingly, these data fit other researchers' reports on North India, where among the upper classes, male children have been found to be favored over female children and to receive preferential treatment in infancy (Miller, 1981; Pettigrew, 1986; Poffenberger, 1981). Leigh Minturn also reported that the Rajput mothers in Khalapur are more apt to neglect girl than boy infants—for example, by procuring less medical attention for the former (Minturn and Hitchcock, 1963). In Khalapur, the sons continue the patrilineage and care for the parents in their old age, while daughters marry into other communities and require a large dowry if the arranged wedding is to a status family. Table 3.3 shows that Khalapur mothers are about twice as nurturant to their young sons as to daughters (7 percent versus 3 percent); however, because the number of interacts is small, this difference is not statistically significant.

Research conducted in the United States has not tended to find clear-cut sex differences in maternal nurturance (see the review in

Table 3.3. Proportion of nurturance received (as a percentage of all social acts received from mothers) by children of different age groups

Community (New Samples)[a]	Age 2–3 years			Age 4–5 years			Age 6–8 years			Mean (across sex/age groups) (%)
	Girls (%)	Boys (%)	Diff.	Girls (%)	Boys (%)	Diff.	Girls (%)	Boys (%)	Diff.	
Kien-taa	20	38	-18**	8	5	+3	—	—	—	18
Kokwet	26	29	-3	23	20	+3	10	8	+2	19
Kisa	24	19	+5	16	10	+6	11	10	+1	15
Kariobangi	14	31	-17**	22	12	+10*	5	[3]	+2	14
Ngeca	25	27	-2	19	17	+2	8	12	-4	18
Bhubaneswar, lower class	57	56	+1	—	[10]	—	[4]	2	+2	26
Bhubaneswar, middle and upper classes	29	37	-8*	16	29	-13*	17	19	-2	25
Mean of 7 groups	28	34	—	17	15	—	9	9	—	19

Community (Six Cultures)[b]	Age 3–6 years			Age 7–10 years			Mean (across sex/age groups) (%)
	Girls (%)	Boys (%)	Diff.	Girls (%)	Boys (%)	Diff.	
Nyansongo	0	2	-2	3	3	0	2
Juxtlahuaca	16	14	+2	10	4	+6	11
Tarong	7	7	0	4	1	+3	5
Khalapur	3	7	-4	0	0	0	2
Orchard Town	6	7	-1	0	—	—	4
Mean of 5 groups	6	7	—	3	2	—	5

Note: The nurturance category for the Six Culture samples includes fewer behaviors than for the New Samples, and thus is not exactly comparable. In the Six Culture Study, mothers were not observed directly and appear in observations only when they happened to interact with the focal (target) child. Maternal nurturance, therefore, was coded primarily when mothers responded to their children's dependency behaviors.

All tests of significance in Tables 3.3 to 3.7 are based on phi tests (derived from chi-squares). Tests are two-tailed: + p < .10, * p < .05, ** p < .01.

a. Kien-taa (Liberia) has been omitted from the New Samples at the 6–8 year age group because there were only one girl and two boys involved in the observations (see total numbers of mother-to-child dyads presented in Appendix B). Similarly, the scores from lower-class Bhubaneswar (India) girls aged 4–5 have been omitted because only one girl was observed. The scores from Kariobangi (Kenya) boys aged 6–8, and Bhubaneswar boys aged 4–5 and girls aged 6–8 have been placed in brackets because in each case only two children were observed.

b. Taira (Okinawa) has been omitted from the Six Culture communities because there were too few acts. Similarly, Orchard Town (U.S.A.) boys aged 7–10 have been omitted because of few acts. (See total numbers of mother-to-child acts presented in Appendix B.)

Table 3.4. Proportion of total compliance by mothers (immediate or delayed) to children's dependent bids

Community (New Samples)[a]	Age 2–3 years			Age 4–5 years			Age 6–8 years			Mean (across sex/age groups) (%)
	Girls (%)	Boys (%)	Diff.	Girls (%)	Boys (%)	Diff.	Girls (%)	Boys (%)	Diff.	
Kien-taa	80	82	−2	77	67	+10	—	—	—	77
Kokwet	80	88	−8	74	68	+6	70	75	−5	76
Kisa	92	33	+59*	33	43	−10	50	29	+21	47
Kariobangi	69	56	+13	64	68	−4	50	[00]	+50	51
Ngeca	64	67	−3	68	80	−12*	58	60	−2	66
Bhubaneswar, lower class	60	44	+16	—	[19]	—	[50]	25	+25	40
Bhubaneswar, middle and upper classes	50	62	−12	56	67	−11	39	45	−6	53
Mean of 7 groups	70	62	—	62	59	—	53	39	—	58

Note: * p < .05.

a. See note a to Table 3.3. Comparable data are not available for the Six Culture samples.

Maccoby and Jacklin, 1974). Some studies have found parents to physically stimulate or elicit gross motor behavior more with boy infants than with girls (Lewis, 1972; Moss, 1967; Parke, O'Leary, and West, 1972; Yarrow, Rubenstein, and Pederson, 1975). Clarke-Stewart's observational study (1973) did not find sex differences in the total amount of mother-child interaction, nor did Pederson and Robson (1969) in their study of fathering. However, Minton, Kagan, and Levine (1971) found boys to receive more total mother-child interaction, and Yarrow, Rubenstein, and Pederson (1975) found boys to receive a greater variety and level of social stimulation. These studies differed in social class, ethnic group, and age of samples.

Charles Super (1984) reports on spot-observation data collected in 13 communities in East Africa. In 7 of these communities, mothers were significantly more likely to delegate care of female than of male infants. Across the entire sample, mothers were observed to be the primary caretaker immediately responsible for the baby's welfare in 66 percent of observations of boys, 54 percent of girls. In terms of "warmth" or "affection," American studies using observational methods have not found mothers to favor boys versus girls, either during infancy or later (Allaman, Joyce, and Crandall, 1972; Baumrind, 1971; Clarke-Stewart, 1973; Hatfield, Ferguson, and Alpert, 1967; Kagan, 1971; Lewis, 1972; Moss, 1967; Stayton, Hogan, and Ainsworth, 1971). However, a number of American studies relying on child or parent interviews have found that preschool and older girls report receiving more nurturance and affection from parents than do boys (Cox, 1970; Hoffman and Saltzstein, 1967; Miller, 1971; Siegelman, 1965). American girls may have a more intimate and outwardly close relationship with parents than do boys during later childhood and adolescence because boys actively dissociate themselves from such emotional expressiveness and closeness (see Chapter 6 and Chodorow, 1978).

In sum, we conclude that there are cross-cultural differences in the style and amount of nurturance that mothers direct to infants and young children versus older ones, but no such clear-cut differences in nurturant treatment of boys versus girls.

Maternal Training

Training constitutes a large proportion of mothers' behavior and increases as children get older. Table 3.5 shows that maternal train-

Table 3.5. Proportion of training mands received (as a percentage of all social acts received from mothers) by children of different age groups

Community (New Samples)[a]	Age 2–3 years			Age 4–5 years			Age 6–8 years			Mean (across sex/age groups) (%)
	Girls (%)	Boys (%)	Diff.	Girls (%)	Boys (%)	Diff.	Girls (%)	Boys (%)	Diff.	
Kien-taa	39	12	+27***	52	43	+9+	—	—	—	36
Kokwet	18	21	-3	24	26	-2	50	61	-11	33
Kisa	43	28	+15	50	37	+13	36	40	-4	39
Kariobangi	36	29	+7	56	40	+16*	65	[46]	+19*	45
Ngeca	27	24	+3	49	46	+3	56	43	+13**	41
Bhubaneswar, lower class	5	5	0	—	[31]	—	[50]	26	+24	23
Bhubaneswar, middle and upper classes	21	18	+3	22	26	-4	38	27	+11*	25
Mean of 7 groups	27	20	—	42	36	—	49	40	—	34

Community (Six Cultures)[b]	Age 3–6 years			Age 7–10 years			Mean (across sex/age groups) (%)
	Girls (%)	Boys (%)	Diff.	Girls (%)	Boys (%)	Diff.	
Nyansongo	62	54	+8	48	63	-15+	57
Juxtlahuaca	39	31	+8	74	46	+28*	48
Tarong	41	33	+8	63	28	+35***	41
Khalapur	19	14	+5	54	45	+9	33
Orchard Town	18	14	+4	14	—	—	15
Mean of 5 groups	36	29	—	51	46	—	40

Note: + $p < .10$, * $p < .05$, ** $p < .01$, *** $p < .001$.
a. See note a to Table 3.3.
b. See note b to Table 3.3.

ing, that is, task commands and suggestions related to proper social behavior, increases with age of the child in every cultural sample (combining mothers' behavior to girls and boys). Averaging across the seven New Samples, the mean proportion of training is 23 percent for mothers of 2- to 3-year-olds, 39 percent for 4- to 5-year-olds, and 44 percent for 6- to 8-year-olds. Similarly, averaging across the Six Culture samples, the mean proportion of training is 32 percent for mothers of 3- to 6-year-olds versus 48 percent for 7- to 10-year-olds.

Not only does maternal training increase in relative frequency as children get older, but the content of the training also tends to change predictably. For younger children the training is focused on manners, hygiene, and socially approved behavior, whereas for older children it is focused more on chores and other socially useful activities. Maternal commands related to proper social behavior (manners and hygiene) increase most steeply between age 2–3 years and age 4–5 years and then level off, while maternal commands related to performance of chores increase at a fairly regular rate throughout the childhood period.

Children's sex is also a factor transculturally in maternal training. In fact, of the four major categories of maternal behavior, training shows the most consistent differences in amount received by girls versus boys. These findings are presented in Table 3.5. Of the 28 son/daughter comparisons that can be made, mothers are seen to favor daughters in 21 cases, sons in only 6 (with 1 tie). This finding would be expected by chance less than 1 percent of the time (by the sign test). Furthermore, 9 of the comparisons in the table are themselves statistically significant (by phi tests); 8 of these involve girls receiving more training while only 1 involves boys receiving more. Overall the findings indicate that mothers begin training daughters earlier than sons, as if responding to a developmental difference in the rate of social maturation.

For the young age groups, much of the sex difference in maternal training has to do with girls receiving a preponderance of hygiene and etiquette commands, in other words, receiving earlier pressure for proper social behavior. For the older age group, however, much of the sex difference has to do with girls receiving the preponderance of task commands. After about age 7 boys receive as much pressure as girls for proper social behavior, but girls now receive considerably more pressure to be responsible in terms of household tasks and child

Grooming, Ngeca (Frances M. Cox, 1975)

care. There is no question that girls are assigned more work than boys during the childhood years; to state the situation in the baldest terms, girls work while boys play. As shown in Chapter 2, these sex differences in maternal training of girls versus boys are corroborated by the systematic spot observations on the children's activities and by numerous other cross-cultural studies. The sex differences in maternal training are important from our point of view both because they are substantial and consistent across cultures and because they indicate the main arena of power in which mothers can differentially shape the social behavior and personality development of their sons versus their daughters.

Maternal Dominance and Control

Mothers' attempts to control their children by reprimanding, punishing, and commanding them egotistically show no general effects for children's age (see Table 3.6). Infants, of course, receive a much lower relative percentage of maternal control than do older children (see Wenger, 1983), but our analysis does not include the transition from infancy to childhood because infants were not the target subjects

Table 3.6. Proportion of controlling acts received (as a percentage of all social acts received from mothers) by children of different age groups

Community (New Samples)[a]	Age 2–3 years			Age 4–5 years			Age 6–8 years			Mean (across sex/age groups) (%)
	Girls (%)	Boys (%)	Diff.	Girls (%)	Boys (%)	Diff.	Girls (%)	Boys (%)	Diff.	
Kien-taa	20	35	−15*	24	39	−15**	—	—	—	30
Kokwet	30	28	+2	27	37	−10	20	6	+14**	25
Kisa	11	17	−6	16	27	−11	28	27	+1	21
Kariobangi	17	24	−7	9	32	−23***	12	[34]	−22**	21
Ngeca	26	27	−1	18	22	−4	17	22	−5	22
Bhubaneswar, lower class	20	19	+1	—	[54]	—	[42]	66	−24*	40
Bhubaneswar, middle and upper classes	34	33	+1	51	37	+14**	43	50	−7	41
Mean of 7 groups	23	26	—	24	35	—	27	34	—	29

Community (Six Cultures)[b]	Age 3–6 years			Age 7–10 years			Mean (across sex/age groups) (%)
	Girls (%)	Boys (%)	Diff.	Girls (%)	Boys (%)	Diff.	
Nyansongo	29	34	−5	36	31	+5	32
Juxtlahuaca	34	49	−15	15	33	−18+	33
Tarong	47	50	−3	25	47	−22	42
Khalapur	47	66	−19+	43	48	−5	51
Orchard Town	43	44	−1	50	—	—	46
Mean of 5 groups	40	49	—	34	40	—	41

Note: + p < .10, * p < .05, ** p < .01, *** p < .001.
a. See note a to Table 3.3.
b. See note b to Table 3.3.

of the behavioral observations. Within the childhood period, age trends are not consistent across cultural samples. Slight increases are found in some samples, decreases in others.

Although age is not a powerful predictor of maternal control, children's sex is more significant: mothers seek to control sons proportionately more than daughters. It can be seen in Table 3.6 that mothers seek to control sons more than daughters in 21 of the 28 paired comparisons; this finding would be expected by chance less than 5 percent of the time (by the sign test). Boys receive significantly more control in two of the African samples, Kien-taa and Kariobangi. Controlling sons is a salient problem for those urban mothers of Kariobangi who bring their older boys with them to the city; the living space is limited, and mothers have few chores (or toys) with which to channel their sons' exuberant energy. Interestingly, one culture in which mothers are found to control daughters significantly more than sons is the middle- and upper-status families of Bhubaneswar, India, where (as already noted) boys are reported to be strongly preferred and to receive more nurturant care. The North Indian community of Bhubaneswar is a highly stratified society, where social relationships are hierarchical and are typified by reciprocal dominance and a demanding style of dependency (even begging) as institutionalized behaviors. In Bhubaneswar, as in much of North India, older women (for example, mothers-in-law) dominate the younger women in the household (for example, daughters-in-law), and even mother-daughter interaction involves more dominance than is seen in the other cultural communities.

The general finding of a transcultural sex difference in maternal control (leaving aside the special case of societies such as North India) is particularly interesting in light of American studies by other researchers. The evidence from American studies on maternal dominance and reprimands is not extensive (Maccoby and Jacklin, 1974). However, Minton, Kagan, and Levine (1971) found that mothers used strong reprimands and other forms of intervention more with 2-year-old boys than girls because weaker forms of intervention proved ineffective; mothers "escalated" their behavior more with boys in order to teach compliance. Similarly, in a respected study of teacher behavior, Serbin, O'Leary, Kent, and Tonick (1973) found that 3-year-old boys, who tended to ignore teachers, received more negative control than girls at school; boys received more reprimands of all sorts, especially "loud reprimands," and more physical restraining. Hetherington, Cox, and Cox (1982) found that the stress of parental divorce initiated a cycle of escalating negative interaction between mothers and preschool-age sons; the boys became difficult for mothers to control, and mothers then became more hostile, authoritarian, and coercive with boys than with girls.

The American research, then, not only tends to corroborate our findings in terms of a transcultural phenomenon but also suggests a causal mechanism: adults (perhaps adult females, in particular) are led to behave in a more dominating and controlling way with boys than girls because boys require or elicit such intervention. Data to be presented in Chapter 4 show that, across cultures and age groups, boys are less obedient and compliant to mothers than are girls. Thus, boys may require more control—firm, strong, and definite "structuring"—perhaps because they are, on average, less sensitive to the needs of others and therefore less compliant or responsive to their mothers' directions. This does not meant that boys are "uncontrollable" but rather that they elicit a more intrusive and power-oriented control pattern from mothers than do girls. Boys may function more optimally with more structuring of their social behavior by caretakers, and mothers may be responsive to their children's functional style and adapt their behavior accordingly.

Maternal Sociability

Sociability constitutes a substantial proportion of mothers' behavior to children. The interesting feature of this category is that neither the age nor the sex of a child influences mothers' behavior in a general way. Table 3.7 shows that children receive about equal proportions of sociability at all age grades—about 13 percent. (The proportion at age 2–3 is slightly higher—14 percent.) Girls are seen to receive the greater proportion of sociability in 13 of the 28 paired comparisons, boys in 13 (with 2 ties). Of the comparisons that are statistically significant (by phi tests), 4 favor daughters, 3 sons.

Maternal sociability, then, is a category of behavior that is not specifically elicited by a particular type of child (as nurturance is elicited by young children and training is elicited by girls). Rather, sociability can be elicited by any type of child. Research indicates that even infants are capable of acting as "reciprocal social partners"

Table 3.7. Proportion of sociability acts received (as a percentage of all social acts received from mothers) by children of different age groups

Community (New Samples)[a]	Age 2–3 years			Age 4–5 years			Age 6–8 years			Mean (across sex/age groups) (%)
	Girls (%)	Boys (%)	Diff.	Girls (%)	Boys (%)	Diff.	Girls (%)	Boys (%)	Diff.	
Kien-taa	9	6	+3	12	8	+4	—	—	—	9
Kokwet	24	20	+4	23	16	+7	20	23	-3	21
Kisa	20	24	-4	9	24	-15	19	16	+3	19
Kariobangi	24	10	+14*	11	12	-1	12	[17]	-5	14
Ngeca	18	16	+2	13	14	-1	16	16	0	16
Bhubaneswar, lower class	5	4	+1	—	[0]	—	[0]	3	-3	2
Bhubaneswar, middle and upper classes	12	6	+6*	10	6	+4	2	2	0	6
Mean of 7 groups	16	12	—	13	11	—	12	13	—	13

Community (Six Cultures)[b]	Age 3–6 years			Age 7–10 years			Mean (across sex/age groups) (%)
	Girls (%)	Boys (%)	Diff.	Girls (%)	Boys (%)	Diff.	
Nyansongo	9	10	-1	14	3	+11*	9
Juxtlahuaca	9	3	+6	0	17	-17**	7
Tarong	3	10	-7**	9	22	-13*	11
Khalapur	21	7	+14+	0	6	-6	8
Orchard Town	26	28	-2	21	—	—	25
Mean of 5 groups	14	12	—	9	12	—	12

Note: + p < .10, * p < .05, ** p < .01.
a. See note a to Table 3.3.
b. See note b to Table 3.3.

to interested adults; their appealing facial expressions, sounds, and gestures draw others to them and make them enjoyable partners for face-to-face interaction. Older children, too, have many strategies for engaging in social interaction with their mothers—strategies that have been shaped by their cultural context.

Other factors, presumably, are more important than children's sex and age characteristics in influencing the percentage of maternal initiations coded as sociable. These factors are cultural ones—for example, mothers' workloads (how busy or pressured mothers feel), their isolation (how many adult partners are available to mothers for friendly interaction), and the number of adults in the household (how disturbing children's interruptions are to adult conversations). It is interesting to note that the Orchard Town mothers, who experience relatively light workloads, much isolation, and little adult companionship in the household, have the highest sociability scores of the Six Culture samples (see Table 3.7).

The possible importance of cultural factors in determining maternal sociability—not in terms of their proportionate sociability but in terms of their overall *rate* of interaction with children—is suggested by the Six Culture study. In the Six Culture sample we were able to estimate relative rates of maternal interaction with boys and girls: the total number of each mother's acts to children was divided by the number of five-minute observations in which each mother was present with the target child. Table 3.8 presents the results, showing the range and median scores for each sample of mothers.

It can be seen that, as with sociability, there is little difference in maternal rates of interaction due to children's sex. However, the cultural differences are interesting. Interaction between mothers and children is highest in Nyansongo and Orchard Town, lowest in Juxtlahuaca and Khalapur, suggesting that household arrangements may be associated with the scores. In Nyansongo, Orchard Town, and most of the households in Tarong, no other adult females share the house with the mother. Although the Nyansongo mothers have sisters-in-law and co-wives who live on the same homestead, and the Tarong mothers have related women living across the yard, these women do not live together in an enclosed space. In Khalapur, India, on the other hand, there are several women who share intimate space, and in Juxtlahuaca related women share a courtyard and sometimes a cook shack. Thus, when women share living space with other women, they seem to interact less with their children. The women of

Table 3.8. Median rate of interaction with mother (based on number of acts per 5-minute interval)

Community	Girls			Boys		
	No.	Med.	Range	No.	Med.	Range
Nyansongo	8	3.0	(.7–6)	8	3.0	(0–6)
Juxtlahuaca	11	1.6	(.87–3)	11	1.6	(0–2.5)
Tarong	12	1.9	(0–3)	11	2.0	(0–6)
Khalapur	11	0.7	(0–2.3)	11	0.0	(0–2)
Orchard Town	6	2.2	(1.6–7)	7	2.4	(1–3.6)

Nyansongo and Orchard Town, whose lives are different in so many respects, have in common the fact that when they are with their children, other women are usually not present as well. The style, or profile, of interaction in Nyansongo differs markedly from that in Orchard Town, but the rate is similar. The Orchard Town mothers are high in sociability and information exchange, while the Nyansongo mothers are high in training—assigning chores and teaching useful skills.

Conclusions

This analysis of maternal behavior suggests that there are great transcultural similarities in the ways in which mothers behave to children of each given age. This eliciting power of children comes from universal constraints on how adults can best promote the well-being of children of each age, as well as on what they need to teach them in terms of socially approved behavior and age-related competencies. To put it simply, mothers emphasize nurturance with lap and knee children, control with yard children, and training with school-age children. The differences found between cultural samples in maternal patternings are associated with mothers' workloads, household composition and support networks, and beliefs about the nature of children.

The transcultural differences in mothers' behavior due to children's sex are certainly far less striking and consistent than the differences due to children's age. One main difference, concerning mothers' attempts to control sons more than daughters, replicates other findings from the United States (see the earlier discussion of maternal dominance and control). We suggest that boys may tend to ignore adult commands until adults escalate to higher levels of overt authority. Our second main finding concerns the higher proportion of training mands to daughters, a finding that was corroborated by the ethnographic and spot-observation data presented in Chapter 2. Thus the data converge to suggest that a major aspect of sex-role development is an earlier and greater pressure on girls for socially acceptable and responsible behavior.

Chapter 4

Mothers as Elicitors and Modulators of Children's Behavior

We have seen that mothers' behavior has similar characteristics all over the world because of the universal needs and desires of young children. We have also seen the kinds of differences that exist in maternal profiles—differences that can be attributed to ecology and culture.

Children's behavior to mothers is the reciprocal of maternal behavior and tells a similar story about the eliciting power of one's social partner. There are universalities in children's interaction with mothers that can be attributed to the way in which children everywhere perceive mothers as a source of the material and emotional resources that they need to grow and thrive. Of course, differences also exist in children's profiles—differences that can be attributed to children's gender, developmental age, and cultural experience.

In analyzing and describing children's interaction with mothers, we have found four main categories of behavior to be of particular importance. These four categories are reciprocals of the summary categories that rank first to fourth in maternal behavior in all of the communities studied. First, dependency behavior is consistently elicited by mothers; it is the reciprocal of mothers' nurturance. Second, obedience or cooperation is a key feature of child-to-mother interaction; it is the reciprocal of the mother's training (prosocially commanding) mode. Third, dominance and aggression, although not of high frequency in child-to-mother interaction, appear in reciprocal relationship to mothers' controlling mode. Finally, child sociability is the reciprocal of maternal sociability.

Mothers as Elicitors of Dependency Behavior

Universal dimensions of the maternal role, then, appear to influence strongly the behavior of children everywhere in predictable ways. The eliciting power of the maternal figure seems to be clear-cut and consistent cross-culturally. First and foremost, the maternal figure elicits dependency or "seeking behavior," as children attempt to gain the satisfaction of various organic needs and pursue the less well understood but equally powerful goals of mastery, body contact, and exploration. The long period of helplessness in the human child necessitates the development of this elaborate set of seeking behaviors on the part of children (and reciprocal nurturant behaviors on the part of caretakers). Dependency behaviors constitute a major category of children's behavior to mothers not because they derive from a unified motivational system (or "trait") in children, but because they form a loosely associated cluster of behaviors related to the universal needs of children and the reciprocal role requirements of their caregivers (see Sears, 1972).

Table 4.1 shows that dependency behavior is indeed a form of behavior that children direct specifically to mothers, more than to any of the other members of their social world. The table is striking in the cross-cultural consistency of the findings. Mothers and older children consistently elicit more dependency than do other social partners, such as infants and other young children of the same age group.

What kinds of specific behaviors are included in the summary category of dependency? The seeking of food, instrumental help, comfort and contact, information, attention and approval, and permission are transcultural elements that can be seen in children's behavior in any community.

The seeking of food from the mother is obviously one of the infant's first learned behavior patterns. In all communities mothers are seen as the main controllers and purveyors of the nutritional resources that first infants and then children desire. Starting from the nursing period, mothers are what Elise Boulding has called "the keepers of the warehouse." Certainly, in all of our sample communities, they are in charge of the daily provision of food and drink, and they plan and supervise the main meals of the family. The cultures differ only in the conscious emphasis that they place on this aspect of the maternal role. In the subsaharan African communities, the

Table 4.1. Percentage of dependency behavior (as a proportion of all social acts) to different partners by children aged 3–6 years

Girls' total dependency[a]	Nyansongo	Juxtlahuaca	Tarong	Taira	Khalapur	Orchard Town
To mothers	63.6	73.6	61.4	85.7	53.2	39.9
To adolescents[b]	33.3	36.8	12.5	50.0	33.3	25.0
To older boys (7–10)	29.2	40.0	13.5	46.2	6.7	45.4
To older girls (7–10)	28.9	17.2	20.0	32.4	16.7	15.6
To younger boys (3–6)	0.0	11.4	10.0	16.2	5.6	10.6
To younger girls (3–6)	7.1	7.1	11.7	25.0	12.5	19.4
To infants	1.2	6.9	1.4	0.0	0.0	0.0
To others	26.3	24.0	23.7	24.6	30.5	35.7

Boys' total dependency[a]	Nyansongo	Juxtlahuaca	Tarong	Taira	Khalapur	Orchard Town
To mothers	11.1	46.7	62.4	40.0	42.9	43.6
To adolescents[b]	6.9	22.2	20.0	25.0	11.1	—
To older boys (7–10)	9.6	12.5	8.8	24.3	16.7	25.5
To older girls (7–10)	27.8	12.0	24.1	21.0	23.1	25.0
To younger boys (3–6)	8.8	10.0	12.0	8.8	3.0	15.6
To younger girls (3–6)	14.3	12.2	9.0	13.8	15.2	27.8
To infants	0.0	4.7	4.1	0.0	0.0	18.2
To others	5.7	23.9	22.8	19.0	21.0	32.0

a. "Total dependency" includes the seeking of proximity, physical contact, help, food, attention, comfort, permission, and any other emotional or physical resources.

b. The scores for male and female adolescents were combined because of low frequencies. Adolescents are not common social partners for young children because of the reduced time they spend in the home setting.

provision of food is the most salient feature of the maternal role and is focal to women's self-definition as mothers (LeVine, 1973). The mothers plant, harvest, process, and cook the food, and children as young as 2 years of age start to participate in aspects of this work. Perhaps because food is not always plentiful, these mothers never withhold food as a punishment, and they feel that a woman who does not work as hard as she can to provide food for her children has seriously violated her role obligations.

Mothers also provide instrumental help to children in all of the communities studied. Young children may need assistance in performing the self-care tasks related to dressing, personal hygiene, toilet training, and eating; they may also need help in the performance of chores or errands. The cultures we studied vary only in terms of the ages when mothers begin to encourage their children to stop or reduce their coming to them for instrumental help. In communities where mothers consider it inappropriate for children past infancy to continue to seek a great deal of help, they pressure children either to become self-reliant early or to turn to older siblings as their major source of help.

Mothers are the caregivers most frequently on hand to care for children when they are ill, hurt, frightened, fatigued, or otherwise in need of comfort. For the very young, contact with the mother's body is the most effective soother of distress or anxiety. Children everywhere seek to touch and be close to their mothers, but variation is seen in how often and in what way mothers allow access to themselves. That is, mothers both elicit and modulate children's proximity and touching; they may limit or encourage access to themselves.

Mothers are a source of information about the world around them. Their attention is sought for the informative interchange that characterizes mother-child interactions in all of our samples. This sociable exchange orients children to the significant features of the social and physical environment and serves as a major source of technical information and knowledge about the values of the community. Cultures vary only in the content of the information and values taught and in normative beliefs about the age at which children are considered old enough to understand and be taught certain kinds of knowledge.

Mothers are also a source of attention and approval; they monitor their children's social behavior and praise or punish when necessary. In all cultures children seek to prove themselves competent and to earn their parents' approval, although the most overt forms of attention seeking may or may not be rewarded depending on cultural values. For example, in many of our sample communities, praise is believed to spoil children. Mothers are apt to communicate their approval of their children's responsible behavior by assigning them more difficult work that involves less supervision. In fact, when children are in the mood to play they tend to move away from their mothers' immediate presence in order to avoid being assigned work; children learn to avoid maternal attention. In Orchard Town, in contrast, young children are encouraged to spend much time in interaction or close company with their mothers; children's attention seeking and "look at me" behaviors are rewarded with parental praise and recognition because they are considered a forerunner of worthwhile striving for achievement.

Finally, mothers act as the major "gatekeepers" whose permission is required for access to desired activities and privileges. Mothers set the limits on physical wandering and assign worktimes and playtimes for children; they decide when a child is old or competent enough to move on to a new stage in terms of family work. When children are competing for desired privileges, mothers decide who deserves or is ready for them and who must wait. Of course, cultures vary in their developmental expectations about when children are considered ready for various privileges and in their moral values about children's rights of access.

Age Changes in Children's Dependency

Children's dependency, then, is a culturally universal phenomenon based on infants' and children's real developmental limitations. Accordingly, this dependency should decrease as children become more mature and competent. Mothers, as we have seen, withdraw their initiated and responsive nurturance as children become older; dependency of children on mothers would be expected to show a parallel developmental path. Findings on age changes in dependency to mothers are presented in Tables 4.2 through 4.5. These tables show the proportion of total dependency as well as the seeking of proximity, help, and attention, broken down by children's sex, age, and cultural community. The proportions are in each case calculated as a percentage of children's total social acts to mothers (see Appendix C).

Surprisingly, total dependency on mothers (Table 4.2) declines with

Table 4.2. Proportion of total dependency (as a percentage of all social acts to mothers) by children of different ages

Community (New Samples)[a]	Age 2–3 years			Age 4–5 years			Age 6–8 years			Mean (across sex/age groups) (%)
	Girls (%)	Boys (%)	Diff.	Girls (%)	Boys (%)	Diff.	Girls (%)	Boys (%)	Diff.	
Kien-taa	62	[68]	−6	51	46	+5	—	—	—	57
Kokwet	59	60	−1	56	56	0	19	39	−20	48
Kisa	53	44	+9	34	48	−14	43	36	+7	43
Kariobangi	39	60	−21**	39	49	−10	36	[27]	+9	42
Ngeca	36	54	−18***	46	57	−11+	40	46	−6	46
Bhubaneswar, lower class	80	82	−2	[39]	48	−9	36	33	+3	53
Bhubaneswar, middle and upper classes	86	70	+16***	79	57	+22*	48	83	−35***	70
Mean of 7 groups	59	63	—	49	52	—	37	44	—	51

Community (Six Cultures)[b]	Age 3–6 years			Age 7–10 years			Mean (across sex/age groups) (%)
	Girls (%)	Boys (%)	Diff.	Girls (%)	Boys (%)	Diff.	
Nyansongo	64	11	+53***	26	36	−10	34
Juxtlahuaca	74	47	+27	40	[78]	−38*	60
Tarong	61	62	−1	31	31	0	46
Khalapur	53	43	+10	54	67	−13	54
Orchard Town	40	44	−4	47	[75]	−28	51
Mean of 5 groups	58	41	—	40	57	—	49

Note: All tests of significance in Tables 4.2 to 4.8 are based on phi tests, derived from chi-squares. Tests are two-tailed: + p < .10, * p < .05, ** p < .01, *** p < .001.

a. Kien-taa (Liberia) has been omitted from the New Sample communities at the 6–8-year age group because only one boy and one girl were involved in the observations (see total number of child-to-mother dyads presented in Appendix C). Scores from Kien-taa, boys aged 2–3, from lower-class Bhubaneswar (India), girls aged 4–5, and from Kariobangi (Kenya), boys aged 6–8, have been placed in brackets because they are each based on two child-to-mother dyads only.

b. Taira (Okinawa) has been omitted from the Six Culture communities because there were too few acts (see total numbers of child-to-mother age only for girls across the communities. The pooled means of girls and boys in the New Samples (shown in the top half of the table) both show declines, as do the pooled girls in the Six Culture samples, but the boys in the Six Culture samples actually show an increase in dependency with age, from 41 percent to 57 percent (see the bottom half of the table). Of course, children's *total amount of contact* with their mothers does decrease from early to later childhood in most communities (see Table 2.7 for data on the percentage of Six Culture observations in which mothers are present). Thus, with increasing age children spend less time with their mother, but when interacting with her, their dependency (as a relative proportion of all social acts) remains high, especially in the case of boys.

Maccoby and Masters in their literature review (1970) similarly found no clear-cut changes in proportional dependency with age, but they did find changes when they looked at particular subcategories of dependent behavior: the more intimate and proximal forms of dependency (clinging, seeking to be near the mother) were found to decrease with children's age, while more verbal modes of dependency (especially help and attention seeking) remained relatively high. The studies discussed by Maccoby and Masters were of American children.

Table 4.3 shows a cross-culturally consistent tendency for physical dependency (proximity seeking) to decline as children get older. The data from the New Samples show the greatest changes to occur between the age groups 2–3 and 4–5. The Six Culture data show that further changes take place between the yard-age and school-age periods: Tarong children and Juxtlahuaca and Nyansongo girls show a marked decrease in physical dependency between middle and later childhood.

Table 4.4 suggests that help seeking similarly tends to decline with children's age, especially for girls. In Bhubaneswar, Khalapur, Juxtlahuaca, Orchard Town, and Nyansongo, 10 percent or more of boys' total acts to mothers are still help-seeking behaviors, even in the oldest age grade.

Attention seeking (Table 4.5) shows no tendency at all for a general age decline in either boys or girls. Societies that actually show substantial increases in attention seeking with age for either boys or girls include two of the subsaharan samples (Ngeca and Nyansongo), one of the North Indian samples (Bhubaneswar middle/upper class), and Orchard Town, U.S.A. (although this latter sample has very few

Table 4.3. Proportion of proximity and contact seeking (as a percentage of all social acts to mothers) by children of different ages

Community (New Samples)[a]	Age 2–3 years			Age 4–5 years			Age 6–8 years			Mean (across sex/age groups) (%)
	Girls (%)	Boys (%)	Diff.	Girls (%)	Boys (%)	Diff.	Girls (%)	Boys (%)	Diff.	
Kien-taa	4	[0]	+4	2	6	−4	—	—	—	3
Kokwet	29	34	−5	21	17	+4	2	11	−9	19
Kisa	26	23	+3	3	21	−18+	12	14	−2+	17
Kariobangi	10	14	−4	11	0	+11+	10	[14]	−4	10
Ngeca	26	15	+11**	8	9	−1	5	3	+2	11
Bhubaneswar, lower class	38	43	−5	[0]	13	−13	18	17	+1	22
Bhubaneswar, middle and upper classes	41	21	+20***	37	14	+23**	19	25	−6	26
Mean of 7 groups	25	21	—	12	12	—	11	14	—	15

Community (Six Cultures)[b]	Age 3–6 years			Age 7–10 years			Mean (across sex/age groups) (%)
	Girls (%)	Boys (%)	Diff.	Girls (%)	Boys (%)	Diff.	
Nyansongo	27	0	+27*	2	0	+2	7
Juxtlahuaca	44	17	+27**	10	[0]	+10	18
Tarong	31	46	−15	6	12	−6	24
Khalapur	8	0	+8	0	0	0	2
Orchard Town	2	1	+1	0	[0]	0	1
Mean of 5 groups	22	13	—	4	2	—	10

Note: [+] $p < .10$, [*] $p < .05$, [**] $p < .01$, [***] $p < .001$.
a. See note a to Table 4.2.
b. See note b to Table 4.2.

Table 4.4. Proportion of help seeking (as a percentage of all social acts to mothers) by children of different ages

Community (New Samples)[a]	Age 2–3 years			Age 4–5 years			Age 6–8 years			Mean (across sex/age groups) (%)
	Girls (%)	Boys (%)	Diff.	Girls (%)	Boys (%)	Diff.	Girls (%)	Boys (%)	Diff.	
Kien-taa	19	[20]	−1	9	8	+1	—	—	—	14
Kokwet	1	4	−3[+]	6	0	+6	2	4	−2	3
Kisa	0	4	−4	3	0	+3	3	0	+3	2
Kariobangi	9	10	−1	5	3	+2	5	[0]	+5	5
Ngeca	5	10	−5	12	8	+4	4	6	−2	8
Bhubaneswar, lower class	25	21	+4	[22]	20	+2	0	17	−17	18
Bhubaneswar, middle and upper classes	22	10	+12**	19	14	+5	3	11	−8	13
Mean of 7 groups	12	11	—	11	8	—	3	6	—	9

Community (Six Cultures)[b]	Age 3–6 years			Age 7–10 years			Mean (across sex/age groups) (%)
	Girls (%)	Boys (%)	Diff.	Girls (%)	Boys (%)	Diff.	
Nyansongo	14	0	+14	5	11	−6	7
Juxtlahuaca	14	20	−6	17	[33]	−16	21
Tarong	20	9	+11*	9	6	+3	11
Khalapur	38	36	+2	23	62	−39	40
Orchard Town	20	26	−6	20	[25]	−5	23
Mean of 5 groups	21	18	—	15	27	—	20

Note: [+] p < .10, * p < .05, ** p < .01.
a. See note a to Table 4.2.
b. See note b to Table 4.2.

child-to-mother acts). This pattern does not lend itself to a ready cultural explanation.

In sum, the cross-cultural findings indicate that dependency may change form and become less intimate and proximal as children grow more verbal and mature, but it does not disappear. Mothers may pressure their children toward maturity by lessening their initiated and responsive nurturance, but children, when interacting with mothers, continue to see their mothers as providers of good things and feelings. They continue to seek material and emotional resources from their mothers as their highest single summary category of observed behavior.

Cultural Differences in Expression of Dependent Style

Although there are universal aspects to children's dependency, there are culturally specific ways in which the expression of dependency is limited or encouraged by caretaking adults. The wants and desires of children are founded in developmental maturity but modulated by culture. Mothers elicit seeking behavior in all the communities studied, but they channel children's styles of seeking in accordance with their theories of natural or acceptable behavior in children. The data have much to say about the intersection of specific cultural expectations, on the one hand, and universal needs and wants, on the other.

Adults in some cultures encourage an active, insistent, almost aggressive style of dependency in their children through a pattern of inconsistent nurturance. Susan Seymour (1974, 1976a, 1976b) has described this pattern in the North Indian mothers of Bhubaneswar (where she did her fieldwork) and Khalapur (studied by Leigh Minturn and John Hitchcock). Seymour claims that North Indian mothers respond intermittently to their children's demands for comfort, care, and attention, often only after delays and persistent crying by their infants or children. This "aperiodic" reinforcement of seeking behavior by the mothers thus increases the strength of their children's seeking behavior. Here is an example from a New Capital middle-class household of a mother offering, then withdrawing, her breast:

> Mrs. S. returned to the back verandah with Giti (girl, 1 year) and nursed her for a moment on her left breast. (This was for the third time that morning during a one-hour period.) Then she stopped Giti from sucking and made her sit up on her lap. Giti sat on her mother's

Table 4.5. Proportion of attention seeking (as a percentage of all social acts to mothers) by children of different ages

Community (New Samples)[a]	Age 2–3 years			Age 4–5 years			Age 6–8 years			Mean (across sex/age groups) (%)
	Girls (%)	Boys (%)	Diff.	Girls (%)	Boys (%)	Diff.	Girls (%)	Boys (%)	Diff.	
Kien-taa	17	[15]	+2	10	15	−5	—	—	—	14
Kokwet	11	4	+7*	4	4	0	2	11	−9	6
Kisa	8	17	−9	17	18	−1	16	8	+8	14
Kariobangi	10	30	−20**	7	24	−17*	8	[9]	−1	15
Ngeca	10	17	−7+	20	28	−8	12	19	−7	18
Bhubaneswar, lower class	0	1	−1	[0]	4	−4	0	0	0	1
Bhubaneswar, middle and upper classes	0	6	−6*	0	16	−16*	13	8	+5	7
Mean of 7 groups	8	13	—	8	16	—	8	9	—	11

Community (Six Cultures)[b]	Age 3–6 years			Age 7–10 years			Mean (across sex/age groups) (%)
	Girls (%)	Boys (%)	Diff.	Girls (%)	Boys (%)	Diff.	
Nyansongo	4	1	+3	15	21	−6	10
Juxtlahuaca	4	0	+4	3	[0]	+3	2
Tarong	3	1	+2	6	3	+3	3
Khalapur	5	7	−2	8	5	+3	6
Orchard Town	12	10	+2	13	[25]	−12	15
Mean of 5 groups	6	4	—	9	11	—	7

Note: * p < .05, ** p < .01, *** p < .001.
a. See note a to Table 4.2.
b. See note b to Table 4.2.

lap crying intermittently and reaching for her mother's breast. Mrs. S. held her saree over the breast so that Giti could not get to it. She laughed and tried to get Giti to smile. Finally, Giti broke into a smile. A few minutes later Mrs. S. pulled her saree back and let Giti nurse some more. She let Giti suck for several minutes and then sat her up again. (Seymour, 1974, p. 5)

Seymour found that maternal responsiveness is especially low in the large joint households of traditional residential areas and in families of lower socioeconomic status, where mothers are busy with economic tasks in addition to housework and child care. In contrast to many of the other sample communities, there is a good deal of confusion in the North Indian families' courtyards because of the large number of people who are usually present. Furthermore, although the workload of the mothers is lighter than in subsaharan Africa, food preparation in North India is much more elaborate than the maize and bean menus that are the main fare of subsaharan Africa and Mexico.

As a result of the inconsistent responsiveness, much of children's attention-seeking behavior in Bhubaneswar is scored as teasing, aggressive, or negative in tone—a pattern that parents referred to as "naughty" but seemed to accept as a stage children must go through and outgrow. In Seymour's view, the active dependency of Indian children is part of a much larger cultural whole: interdependence of people is the ideal in India and has been institutionalized in the joint family system, intercaste relations, begging of the destitute and "holy men," and so forth.

Another dimension of dependency affected by culture is its usual modality—verbal or nonverbal. During infancy, caretaking practices influence whether children come to express their needs more through motoric or through vocal signals. Infants who are carried on their caretakers' front, back, or hip much of the day develop a more motoric style, originally based on subtle, tactile communication with caregivers. Many anthropologists who have worked in societies in which infants are frequently carried have commented on the low amount of infant crying heard, noting that mothers often respond to infants' needs before they break into actual crying. In contrast, cultural expectations are different where infants spend much time in beds, cradles, or playpens: infants then develop a vocal style of dependency based on crying or calling for their caregivers (J. Whiting, 1971, 1981a).

The findings that test this idea can be seen in Table 4.3. Proximity seeking, the physical style of dependency, is expected to continue into the knee-child period for lap babies who have been carried on the front, back, or hip. These lap children, who are used to communicating through bodily movements and touch, are expected to remain high in proximity seeking through the knee- or yard-child periods, since this is their preferred and most practiced method of eliciting nurturance and interaction. In contrast, proximity seeking is expected to be low during the knee- or yard-child periods for lap children who spend more time in beds, cradles, playpens, and the like.

In Table 4.3, which shows the proportion of mother-directed behavior that was coded as seeking proximity (or touch), the data are seen to support our hypothesis for 11 of the 12 communities. For example, the young children of Orchard Town and Khalapur, as expected, score low in proximity seeking; they are the lap babies who spend the least time in physical contact with caregivers. Likewise, the knee or yard children of the subsaharan African communities (Kokwet, Kisa, Ngeca, and Nyansongo) score high, as expected, in proximity seeking. As lap babies they sleep with their mothers and are usually carried around during the daytime on their caretaker's front, back, or hip. The knee or yard children of Tarong, Juxtlahuaca, and Bhubaneswar also score high in proximity seeking. As lap babies they are carried and held more than the infants of Orchard Town, but they tend to spend part of the day placed in cradles, family beds, or mats on the floor. Finally, the knee children of Kariobangi, as expected, score low in proximity seeking; Kariobangi mothers, not involved in subsistence agriculture, live in small city apartments and do not carry their babies as frequently as they do when dwelling in rural Kisa. Only the findings for Kien-taa fail to support our prediction; these children are carried in infancy and sleep with their mothers but score low in proximity seeking.

A verbal rather than physical side of dependency is expected in children who receive less physical contact and carrying as lap babies. Because attention and help seeking were coded for both the New Samples and the Six Culture samples, these two behaviors have been used to examine cultural differences in the vocal style of dependency. In a parallel vein, Bronson (1971) compared preference for verbal versus physical modalities in a reanalysis of observational data on seventeen 2-year-olds in Burton White's American sample (Brookline,

Massachusetts) and fourteen 2-year-olds in Beatrice Whiting's Kenyan sample (Ngeca). Bronson showed that the Ngeca 2-year-olds had significantly higher ratios of physical to verbal imitation, as well as physical to verbal aggression, when adult-directed behavior and peer-directed behavior were combined. We similarly expect the subsaharan African children to have relatively low amounts of verbal dependency.

Table 4.4 shows that help seeking is, as expected, high in Orchard Town, Khalapur, and Bhubaneswar and low in the subsaharan African communities. However, the findings on attention seeking do not fit our predictions. Table 4.5 shows that attention seeking is, as predicted, high in Orchard Town and low in Tarong and Juxtlahuaca. However, attention seeking is not high in North India, as was predicted. Most puzzling of all, attention seeking is surprisingly high in the subsaharan African samples, especially for boys, even though maternal values in these communities are not in the direction of encouraging vocal dependency. In the African sample communities, mothers and surrogates carry lap children a great deal; moreover, they do not unconsciously reinforce attention seeking (as do the mothers of North India) by giving children inconsistent attention, that is, by responding reluctantly or only after delays to young children's crying and whining. The attention-seeking findings, in sum, do not support our hypothesis about the cultural encouragement of a vocal style of dependency.

Sex Differences in Style of Dependent Behavior

What about sex differences in either total amount or preferred modality of dependency? American cultural stereotypes would have it that girls are allowed or encouraged to express greater dependency needs of all kinds than are boys—needs for affection, help, and approval (see Edwards and Whiting, 1974; Whiting and Edwards, 1973). These stereotypes are not supported by the cross-cultural data, however, with the possible exception of proximity seeking. Attention seeking may be higher in boys.

Returning to Table 4.2, one sees no hint of a tendency toward a feminine preponderance in total dependency. In 18 of the 30 paired comparisons, boys score higher, while girls score higher in only 10 (with 2 ties). Nine comparisons are statistically significant, with 4 favoring girls and 5 boys. Overall, it is boys who are slightly more dependent on mothers than are girls.

Sex differences in proximity seeking (Table 4.3) are also not great, but where the differences are statistically significant, it is girls who score higher. Of the 30 paired comparisons, 15 favor girls and 13 favor boys (with 2 ties), and all of the 5 comparisons significant at the 5 percent level or better have girls as the higher group. In an earlier paper (Whiting and Edwards, 1973), we concluded that proximity seeking may be a feminine form of physical contact, contrasting with rough-and-tumble play (roughhousing, or playful aggression), which appears to be a masculine modality—higher in boys than girls throughout the world (with a few exceptions, as in Ngeca.)*

Help seeking (Table 4.4) does not show consistent sex differences. Of the 30 paired comparisons, 15 favor girls and 15 boys, and few are significant. Of the 30 attention-seeking comparisons, 11 favor girls and 17 boys (with 2 ties). Of the 5 significant comparisons, 4 favor boys. The age grade where sex differences appear most consistently is the "transitional age" of 4–5 years. At this age, when American psychologists have hypothesized that children are forming their gender identity, boys engage in consistently more attention seeking, girls in consistently more help seeking. Attention seeking is a behavior that contains elements of dominance and self-assertion and may be a way in which young boys express their masculinity when interacting with their mothers, especially in the subsaharan African and North Indian communities where adult men are expected to dominate their wives forcefully. Help seeking, in contrast, may occur in girls because they receive earlier and stronger maternal pressure to engage in responsible household work; their help seeking may represent a way of gaining maternal guidance as they go about the challenging problem of accomplishing tasks in a responsible and correct way. We will show in the next section that girls are consistently more cooperative or compliant to their mothers' commands, and their greater help seeking at age 4–5 is as much an aspect of growing maturity as it is of residual infantile dependency.

Mothers as Elicitors of Obedient or Cooperative Behavior

As the primary physical and emotional nurturers of children, then, mothers elicit a great deal of seeking behavior, the primary goal of

---

*Rough-and-tumble play among children is also evidence of dominance struggles, as will be discussed in Chapter 7.

which is maternal care and attention. This seeking behavior is self-initiated on the child's part, not instigated by the mother, though its content and frequency are influenced by children's learning histories.

In addition to the self-initiated seeking behaviors, a second class of children's behaviors with mothers has sometimes been labeled as "dependent." This class includes the obedient or compliant behaviors that occur when children obey or follow maternal commands or requests. Obedient behaviors are not self-initiated; they occur as responses to maternal instigations. Why, then, have they been called dependent? They are not dependent in the sense of "succorant" (seeking nurturance), but they do derive from the dominant-dependent relationship of mother and child. Mothers, as the household managers responsible for their children's day-to-day well-being, protection, and health, must issue many training commands and requests that relate to the immediate and long-term interests of the children or the household as a whole. These "dominant" or "training" aspects of the maternal role require a complementary readiness to obey on the part of the child. Thus it can be said that mothers *elicit* children's obedience as part of their reciprocal relationship.

It may be that obedience, especially in reference to older children, should be relabeled "cooperation." The process of working with other people may teach children not just to obey passively, but also to cooperate actively. Within the household, the routine tasks of food preparation, cooking, cleaning, and child care are facilitated by the development of a mother-child choreography in which children not only respond to their mothers' stated requests but also come to anticipate their unstated desires and act with few commands or promptings. The goals of the children's efforts are set by the mother, who schedules the activities and when necessary demonstrates techniques or assists children who seek information or help. However, once children have mastered the necessary techniques and skills, then adult and child can work together with each person monitoring the other's actions and helping when help is called for. The asymmetric dominance/dependence relationship of mother and child evolves into a more symmetrical manager/executive assistant relationship, in which the child's obedience and compliance have grown into a mature cooperation.

This type of cooperative relationship is clearly illustrated in many of our subsaharan observations focused on mothers and children working together. For example, when a group of mothers and daughters in Kenya work together to prepare a feast, one can observe the

Three-year-old girl helping older sister to clean blossoms of nim tree, Bhubaneswar (Susan Seymour, 1966)

perfect and intricate choreography of undirected cooperation in action. That such a choreography is achieved through a long learning process is evident to those of us who as adult American women have tried to share a kitchen with a new housemate. In contrast, we have noticed that when the visitor to our kitchen is our own mother, daughter, or sister, a different outcome occurs; as we have seen in Kenya, the mutual coordination of action and the responsiveness to unspoken cues make the cooperation smooth and effective. The "owner" of the kitchen, no matter what her age, becomes the managing director, and the mother, daughter, or sister takes the complementary role of assistant.

Cooperative and obedient behavior thus indicates that the child helper has internalized a common goal with the adult and has learned to monitor the activities of co-workers in order to cooperate most effectively in the accomplishment of the task. However, this kind of mother/child cooperation is not one that allows the child much opportunity to suggest new strategies or to renegotiate the goal. The goals and techniques of housekeeping and child care derive from routine cultural patterns; the task demands are usually immediate and nonnegotiable, and there is little room for discussion of alternative strategies. Sometimes when a particular problem is encountered, a child may be allowed to make suggestions, but in general the sequence of steps is predictable and the solution routine.

Cultural, Age, and Gender Differences in Obedience and Cooperation

Thus interaction with mothers, especially in the context of task performance, should heighten the values of cooperation and obedience in children. Older children would generally be expected to be more able to control and channel their behavior and to respond compliantly. In terms of culture, children who live in communities where they and their mothers are busy with subsistence and child-care tasks would be expected to receive special pressure and practice in the act of cooperation. In addition, because girls in all communities spend more time working under the authority of their mothers than do boys, they would be expected to receive relatively more practice in cooperating with their mothers. Of course, boys theoretically could gain a comparable kind of practice through work with their fathers, but ethnographic information and the spot observations discussed in Chapter 2 indicate that preadolescent boys spend far less time with men than girls do with women and that overall boys engage in less work than girls. Boys are generally not assigned "men's work" until their early teens, except in societies where young boys are involved in the care of large animals.

Our theory thus predicts that older children, girls, and children who live in certain cultural communities, those featuring the training mothers (see Chapter 3), should be relatively obedient to their mothers' commands and suggestions. The findings regarding these hypotheses are presented in Table 4.6. This table shows, for twelve cultural samples, age and gender differences in the percentage of children's compliance to maternal commands or suggestions. "Compliance" is measured as the percentage of occasions when the child obeys either immediately or after an initial delay or refusal. For each sex/age group, the number of compliant acts is divided by the number of total events (compliances plus noncompliances) to form the ratios presented.

The table indicates that children show generally more cooperation as they grow older, although the overall changes are not great. The children in the New Samples range from 72 percent total compliance

Table 4.6. Percentage of children's "total compliance" (immediate or delayed) to mothers' prosocial commands and reprimands

Community (New Samples)[a]	Age 2–3 years			Age 4–5 years			Age 6–8 years			Mean (across sex/age groups) (%)
	Girls (%)	Boys (%)	Diff.	Girls (%)	Boys (%)	Diff.	Girls (%)	Boys (%)	Diff.	
Kien-taa	70	[73]	−3	89	83	+6	—	—	—	79
Kokwet	91	75	+16*	84	84	0	96	89	+7	87
Kisa	83	62	+21	91	83	+8	83	76	+7	80
Kariobangi	76	95	−19	87	76	+11	86	[92]	−6	85
Ngeca	81	70	+11*	86	84	+2	96	92	+4*	85
Bhubaneswar, lower class	62	67	−5	—	68	—	77	62	+15	67
Bhubaneswar, middle and upper classes	57	53	+4	63	50	+13	78	58	+20	60
Mean of 7 groups	74	71	—	83	75	—	86	78	—	78

Percentage of "total compliance" (immediate or delayed) to mothers' instigations (of any type)

Community (Six Cultures)[b]	Age 3–6 years			Age 7–10 years			Mean (across sex/age groups) (%)
	Girls (%)	Boys (%)	Diff.	Girls (%)	Boys (%)	Diff.	
Nyansongo	71	53	+18	63	45	+18*	58
Juxtlahuaca	69	79	−10	78	[44]	+34**	68
Tarong	68	48	+20**	77	61	+16+	63
Khalapur	51	60	−9	67	50	+17	57
Orchard Town	48	53	−5	76	—	—	59
Mean of 5 groups	62	59	—	72	50	—	61

Note: + p < .10, * p < .05, ** p < .01.
a. See note a to Table 4.2.
b. See note b to Table 4.2.

at ages 2–3, to 79 percent at ages 4–5, to 82 percent at ages 6–8. Furthermore, as predicted, the subsaharan African children from communities with busy training mothers are relatively more compliant than the children from the other communities. (Nyansongo appears to be the exception to the rule, but it has very small numbers of compliant versus noncompliant acts.)

The table also supports the hypothesis that girls are generally more obedient to mothers than are boys. Of the 28 boy/girl comparisons in Table 4.6, girls score as more compliant in 20, while boys score higher in only 7 (with 1 tie). The sex differences are statistically significant at the .05 level for six of the individual comparisons, and in all cases girls outscore boys. The gender difference is consistent across the three age groups. Bronson (1971) likewise found in her comparison of Brookline and Ngeca 2-year-olds that girls were significantly more compliant to adults than were boys; she did not discover cultural differences among children of this young age, but the gender difference was consistent across both American and African groups.

A complementary interpretation for the sex difference seen in Table 4.6 concerns how obedience conforms with children's emerging sense of gender identity. Starting around age 4 or 5, when children are said to develop an identity as masculine or feminine, boys become more conscious of the relative superiority of men's status in their society and may begin to see obedience to mothers as "unmanly." Because boys are less involved with their mothers' work goals than are girls, they may experience obedience as an unwilling "giving in" to the mother, whereas girls may experience the same obedience as an act of willing cooperation. Thus, obedient behaviors with the same outward form may have different inner meanings for boys versus girls and be striven for by the one, avoided by the other.

Mothers as Elicitors of Dominant/Aggressive and Sociable Behavior

Dependency and obedience have been shown to be elements of the complementary mother-child relationship. Because of the greater age, maturity, authority, and power of the mother, this reciprocal relationship is largely asymmetric. The mother's role is to be nurturant and prosocially commanding; the child's role is to be dependent and obedient or cooperative.

Not all aspects of the mother/child relationship are asymmetric, however; at least two kinds of children's behavior would be expected to occur in a symmetrical fashion to maternal behavior. One of these is children's *dominance and aggression,* the counterpart of maternal control (defined as egoistic dominance and reprimanding). Dominance/aggression behaviors are comparable to dependent behaviors in that their judged intent is to satisfy the actor's own needs, but they are distinguished from dependency in involving an assertive, ascendant, or commanding style rather than a seeking or supplicant style. The other type of symmetrical mother/child interaction is *sociability,* defined as greeting, chatting, and other behaviors whose apparent goal is pleasurable interaction with another human being.

Dominance and aggression are never the most frequent categories of children's behavior to mothers. Table 4.7 presents the scores of children's dominance/aggression behavior as a proportion of total behavior to mothers. A comparison of Table 4.2 and Table 4.7 shows that dependency in every instance surpasses dominance/aggression (usually by many times over).

Table 4.7 does not indicate any consistent sex or age trends in children's dominance/aggression to mothers. However, the cultural differences are interesting. The cultural samples with the highest dominance/aggression scores form an obvious cluster: the children of the three North Indian communities and Orchard Town, U.S.A., rank first to fourth. This exactly mirrors the findings on maternal control, because these are the very four communities with the largest proportions of maternal control. Thus, mothers who engage in large amounts of dominating and reprimanding have children who engage in large proportions of dominance/aggression (mostly verbal aggression and commands coded as "seeks submission"). As we have noted, the mothers in these four communities do not work outside the home. Indeed, in the North Indian communities the mothers are confined by the custom of *purdah* to their enclosed and often crowded courtyards, and they have fewer means of channeling their children's energy than do the subsaharan African women who work in the gardens. As a result, the North Indian children are often underfoot, interrupting their mothers' housework and adult sociability and arousing maternal reprimands (rather than commands to perform prosocial activities). Similarly, the Orchard Town mothers are confined in the house for many hours each day with their preschoolers, especially when the weather is cold. The mothers' controlling behav-

Table 4.7. Proportion of dominance and aggression (as a percentage of all social acts to mothers) by children of different ages

Community (New Samples)[a]	Age 2–3 years			Age 4–5 years			Age 6–8 years			Mean (across sex/age groups) (%)
	Girls (%)	Boys (%)	Diff.	Girls (%)	Boys (%)	Diff.	Girls (%)	Boys (%)	Diff.	
Kien-taa	8	[2]	+6	8	15	−7	—	—	—	8
Kokwet	6	2	+4	2	6	−4	2	4	−2	4
Kisa	2	0	+2	0	0	0	4	3	+1	2
Kariobangi	3	2	+1	4	3	+1	3	[4]	−1	3
Ngeca	2	0	+2	2	3	−1	0	1	−1	3
Bhubaneswar, lower class	13	10	+3	[56]	50	+6	36	58	−22	37
Bhubaneswar, middle and upper classes	9	25	−16***	14	29	−15+	45	12	+33***	22
Mean of 7 groups	6	6	—	12	15	—	15	14	—	11

Community (Six Cultures)[b]	Age 3–6 years			Age 7–10 years			Mean (across sex/age groups) (%)
	Girls (%)	Boys (%)	Diff.	Girls (%)	Boys (%)	Diff.	
Nyansango	4	17	−13	10	0	+10	8
Juxtlahuaca	4	17	−13*	7	[1]	+6	7
Tarong	6	7	−1	0	0	0	3
Khalapur	18	21	−3	0	0	0	10
Orchard Town	22	17	+5	13	[0]	+13	13
Mean of 5 groups	11	16	—	6	0	—	8

Note: + p < .10, * p < .05, *** p < .001.
a. See note a to Table 4.2.
b. See note b to Table 4.2.

ior escalates as the noise and activity level of the children increase, particularly when siblings begin to squabble and engage in dominance battles.

Given this interpretation, one might also expect Kariobangi (the urban locale for the Kisa migrants) to show high levels of child-to-mother dominance and aggression. The children of Kariobangi do in fact show a pattern of increased aggression and disruptiveness, but the disruptiveness is not directed toward mothers. Weisner (1979), who analyzed child-to-child dominance and aggression for children in the rural and urban samples, showed increases for children's disruptiveness in the city. However, the Abaluyia cultural patterns of maternal control (strong prohibitions against overt aggression by children toward adults) mean that children's dominance and aggression are directed toward other children, not adults.

In understanding the pattern of the North Indian samples, it is also worth considering the central importance of caste and age/gender hierarchies in the organization of larger Indian society and in the small routines of daily life. By their behavior, Indian mothers may be introducing themes of hierarchy and dominance/subordination to their children and unconsciously allowing, or even encouraging, their children to begin to practice dominance and controlling behaviors. The Orchard Town pattern, in contrast, may derive from a different ideological basis. Orchard Town mothers believe strongly in equality and achievement as social values, and they may unconsciously allow or encourage their children to practice dominance behavior as a part of striving for achievement and success in a competitive society.

Table 4.8 presents the proportion scores of children's "verbal sociability" to mothers. (Note that proximity seeking, though originally coded as "physical sociability," was analyzed as part of the summary category of children's "total dependency.") Although verbal sociability is found to be a sizable proportion of children's behavior, it does not show interpretable culture or gender differences. When boys' and girls' scores are pooled, there is a suggestion of an increase with age (from 4 percent at ages 2–3 to 9 percent at ages 6–8 for the New Samples, and from 22 percent at ages 3–6 to 27 percent at ages 7–10 for the Six Culture samples). Thus, sociability is seen to increase as a relative proportion of children's behavior to mothers as children become more socially competent and less dependent toward their mothers.

Table 4.8. Proportion of verbal sociability (as a percentage of all social acts) that children initiate to mothers

Community (New Samples)[a]	Age 2–3 years			Age 4–5 years			Age 6–8 years			Mean (across sex/age groups) (%)
	Girls (%)	Boys (%)	Diff.	Girls (%)	Boys (%)	Diff.	Girls (%)	Boys (%)	Diff.	
Kien-taa	1	[2]	−1	2	3	−1	—	—	—	2
Kokwet	6	5	+1	4	2	+2	2	0	+2[+]	3
Kisa	15	6	+9	17	27	−10	27	28	−1	20
Kariobangi	16	4	+12	12	8	+4	7	[18]	−11	11
Ngeca	5	7	−2	9	6	+3	14	16	−2	10
Bhubaneswar, lower class	0	0	0	[0]	0	0	0	4	−4	1
Bhubaneswar, middle and upper classes	1	1	0	0	6	−6	2	0	+2	2
Mean of 7 groups	6	3	—	6	7	—	8	11	—	7

Community (Six Cultures)[b]	Age 3–6 years			Age 7–10 years			Mean (across sex/age groups) (%)
	Girls (%)	Boys (%)	Diff.	Girls (%)	Boys (%)	Diff.	
Nyansongo	18	44	−26[+]	38	36	+2	34
Juxtlahuaca	15	33	−18*	33	[0]	+33*	20
Tarong	16	24	−8	34	53	−19	32
Khalapur	20	7	+13	8	19	−11	13
Orchard Town	26	21	+5	20	[25]	−5	23
Mean of 5 groups	19	26	—	27	27	—	25

Note: [+] p < .10, * p < .05, ** p < .01.
a. See note a to Table 4.2.
b. See note b to Table 4.2.

Conclusions

The findings on children's behavior indicate that there are large transcultural similarities in the ways in which children of each age grade behave toward their mothers. The eliciting power of mothers derives from the universal needs of children and the nurturing, training, and guiding dimensions of the maternal role. All children need food, protection, comfort, physical contact, attention, information, guidance, and social interaction, and especially during their children's infancy, mothers are the people in most cultures who are the primary caretakers. As children grow older, other caretakers may play an increasingly greater role in meeting their needs, but when children are in the presence of their mothers, they still continue to direct many dependent acts to them (as a proportion of their total social acts). The findings presented in this chapter suggest that children's dependency toward mothers does not so much decline as it changes in modality during the early and middle childhood years. As children move from infancy through childhood, they become more verbal, more competent in motor skills, and more able and eager to acquire cultural values and information. As a result, their preferred style of dependency tends to shift from the more physical and intimate modes toward the modalities that rely more heavily on verbal skills and relate more to competence in socially approved behaviors. For example, older children tend to seek attention and approval for their performance, help in performing chores or completing self-care tasks, information about happenings that they have observed or heard about, and permission to leave the home and explore the greater environment or to participate in desired activities.

Cultural differences are seen in the ways in which mothers encourage or limit the expression of their children's wants or demands. By carrying or holding children a great deal during infancy, mothers in some cultural groups influence their children to retain a physical style of expressing dependency throughout the knee- and yard-child periods. In contrast, mothers in other groups, by distancing themselves from their infants with the use of such holding devices as cribs, cots, hammocks, or cradles during much of the day or night, ensure that their children will move early toward more verbal and distal styles of dependency, based at first on crying or calling out for the mother. Furthermore, in communities where mothers are especially involved in subsistence work and reliant on their children's assistance, they genuinely need children's cooperation and encourage obedience and responsibility as desired traits in children. Finally, in cultures where mothers engage in relatively high levels of controlling behavior (dominating and reprimanding), they encourage their children to express their egoistic needs in dominant/aggressive modes—to engage in relatively high levels of submission-seeking and insulting behaviors.

Chapter 5

Learning Prosocial Behavior

Interacting with and caring for lap and knee children provide older children with an important opportunity to learn prosocial behavior. These younger children, by their very nature and behavior, elicit prosocial behaviors. In the settings that these children frequent, mothers may also be present, and they model and teach appropriate behavior if they assign caretaking roles to the older children. When the older children then function as caretakers in their mothers' absence, they learn more of the requisite skills by trial and error. Thus girls and boys who frequent social settings that include lap and knee children have the chance to learn and practice nurturance and prosocial dominance, behaviors that are characteristic of the maternal role. Since girls are more frequently in the presence of lap children and are assigned the care of both lap and knee children more frequently, they have more opportunity than boys to learn and practice these behaviors.

Nurturance, as defined here, consists of all those helping and supporting behaviors offered to an individual who is perceived by the actor to be in a state of need. The field observer notes a nurturant act when she records an individual's responsiveness to the succorant demands of another, or observes an actor anticipating what he judges to be another's needs and desires. The nurturant acts may include offering food, material goods, emotional comfort, support and approval, or rights and privileges when the actor controls any of these resources that the other individual needs. Thus, a young child who attempts to distract a crying baby by offering it food or a toy, or by attempting to make it smile, is judged to act nurturantly to the baby; or a child may nurture a friend who is encountering difficulty by helping him to carry a heavy basket. A nurturant child responds to the requests of others for help.

The essence and prototype of nurturance are what has traditionally been called "maternal" behavior, a term used here with the recognition that both males and females, adults and children may behave in maternal ways. In societies that assign the care of younger siblings to children, this nurturant behavior is approved by the elders. Since in most of the nonindustrialized countries children of ages 6 to 8 act as child nurses, nurturant behavior is expected, rewarded, and practiced in childhood. Because these children are members of an extended family or interdependent community, the concept of concern for others and concern for acceptance by one's social group is inculcated; they are trained to be responsible members of their family and kin group.

We assume, in accordance with the sociobiologists, that maternal behavior serves the phylogenetic purpose of helping individuals to reproduce themselves. To this end, parents (not necessarily consciously) invest time and energy in their offspring with the goal of raising them to maturity. To reach this goal, parents and their surrogates must act in nonegoistic ways, putting aside immediate self-gratification in the interest of the welfare of other human beings.

Maternal behavior in all societies is geared to the developmental age of the offspring. In the earliest years of an infant's life, the physical well-being of the child is paramount, and nurturance predominates over other categories in parental behavior. During the infant's preverbal stage, successful nurturance requires that the caretaker be capable of judging and satisfying the needs of the infant. We use the term *needs* here in the true sense of the word, meaning those things essential for physical survival, including food, oxygen, temperature control, protection from noxious environmental elements and disease, relief from fright and anxiety through physical contact, and both stimulation and rest. In most of the world, especially in preindustrial societies where infant mortality is high, the focal concern of the parents of infants is their physical survival— meeting the universal basic needs.

With age, the child develops *wants* (desires) as well as needs. These are the products of social living and are shared by the majority of members of a society. Nurturant behavior will include acts judged to have the goal of satisfying these wants. Although differing in content from society to society, these wants can be categorized into a transcultural typology. In our model we include in the transcultural list

Brother entertaining 2-year-old, Bhubaneswar (Susan Seymour, 1966)

the desire for responsiveness from the physical and social environment, which encompasses desires for social interaction, responsiveness, stimulation, predictability, reassurance, physical contact, verbal comfort, emotional support, approval, self-esteem, and, at various times, autonomy and freedom to explore the social world (B. B. Whiting, 1980).

We have thus defined a nurturant act as a behavior whose judged intent is to satisfy another person's need or want for any type of concrete or emotional aid. *Summed nurturance* includes all offers of food and drink, toys, help, comfort, protection, attention, approval, helpful information, and so on. In the analysis of the Six Culture data, nurturance includes both acts initiated by the actor (initiated nurturance) and acts in response to the seeking behavior of alters (responsive nurturance).

Interaction with Lap Children as Training in Nurturance

Our data on social interaction demonstrate that in all the cultural communities studied, lap children receive a higher percentage of nurturance in all dyadic interaction than do other age groups. Table

5.1 presents these findings for the subsaharan African cases in the New Samples, detailing the proportion of initiated nurturance received by four classes of individuals from children aged 2–10 years. It can be seen that lap children in Nyansongo, Juxtlahuaca, and of age, receive the highest proportion of nurturance: twice the amount of any other type of partner; six to ten times more than children close in age or older children. Children more than three years younger than the actor receive the next highest proportion of nurturance, but less than half that received by lap children.

Table 5.1 also presents comparable data from three of the Six Culture communities where we can identify the age of the lap child. It can be seen that lap children in Nyansongo, Juxtlahuaca, and Tarong receive, on average, four to five times the amount of nurturance received by all younger children, older children, or mothers.

Nurturance is not the only positive behavior of children to lap babies. We summed the percentage of friendly interactions with the percentage of nurturance and compared the summary score with the total percentage of behavior to lap children that is judged to be

Table 5.1. Percentage of nurturance (as a proportion of all social acts) by children of different ages

Community (New Samples)[a]	Percentage of nurturance by children aged 2–10 years				
	To lap children (0–18 mo.)	To children more than 3 yr. younger	To near-age children (± 2 years)	To children more than 3 yr. older	To mothers
Kien-taa	36	14	7	8	2
Kokwet	31	15	8	2	3
Kisa	37	13	3	3	3
Kariobangi	38	17	6	4	4
Ngeca	33	13	6	3	2

Community (Six Cultures)[b]	Percentage of nurturance by children aged 3–10 years			
	To lap-child sibling (0–18 mo.)	To younger children	To older children	To mothers
Nyansongo	48	9	6	8
Juxtlahuaca	50	13	15	7
Tarong	49	11	5	8

a. Nurturance in the New Samples includes only initiated nurturance. In the Six Culture samples it includes both initiated and responsive nurturance.

b. Only the communities where the age of the lap child could be identified are included in this table.

egoistically dominant (the sum of "seeks submission," "assaults," and "insults" or "reprimands"). Only 10 percent of the behavior toward lap children in the subsaharan African samples and 13 percent in the Six Culture samples is judged to be subsumed in this nonpositive category. An additional 7 percent and 5 percent, respectively, is judged to be sociable teasing. In sum, between 70 and 80 percent of the interaction of older children with lap children is judged to be positive, only 17 percent antagonistic. This profile of positive interaction with lap children is true of even our youngest actors. Although our total sample of 2- to 3-year-olds is small (12 girls and 4 boys in child/infant dyads), more than 80 percent of their recorded acts are positive, only 8 percent nonpositive.

The comparatively high proportion of nurturance directed toward lap children, and its appearance in the youngest age grade, suggest that lap children have the ability actually to call forth or *elicit* nurturance. Konrad Lorenz (1943) has argued that there are certain characteristics of infants (lap children) that trigger the release of nurturing behavior in humans and other mammals. In all of our samples even the youngest children, 2- and 3-year-olds, are seen to smile at, pat, or imitate lap babies, to give them objects, play peek-a-boo games, tickle them, make faces to entertain them, and try to guess their needs or wants when the infants show distress. Lorenz lists as among the important releasing features of infants their "babyish" characteristics, such as a relatively large head, predominance of the brain capsule, large and low-lying eyes, bulging cheek region, short and thick extremities, a springy elastic consistency, and clumsy movements (Lorenz, 1943). John Bowlby (1969), in discussing the eliciting ability of infants, focuses not so much on their appearance as on their attractive and appealing "attachment" behavior, which actively serves to maintain their proximity to caretakers. These findings suggest that lap children are biologically equipped with behaviors that elicit and maintain caretaker involvement. Lap children smile, look, vocalize, and (when older) follow, all in the service of keeping people both near to them and socially engaged. They squirm, wince, frown, whine, and cry to elicit nurturance, and they smile, laugh, and wave their arms and legs to respond to friendly overtures.

Thus it appears that adults and children are "prepared" to respond positively to the lap baby's eliciting powers, just as it appears that lap children are "prepared" to respond to the friendly overtures of adults and children. If one accepts the hypothesis that humans share the desire for responsiveness from others, a responsive lap child is good company.

To illustrate how older children in many of our observations spontaneously offer nurturance and positive attention to lap children and seem to enjoy doing so, we present an excerpt from an observation made in Tarong.

> Marina (girl, age 10) is holding her infant sister, Leonida, while she stands watching the younger children running about. She swings the baby up in front of her until their faces are on a level. Grinning, she rubs noses with her. Puri (girl, age 12) wanders past Marina, carrying a baby. As she passes, she leans over and says, "Ba, ba, ba" to Leonida. Marina smiles at Puri. Marina pulls a nursing bottle from her pocket and presents it to Leonida, who seems interested. She squats down and, cradling the baby in her lap, holds the bottle for her. Dominga (older girl) crouches next to Marina, and the two smile as they watch the younger children, encouraged by Puri, chasing each oher. The baby stops eating and yawns. Dominga says, "Perhaps she is sleepy." Marina, tickling the baby's neck, replies, "She just woke up." Marina watches Leonida, who is playing with the nipple of her bottle and cooing. She moves across the yard toward Corazone (girl, age 9) who is holding a baby. Corazone looks, smiles at Leonida, and asks, "Has she teeth already?" Marina answers, a bit proudly, "Yes." Corazone asks, "How many?" Marina answers, "Two." Marina laughs as she watches the children playing. Jiggling Leonida, she says, "Hee hee, hee" to her. (Nydegger and Nydegger, field observations, 1955)

As noted in Chapter 3, mothers entrust lap babies to children as young as 4 years, but favor children between the ages of 6 and 10 as nurses. The 6- to 8-year-old nurses in Tarong, Taira, and Juxtlahuaca are good caretakers. In many of the observations the girls, in particular, seem to accept their role and enjoy it. The following observations made in two different parts of the world present a picture of a competent child nurse.

> Yuriko (Tairan girl, age 6) carries her sister on her back and walks around a banyan tree where a group of girls are playing. Although the baby is quiet, Yuriko lightly pats the baby's behind to pacify her. The girls by the tree are all looking at a book, but Yuriko merely looks in their direction and continues to walk around. The baby coughs a little, and Yuriko says, "Don't cry," and hops up and down in order to calm the infant. She walks back with rapid steps. As she walks up the road

Girl carrying brother, Tarong (1955)

past the store, Yuriko hums to herself and taps the baby's behind again. On the way she meets Kazufumi (boy, age 5), who is also carrying a baby on his back. His baby is crying. "Attend to the child," she shouts as he passes by. Kazufumi walks on, without looking back. (Maretzki and Maretzki, field observations, 1955)

Juanita, a Juxtlahuacan girl, has a similar nurturant interaction with her infant sister. The baby is tied on her back with her *reboza* (shawl) and Juanita supports the infant with her hands held behind her.

Juanita (girl, age 8) gently rocks back and forth, singing in a low voice. There are no words to the song. The infant begins to cry. Juanita stops singing, resettles the baby by bending her body forward and then standing up. She sings again, and once again begins to rock. When the little girl is quiet, Juanita very slowly sits down by her 6-year-old sister. The two girls look at each other and take hold of hands at the same time. (Romney and Romney, field observations, 1955)

Juxtlahuacan child nurse (1955)

Even in observations where infants are cared for by older siblings who seem quite uninterested in the task, the infants usually manage to be quite successful in eliciting nurturance. For example, consider the following observation made in Tarong of a 7-year-old boy with his 1-year-old brother. The brothers are sitting on a sled in the courtyard. Crescencio, the older brother, bored and yawning, is watching other children play tag. As we interpret the events of the observation, baby Pico uses considerable ingenuity to engage repeatedly his older brother's flagging attention. By accident Pico discovers that his older brother will retrieve his stick, so Pico drops it again and again.

Baby Pico (boy, age 1) starts to fuss. Crescencio (boy, age 7) turns to look at him, apparently surprised by the fussing, and picks up the stick Pico has dropped. "This is your toy," says Crescencio, then turns away to watch the other children. He notices Pico crying again and says (annoyed but not yet angry), "Stupid! You keep dropping it! And then you let me pick it up!" Crescencio picks up the stick and hands it to Pico, who immediately throws it to the ground. "No! Do not!" Crescencio angrily shouts and lightly slaps his brother's bottom. Then he breaks into a smile and returns the stick to Pico, who starts to throw it yet again. "You want me to put you there in the manure pile? I'll slap you, huh?" says Crescencio, lightly slapping Pico's bottom again. Pico starts to cry, dropping the stick. Crescencio, looking resigned but a little concerned over Pico's crying, hands Pico the stick. Then Crescencio settles himself to look over the yard. Pico again drops the stick. Crescencio sees the stick fall but does not move to get it. Pico starts to whimper and Crescencio imitates his whimpering sounds, "Uh, uh, uh." Then Crescencio pushes the stick to Pico with his foot. Pico now fusses loudly and Crescencio resignedly picks up the baby and walks off with him toward the older children. (Nydegger and Nydegger, field observations, 1955)

Our data do not, of course, directly address the issue of whether or not nurturant behavior is actually elicited through the kind of instinctual mechanisms postulated by Lorenz. However, the degree of similarity across cultures in the high proportion of nurturant behavior directed to very young children by social partners suggests to us the possibility of some such mechanism. In addition, the high percentage of positive behavior of the 2- and 3-year-olds suggests that this type of behavior is not learned.

American psychologists have also recently become interested in the power of very young children to elicit and maintain caretaking and attachment behaviors (see Stern, 1977). However, their studies have focused on adult-infant interaction, whereas our research extends the observation to include child companions and caretakers. Much of the recent research interest has arisen as a result of detailed micro-analyses of videotaped observations of parents interacting face-to-face with young infants (Brazelton, Koslowski, and Main, 1974; Brazelton et al., 1975). Cross-cultural studies (Field et al., 1981; Nugent, Lester, and Brazelton, 1987) using similar methodologies have revealed that styles of nurturing behavior by adults do vary considerably from one culture to another, though they retain certain cultural universals. For example, the *en face* position, characterized by mutual eye gaze, high levels of positive affect, and reciprocal vocalization, is found in other societies but favored more in our own. The Fais islanders of Micronesia, for instance, are more apt to position their infants on their laps facing outward rather than inward, perhaps because Fais mothers spend more time than do typical American women in social groupings including other adult companions (Sostek et al., 1981; see also Martini and Kirkpatrick, 1981, for similar findings in a study of Marquesas Islanders). Nyansongo mothers in Western Kenya are seen to resort to the en face position less and less after the infant reaches the age of 3 months, and even when interacting en face, they contrast with American parents by appearing to dampen or diffuse, rather than intensify, their infants' excitement through careful use of pauses and modulated responses (Dixon et al., 1981).

The most notable difference between American society and the other cultures studied in this book is the amount of time during which lap babies are in eye-to-eye contact with individuals other than their caretakers. In subsaharan Africa, Taira, and Juxtlahuaca, lap children are strapped to the backs of their caretakers for the major part of the day. These societies do not have cribs, baby carriages, playpens, or other means of confining lap children, and mothers and caretakers carry babies in shawls on their backs in order to free their hands for work or play. In all these societies, as soon as lap children are able to hold up their heads and look around, they can observe from their perch the behavior of their caretakers. From their mothers' or siblings' backs they can vicariously participate in the caretakers' activities—a fact we will return to in our discussion of knee children. The lap children receive greetings on an eye-to-eye level from many adults and children, who stop to elicit a smile or other positive response. In contrast, in societies such as the North Indian and North American communities, where lap children spend much time in a carriage, playpen, cot, or crib, interaction with others requires that an adult or older child stoop over to come into eye contact. These lap children, as a result, view a world full of legs; they are less able to witness the interaction of their caretakers or to hear their conversation with other individuals and thus vicariously participate in social interaction.

Since the lap children in most of our samples are in close physical contact with their mothers during both day and night (they sleep in

Boy nurse with toy car, Ngeca (Frances M. Cox, 1975)

body contact with their caretakers), much of their communication with caretakers is nonverbal. Caretakers learn to read the cues of their charges and to change their walking rhythm or to rock back and forth, jounce up and down, pat the baby's bottom, or change its position. The best demonstration of this kinesthetic style of communication is the caretaker's ability to foresee the lap child's need to urinate or defecate; the caretaker then holds the baby out before it soils the caretaker's clothes. In contrast, the style of communication of American mothers is more verbal and less kinesthetic.

Among our samples, Juxtlahuacan mothers and child caretakers are exceptional in their extensive use of nonverbal techniques—touches, gestures, and glances. This nonverbal type of communication can be seen in the following observation of Juanita, the eldest of four sisters.

> Juanita (girl, age 8) is sitting under a large shady tree in the courtyard with her sisters and two young boy cousins. She is holding her new baby sister wrapped in a *reboza* (shawl) on her lap. Another sister (age 2) pats the baby's head rather hard, knocking it to one side. Juanita pulls the baby back up against herself but says nothing to her little sister. Juanita jounces the baby up and down and talks in a murmuring tone to her. She watches the boys' play while patting the baby's neck continuously. Juanita's 6-year-old sister hits the 2-year-old with a piece of cloth and then looks at Juanita, who says nothing. The 6-year-old hits again, and the 2-year-old whimpers but does not say anything or move way. Juanita puts out her hands in a protective gesture, and the 2-year-old leans up against her.   (Romney and Romney, field observations, 1955)

Cultural groups clearly differ in their styles of expressing nurturance to infants. Nevertheless, we claim that a transcultural behavior system, readily and reliably recognizable as "nurturance," exists as the salient form of behavior directed to, and elicited by, lap children throughout the world.

The social-policy implications of studying infants' eliciting capacities are underscored by recent research findings that some infants, especially those born "at risk" because they are premature or handicapped, are less well equipped than normal infants to stimulate and maintain the attachment behavior of adults. These infants not only may be less physically attractive (by Lorenz' "babyish" criteria) but also may be less able to respond contingently to their caretakers and thus keep an interaction going. When their caretakers attempt to soothe them, they do not cease crying as immediately or completely; when their caretakers attempt to stimulate them by smiling and playing, they do not respond as quickly or positively (Lamb, 1978). Often they are inconsolable; their moods are labile and not often positive (Zeits and Prince, 1982). Perhaps these findings explain why "sickly" or deformed infants are more vulnerable to rejection, neglect, or inadequate care in many cultural contexts besides our own (Johnson, 1981, p. 64; Korbin, 1981, p. 208).

Age Changes in Children's Behavior to Infants

The responses triggered by the young child's immature appearance and behavior are surely not the only important antecedents to nurturant behavior; the physical and cognitive maturation of the caretaker, as well as his or her experience in caretaking, should have an important effect. An analysis of the proportion of nurturance of 4- to 10-year-olds in the subsaharan sample, however, does not indicate that either the age or sex of the actor is an important predictor of the nurturance of these children to infants (see Appendix D). There is a weak tendency for older children to be more nurturant than younger children, but the wide range of scores (ranging from 0 to 100 percent in the subsaharan sample and 22 to 80 percent in the Six Culture sample) and the small sample sizes preclude any conclusion from the data.

Although the quantitative data are not definitive on the effect of age, our qualitative data (observations) suggest that learning to moderate playfulness comes with maturation. Young children tend to overstimulate infants. Delighted when infants smile, laugh, or express pleasure by thrashing with their arms and legs, the 2- to 5-year-olds try to prolong the mirth and often overdo their playfulness. There is evidence in some of our data that the proportion of behavior to infants coded as sociability decreases with the age of the actor. This pattern emerges clearly in an analysis of the Ngeca data (Wenger, 1975; Wenger and B. B. Whiting, 1980). A comparison was made of the rates of nurturance, sociability, egoistic dominance (including aggression), and prosocial dominance for three age grades of children observed interacting with 2-year-olds. The three age grades of child actors were 3- to 4-year-olds, 5- to 7-year-olds, and 8- to 10-year-olds. The rate of nurturant behavior was found to increase linearly with age, significantly so between the youngest and oldest age grades ($p < .007$), while sociability and egoistic dominance declined.

These findings suggest a cognitive-developmental increase in impulse control and the ability to understand the perspective of another and to assess his needs and wants, developmental changes that have been documented by psychologists (Selman, 1980; White, 1965,

1970). These changes in behavioral profile are associated with increased age of the caretaker and also with increased experience interacting with lap children, especially in the role of child nurse. Unfortunately, we cannot at present separate out the relative contribution of maturation versus caretaking experience in causing the age changes in the nurturance of the Ngeca children, because age and experience are necessarily interdependent. We can, however, use our rich corpus of observational material to illustrate the qualitative nature of the age changes.

In most of our samples, 3- and even 2-year-olds are encouraged by mothers to entertain babies for short periods of time and to help stop their fussing. The children usually comply happily, playing peek-a-boo, imitating the lap child, and eliciting smiles and laughter. The problem with 3-year-olds as baby tenders is that they frequently misperceive the lap child's wants and needs or do not have the resources to meet them, and therefore they are unsuccessful in their attempts to nurture. For example, as already noted, they are particularly prone to overdo their hilarious play and overstimulate the lap child, which causes crying that the baby tender is then unable to quiet. Frustrated, the children may then become impatient and antagonistic—shaking, punching, or slapping the baby in exasperation. Thus their profile of behavior is both overly sociable and overly punitive, relative to that of older, more mature baby tenders. Mothers in many of our samples discourage the overstimulation of lap children by young children. The mothers forbid play accompanied by laughter if they think it will eventually lead to the lap child's crying or the older child's becoming too rough. This instruction by the mother (and the experience of attempting to care for an overexcited lap child) can explain the decrease in the proportion of sociability reported earlier.

Three-year-olds are also likely to go too far in their explorations of the lap child's responses; they may hurt or annoy the baby and then ignore its cries. For example, here is an illustration from Ngeca:

Wanjiru (girl, age 3) is told by her mother to sit beside her baby sister (age 6 months) and entertain her. Wanjiru approaches the baby, puts two fingers in the baby's mouth, pulls the lips apart, and looks in the baby's mouth. The mother notices and tells her not to do it anymore and that it is bad for the child. Wanjiru obeys, but after the mother leaves she repeats her actions. The mother returns and warns her again. Wanjiru now tries to put the baby's fingers in its mouth. This annoys the baby and it cries. (B. B. Whiting, field observations, 1973)

However, unless the lap children protest loudly, in general most of the mothers in our sample do not halt curiosity and exploration. Exceptions are the mothers of Orchard Town, who seem to stop older children's exploration of the lap child sooner than do the mothers of the other communities.

One type of situation that seems to call forth intentional aggressive behavior of 3-year-olds toward lap children occurs when the baby has an object that the other child wants or when the baby snatches something from the 3-year-old. Even more provocative is the situation in which the baby has food in its hand or is being fed by the mother or caretaker.

Mothers in all societies recognize aggressive behavior by the young child toward its follower as rivalry or jealousy and expect some such feelings in the displaced child. In fact, in the Kikuyu language, the word for the adjacent younger child has a stem meaning "rival." However, mothers in the different societies vary in their responses to jealous behavior. It is our impression that the New England mothers are most tolerant of jealous feelings, most apt to soothe rather than punish the displaced older child. The mothers of Tarong and Taira, in contrast, often resort to teasing the older child as a way of coping with sibling rivalry.

In an attempt to understand the variation in the nurturance scores of individual children, we reviewed the individual case material on children who had high scores for nonnurturant behavior. We found that such children were overrepresented in the sample families that expected young children to act as caretakers before the age of 6 to 8. In the subsaharan Kenyan samples, particularly Nyansongo and Ngeca, mothers who were involved in farming and had several small children but no hired help were forced to depend on very young children to act as surrogate caretakers. We have, for example, the case of a mother who had only a 3-year-old daughter to leave in charge of her 6-month-old and 2-year-old children when she left the house to bring the cow in from the pasture or to perform some other brief errand. Unlike her own mother's generation, this mother did not live in an extended or polygynous compound where other adults could have helped out or supervised the baby tender. The 3-year-old was not capable of sustained nurturant behavior; in fact, she was rough and dangerously negligent, and her charges frequently ended up in tears. On one occasion when her mother was gone, the child lay down beside the lap baby, sucked a bottle containing cough medicine, and then gave some to the baby.

Mothers in different societies vary in choosing the age of children to whom they are willing to delegate infant care and the amount of responsibility they are willing to assign. When interviewed, even the hardest-working mothers in subsaharan Africa stated that they preferred child nurses to be 7 or 8 years of age and that they used younger children only when there was no adult or sibling of the appropriate age. Orchard Town mothers seldom had baby sitters younger than 12 years of age. Given the small family size in Orchard Town, it is not surprising that only one child in the sample had any experience caring for a lap-child sibling.

In both Nyansongo and Ngeca, children designated as responsible caretakers might be expected to care for lap babies for 2 to 4 hours daily while their mothers worked in the garden or performed household chores. In the other communities, none of the child nurses were expected to work such long hours. Usually the child nurse kept the baby, who was at least 4 or 5 months of age, in the homestead where uncles, aunts, co-wives, or grandparents typically could be called upon if an emergency arose. However, if the homestead did not include these relatives, the child nurse might be as far as a quarter-mile away from the nearest adult. We have many observations of child nurses with their charges, and we can readily discern the behavior of those children who are overtaxed.

Comparing the behavior of 5- versus 8-year-old child nurses convinces us that the culturally universal preference for 8-year-olds is wise. The younger caretakers are inconsistent in their treatment of lap children: one minute they kiss and hug their charges, the next they pinch, slap, or strike them in irritation, or threaten and handle them roughly. The following observation of a 5-year-old Nyansongo girl illustrates the child's inability to cope with the frustration entailed in caring for a lap baby as well as her inability to put the needs of the baby before egoistic desires.

Rebecca (girl, age 5) is observed hoeing in a field with her aunt and cousins. Moriasi (brother, age 1) is also there. Rebecca interrupts her hoeing and goes and picks up the whining infant. She jounces him around a lot, and he begins to cry. "Why do you cry now?" she asks, "I've nothing to give you." She slaps him on the head and pushes him hard. When he cries, Rebecca puts him on her back. She carries the infant over and sits him by another baby who is in the shade at the front of a bigger house and says to the second baby, "Are you unable to walk to your mother?" She lifts up this baby, kissing it, singing to it, jouncing it up and down, and making it dance as she holds it. She sits it back down near her brother. Mokeira (girl cousin, age 5) starts wrestling with Rebecca. They continue wrestling and laughing, and while doing so move quite a distance away from the babies. The aunt sees this retreat and says to the girls, "Why are you leaving these babies?" Rebecca immediately comes running back and proceeds to amuse the babies by singing and dancing. (LeVine, field observations, 1956)

In another observation, Rebecca is seen actually eating her baby brother's food (a banana) while he cries. At the time of the observation food was especially scarce in Nyansongo, and child nurses often ate part of their charge's food.

Although the 6- to 8-year-old Nyansongo child nurses are considered by their mothers to be competent, as a group they are above the mean of Six Culture samples on nonpositive behavior. These children are expected to do some cooking, tend the fire, wash clothes and dishes, carry water, and run errands, in addition to acting as nurses for extended periods of time. Perhaps it is not surprising that they show mood swings toward the babies—sometimes affectionate, sometimes threatening and physically restraining.

The scores of dyad types do not reflect the individual variation that is found in all the samples. It is often possible, when we know families well, to understand why one child is more nurturant than another. The number of children in a family and the amount of help a mother has in child care and in her other work are important predictors. Njeri, a 5-year-old Ngeca girl, was particularly impressive for her age, as the following observation illustrates. Njeri was observed over a three-year period and at all times was a comparatively nurturant caregiver. She was the child of an extended, polygynous homestead where the co-wives were especially friendly and cooperative with one another. They were able to share work in such a way that both they and their children were less burdened and harried, and this was reflected in Njeri's behavior. During the following hour-long observation, Njeri remained nurturant even though she was obviously tired.

Njeri (girl, age 5) is lying on her stomach talking to her niece, Wanjiku (girl, age 5) while the 4-month-old baby sleeps on her back. Her mother's co-wife comes into the yard bringing water. She asks the girls to wash a pair of sneakers, and she admonishes Njeri to be careful of the baby. Njeri sits up carefully. The girls scrape the shoes and soak them in the water, talking and singing. They then begin to play, and the baby begins to awaken. The niece, Wanjiku, bites Njeri and she bites back, causing Wanjiku to cry. Njeri's mother calls to the girls that she does not want to hear any quarrelling. The infant is whining, and Njeri goes into the kitchen to try to get her mother to take her. However, her mother is too busy getting lunch and ignores Njeri. Although upset, Njeri places the baby on the bed and plays with her. She talks comfortingly until the child stops crying, holds her, licks her little hand, and talks to her. The mother tells Njeri in a firm tone that Kangethe (older brother) will be annoyed if he learns that she played on his bed. Njeri ignores this and goes to look out the door, leaving the baby on the bed. The baby fusses and the mother says (teasingly) to the baby, "I want you to cry louder before I pay attention to you." (Actually the mother is still too busy.) Njeri returns to play with the baby, and her mother instructs her to be careful that the baby doesn't fall off the bed.   (B. B. Whiting, field observations, 1969)

Thus it can be seen that the proportion of nonpositive behavior by children to lap babies is high in Nyansongo and Ngeca in those families where the mother has a heavy workload and no network of supporting women and asks her young child to care for a lap baby for an extended period of time. In Taira and Tarong, children are usually asked to care for lap babies only after school or on weekends. In Taira the mothers do not encourage the children to take the babies off their backs; hence the nurses serve primarily as baby carriages, and there are few observations in which the nurse interacts with her charge. In Juxtlahuaca mothers prefer child nurses to be older than 6; most of the baby tenders are 10-year-old girls. In Orchard Town baby sitters are usually 12 years of age or older.

To summarize, older children's interaction with lap children provides an excellent situation in which to study the development of nurturant skills. Although the quantitative data on interaction with lap children 18 months and under does not show significant effects of the nurse's age, the Wenger study of interaction with 2-year-olds and the illustrative case material from all the samples suggest that with increasing age and experience, children become more consistently and appropriately nurturant and less overstimulating, egoistically dominant, and aggressive. With age, the child nurse can sustain nurturant behavior for longer periods of time. Too much responsibility, however, even at age 7 or 8, increases the likelihood of nonpositive behavior.

Thus, in the majority of the communities, mothers prefer child nurses in the 6–10 age group, and preferably girls rather than boys if both are available. Just why mothers prefer this middle-childhood age group over adolescents is an interesting question. It may well be that in those societies where women work in subsistence activities and depend heavily on children's help, adolescents can contribute most usefully to the economic activities that require real physical strength and endurance. Furthermore, it appears from our observations that the 6- to 8-year-old child nurses are more willing than adolescents to engage in activities that interest lap (and knee) children, perhaps because, having recently been little themselves, they are better able to intuit young children's wants. In addition, girls of 6, 7, and 8 are eager to model their mothers' behavior and less interested than adolescents in establishing their own identity away from the homestead. Adolescent girls appear more interested in entering the adult world, where they will soon have their own babies. Thus, the younger child nurses are less frustrated by being at home than the adolescents, who have been granted the privilege of ranging farther from home and engaging in activities not supervised by adults.

Sex Differences in Children's Caretaking Abilities

It is interesting to speculate about why mothers in so many different types of societies say they prefer girls rather than boys as caretakers for their young children. Is it something about the girls themselves, in contrast to their brothers? For example, do mothers recognize that girls possess some innate (prepared), gender-linked capacity that makes them more sensitive and responsive to lap children than boys? Or are the mothers responding to the fact that girls generally tend to be more interested and attracted to babies? (See Berman, 1980, and Fogel, Melson, and Mistry, 1986, for a discussion of gender differences in interest in babies.) Or do mothers choose girls not because of something about the girls, but rather because they consider it inappropriate for male children to play the caretaker role?

There is evidence from some of the communities that mothers may consider girls more apt students of the maternal role. When interviewed about the characteristics of girls and boys, some mothers noted that girls were more responsible than boys, more apt to do what they were assigned. In fact, as we have noted, girls are more compliant to their mothers than boys. However, we know of no statement made by the mothers that girls are more nurturant to infants than are boys.

We have too few observations to make any final statement about the relative nurturance of boys and girls. Our theory would suggest that since infants elicit nurturance, both boys and girls should behave nurturantly. Table 5.2 presents the mean proportion of nurturance in dyads in which 4- to 10-year-old girls and boys interacted with infants. It can be seen that in six of the eight comparisons, girls are relatively more nurturant than boys, in some cases substantially so. When one looks at the individual scores in Appendix D, however, the range of these scores is seen to be great.

Although there is only weak evidence for greater nurturance by girls than boys to lap children, our data also suggest that girls interact more often with them than boys do. Table 5.3 presents the percentage of all the acts of girls and boys that are directed to lap children. It can be seen that in six of the eight samples, girls interact with babies

Table 5.2. Sex differences in mean proportion of nurturance to lap children by girls and boys 4–10 years of age

Community	No. of dyads (No. of all social acts to lap children in parentheses)		Percentage of nurturance (as a proportion of all social acts to lap children)		
	Girls	Boys	Girls (%)	Boys (%)	Diff.
New Samples[a]					
Kien-taa	5 (108)	3 (69)	38	25	+13
Kokwet	8 (89)	6 (48)	27	31	−4
Kisa	3 (16)	1 (5)	49	0	+49
Kariobangi	8 (131)	3 (27)	39	29	+10
Ngeca	10 (109)	4 (36)	47	29	+18
Six Culture samples[b]					
Nyansongo	6 (174)	3 (35)	45	51	−6
Juxtlahuaca	5 (72)	4 (33)	62	36	+26
Tarong	6 (173)	4 (186)	52	41	+11

a. Nurturance in the New Samples includes only initiated nurturance. In the Six Culture samples it includes both initiated and responsive nurturance.

b. Only the communities where the age of the lap child could be identified are included in this table.

more frequently than do boys. This finding recalls the spot-observation and other findings presented in Chapter 2 that show girls to be present more often than boys with lap children and to be found caring for them more often. Thus, although lap children elicit nurturance from both girls and boys, we conclude that either maternal assignment or children's own choices of what they like to do result in girls' getting more practice in maternal behavior.

It seems clear, then, that regardless of gender differences in nurturance, both boys and girls tend to be nurturant to lap children, more nurturant than to any other individuals with whom they interact. It is also evident that nurturance and sociability predominate in social interaction with lap children. Aggressive behavior tends to be observed in the interaction between older children and lap babies only when caretakers spend too long a period of time being responsible for the baby. Even knee children (2- to 3-year-olds) who have been displaced by a lap-child sibling are more positive than negative in their interaction with lap children.

There is some evidence of differences in the *style* of caregiving by male and female child nurses: girls appear to be more involved in the caretaker role and less reluctant to be caregivers. The comparison is clearest in Juxtlahuaca, where the girl nurses are the most consistently nurturant. By age 8, when the girls are called upon to be child nurses, they are expected to take full responsibility for lap babies

Table 5.3. Percentage of total acts of all children that are to lap children

Community	Girls (%)	Boys (%)	Diff.
New Samples			
Kien-taa	12	9	+3
Kokwet	5	3	+2
Kisa	4	1	+3
Kariobangi	11	11	0
Ngeca	5	1	+4
Six Culture samples[a]			
Nyansongo	38	16	+22
Juxtlahuaca	23	17	+6
Tarong	23	34	−11

a. Only the communities where the age of the lap child could be identified are included in this table.

and young siblings. They also perform many other chores and in many ways behave like adult women. Juxtlahuacan boys, in contrast, only care for younger siblings if there is no girl available. Jubenal, a 7-year-old and the eldest of four, was the only boy in our sample whose mother expected him to care for his siblings frequently. Although Jubenal appeared to be quite competently nurturant when necessary, in most observations when he was in charge he climbed trees, played games, called to his friends, and paid little or no attention to his siblings unless they cried or were in an obvious state of need. Unlike the typical Juxtlahuacan girl, who was most often observed combining child care with chores or casual sociability and gossip, Jubenal always tried to combine child care with active play with peers. This was a style more frequently found in Taira, where both boys and girls attempted to play all types of games with babies tied to their backs. However, Taira girls were unusual when compared with those in the other samples.

Across the samples, if one reads through the observations and makes a clinical judgment, girls seem to enjoy interacting with lap children more than boys do. In the following observation, Romulo, a Tarong boy caring for his younger brother, speaks out about his preference for children who can stand up and do things. Romulo's brother, Jimmy, is just learning to stand up by himself.

Romulo (boy, age 7) stands with Jimmy, the baby. He carries him to the middle of the yard. He stands Jimmy up by holding one of his hands and saying, "Stand. Balance yourself." Jimmy stands for a moment and then squats. Romulo again helps Jimmy stand, holding his hands and saying, "Stand, stand! You stand!"

Romulo slowly lets go of Jimmy's hand and backs off laughing as Jimmy stands alone staring at him. Romulo says, "Stand and do not open your eyes wide."

Romulo spreads his arms wide and makes noises at Jimmy. Then he notices his sister and a friend rolling a large empty oil drum. He goes over and tries to stand on it. He starts to sing loudly.

Jimmy, who has been watching, suddenly sits down hard and whimpers slightly. Romulo slides from the drum, laughs, notices Jimmy and runs back across the yard and helps him to his feet. He says "You stand" three times as he gets Jimmy up. Then he smiles and admonishes, "Standing is what I like." He leaves Jimmy standing and runs back to the drum.

All get on top of the drum. Romulo stands on the drum singing loudly. Jimmy sits down hard, whimpers once.

Romulo jumps off the drum and goes to Jimmy. He helps Jimmy stand, saying, "You balance yourself. I do not want one that cannot balance itself."

Jimmy starts to yowl loudly, and Romulo picks him up and carries him to the drum, sets him on it and climbs astride it behind him.

The girls watch, laughing. Romulo says, "Good! A bicycle!" (Nydegger and Nydegger, field observations, 1955)

To sum up, there is no question that lap children elicit nurturance and other positive, friendly responses from all ages of children and from both sexes. Eighty percent of the behavior of even our youngest class of children to lap babies is positive. We favor a hypothesis that lap children (from 3 months on) are biologically prepared to elicit nurturance and positive responses, and that adults and children are prepared to be responsive to these elicitations. Our data suggest the possibility of a trend across the samples for girls to be more nurturant to lap children than boys, but in our small sample the differences are not robust or consistent and are based on few data (since boys interact with lap children infrequently). However, even if one accepts that there is evidence of a difference, there is no way of separating the possible innate preparedness of girls to be nurturant from their experience. Girls receive more experience in interacting with lap children and therefore, since lap children elicit nurturance, more practice in nurturant behavior.

Thus, although we do not preclude the possibility of an innate preprogramming in females that makes them especially apt pupils in responding to lap babies, more interested in them, and more eager to imitate mothers as a function of identification, we have no conclusive data to indicate that girls are in fact greatly more nurturant to lap children than are boys. For this reason, our finding in subsequent chapters that girls are more nurturant to other classes of social partners than are boys may be the result of girls' training as child nurses. The difference in style between girl and boy child nurses may be a reflection of the boys' preference for physical activity, which may make them more reluctant than girls to be caregivers.

It is also important in considering the stereotypes of male and female behavior to remember that training in nurturance to nonverbal humans is training in intuition, a trait that, according to Western stereotypes, is considered to be characteristic of females. The caretaker of the preverbal child must guess the needs and wants of someone who cannot communicate by speech. Being able to intuit the child's desires requires that the individual draw on empathy, consciousness of her own wants in similar situations, or previous experience. Since girls have more experience than boys in caring for preverbal children, they receive more opportunity to develop this kind of intuition or empathy.

In many of the communities in the United States, few children have the opportunity to practice nurturance by interacting with lap children. In the Orchard Town sample, for instance, only 3 percent of children's interaction was with lap children, in comparison with an average of 19 percent in the four societies in the Six Culture study where children regularly cared for lap children (Nyansongo, Tarong, Juxtlahuaca, and Taira). In later chapters we will compare the nurturance of these Orchard Town children when they are interacting with knee children, older children, and peers to see if we can discover any differences that might be attributed to this lack of experience in caretaking.

Interacting with Knee Children as Training in Dominance

As the preceding observations indicate, child nurses are not only nurturant but also occasionally dominant. Knee children rank second only to lap children in the relative proportion of nurturance that they receive from children 4–10 years of age, but they receive much more dominance.

Two different types of dominance are commonly received from older children—egoistic dominance and prosocial dominance. *Egoistic dominance* is behavior judged to have the intention of changing the behavior of another to satisfy the actor's own desires without consideration for the needs or wants of the alter. An egoistically dominant actor may use simple commands or coercive techniques of persuasion (for example, seeking submission by direct commands or threats; assaulting or insulting; competing; or seeking freedom from social interaction in order to obtain personal goals). In contrast, *prosocial dominance* includes mands that attempt to persuade the social partner to behave so as to benefit the group or to behave in a socially approved manner.

All children younger than the actor elicit both types of dominance. Prosocial dominance is most frequent in the behavior of individuals who are responsible for the care and socialization of others, and, not surprisingly, mothers have by far the highest proportion of prosocial mands. Children also use this form of dominance as a technique for controlling the behavior of others: appealing to them to abide by the family's rules for appropriate behavior, asking them to do their share of the family work, or reprimanding them for deviations.

Once children can walk and talk—that is, once they become knee children—they elicit prosocial dominance. In all the countries we have studied, older siblings are expected to help care for knee children. Even when older children are not actually assigned the responsibility, it is assumed that they should monitor their younger siblings' behavior if no older member of the family or designated child nurse is present. Although caring for a lap child (an infant not yet able to walk) elicits nurturance and trains children in responsiveness and in intuiting the needs of a preverbal child, interacting with motile knee children also elicits prosocial dominance—that is, innumerable commands and proscriptions whose intent is to see that the exploring child does not harm himself or others.

The following interaction illustrates the type of behavior that is coded as prosocial dominance. The observation takes place at 4:00 P.M. in Taira, when the older children have returned from school to take over supervision of the younger ones while the mothers and grandmothers go about finishing the day's chores and preparing dinner.

> Toshiko (girl, age 7) and Satoshi (brother, age 2) are playing near the hedge of a neighbor's house. There is a pole leaning against one of the trees. Satoshi starts to climb up the pole and Toshiko says, "Don't, you'll fall!" The little boy giggles hilariously and answers, "No, I won't." Toshiko goes over and puts her arms around him and lifts him down gently.
>
> Later while Toshiko is climbing a tree with her friend, Satoshi again tries to shinny up the pole. Toshiko again tells him to get down and when he does not comply, she lifts him down, again gently. Toshiko then tells Satoshi, "You stay here for a moment. I am going home. OK?" Satoshi giggles and answers "yes," but when she leaves, he runs around the house and down to the beach. (Maretzki and Maretzki, field observations, 1955)

Caring for a knee child who does not choose to be confined is a much harder task than caring for a lap child. Anyone who has watched a 2-year-old will know that being responsible for a child of this age is time-consuming and requires the caretaker to be continually alert. The young charges are constantly on the move exploring the physical and human environment; they embark on many fool-hardy adventures and call forth many interventions, warnings, pro-hibitions, and reprimands—behavior we classify as prosocial domi-nance. These mands are judged to have the intent of protecting the knee child from harm.

Supervising a lap child is not so difficult. As we have seen, in most of the Third World cultures they are seldom put down on the ground and spend most of the day on the lap or back of their caretakers. In the tropics there is danger from infection from the numerous parasites that are present in the ground surrounding the houses, especially if animals are allowed in the yards. But 2-year-olds are too heavy to be carried all the time. Even when there are walls or fences that confine them, the bare ground is still a source of potential infection, and there are many objects that the child should not touch. With the exception of Orchard Town and New Capital, Bhubaneswar, all the houses in our sample communities have open fires, and being burned is an ever-present danger. In all of the societies except Orchard Town, where families have fenced-in yards and playrooms from which all dangerous articles have been removed, knee children must be super-vised. When adults are busy, as is frequently the case, older children must be called upon to supervise.

Knee children must be socialized into becoming acceptable mem-bers of their group as well as being protected from physical danger or infection. They are frequently advised as to hygiene, etiquette, and other social rules. Such remarks have been coded as pro-etiquette mands. "Don't play in the water, it is for drinking"; "Don't play on your brother's bed"; "Greet your grandmother"; "Don't climb on father's chair"; "Don't make so much noise"—these are typical kinds of prosocial/pro-etiquette mands issued to knee children by the care-taker. Suggestions and commands such as "Give the baby part of the banana" and "Give the baby that stick it wants" are also coded as prosocial (pro-child) mands. Although the details of the socialization process and the content of the rules differ from one society to another (and within a society from one family to another), the cross-cultural similarities in the lessons taught to young children are nevertheless striking.

In addition to pro-etiquette and pro-child mands, knee children begin to receive task commands (prosocial/pro-chore mands). Soci-eties differ in the age at which they begin assigning work to children, but in all of our sample communities, mothers assign errands to 2-

and 3-year-olds: the children are asked to feed chickens, gather fruit from under trees, carry firewood into the house, and many other simple tasks. In Khalapur and Juxtlahuaca, 3-year-olds are sent to the local store to make small purchases; in Juxtlahuaca, they deliver tortillas to be sold. These errands teach children vocabulary words for objects and appropriate labels for the individuals in their environment. In all of the Kenyan communities, 3-year-olds are assigned many little errands and tasks. After the birth of a new baby, these tasks are a way of keeping knee children busy and making them feel important, distracting them from their desire to regain their lost place with their mothers (LeVine and LeVine, 1963). In Ngeca, a mother returning from the field to greet her knee child who was left alone with older siblings was heard to say in a nurturant manner, "So no one has taken care of you all day." Soon she was dispatching the small child off to carry potato peels to the compost pile. It is clear from the observation that the child enjoyed performing the chore. In societies where the 4- and 5-year-olds are beginning to have assigned work, the knee child feels grown up when included in the work force. Our Kenyan student observers remembered from their childhood that to be assigned a chore was to be part of the family, to be important in the mother's eyes. To be overlooked when work was handed out was interpreted as disapproval—what some might call withdrawal of love.

In all of the communities 3-year-old knee children show a great desire to imitate the work activities of their parents and older siblings, and they are often found participating on the periphery of household or agricultural tasks. Nurturant adults and siblings allow them to "help" without being too critical of their mistakes. However, the children show their concern for competence and for performing successfully like their elder siblings. The following observation from Tarong is illustrative of both the tolerance of older siblings and the knee child's concern for competence.

> Zosima (girl, age 6) is carrying rice bundles into the house to dry, grunting with the strain. Her younger sister, Luziminda (age 3), is imitating Zosima but drops her bundle on the porch.
> "Bring them all the way to the house, all right?" says Zosima. Luziminda tries to comply but drops her bundle, breaking it. "Bundle broke, bundle broke, bundle broke," she repeats with a worried expression. Zosima, returning with more bundles, comes to look, but just shakes her head.

"Let's move those ones also," suggests Zosima, leading the way to some bundles drying across the road. The girls each carry two more bundles onto the porch. Pausing to rest, Zosima looks again at the broken bundle, saying, though not angrily, "Ala! It broke. Ala! It broke." Then she goes off to say hello to a neighbor child and to climb a tree. Luziminda, obviously worried by the broken bundle, keeps trying to push the stalks together, and takes a handful of stalks to where Zosima had placed her bundles.

The mother appears on the porch, carrying the baby. She comments on the scattered bundle and instructs the elder, Zosima, to gather up all the loose pieces. Zosima begins to do so, and little Luziminda joins her, helping. The mother watches the girls for a minute, smiles, then goes back into the house.   (Nydegger and Nydegger, field observations, 1955)

The contrast in the behavior elicited by lap versus knee children is illustrated in the following observation of an 8-year-old Juxtlahuacan girl caring for her 3-year-old brother and her 1-year-old sister. The girl is more nurturant to the lap child, more apt to reprimand the knee child:

Teresa (girl, age 8) is sitting by her mother shucking corn. The baby toddles by and gets dangerously near the fire. Teresa grabs the baby saying, "No, no, you're going to burn yourself."

The mother puts on her shawl and prepares to leave the house. The baby, seeing this, begins to cry, and Teresa comforts her, plays with her, shows her how to blow a toy flute, and imitates the baby's expression.

The mother leaves, first asking Cirilio (boy, age 3) if he wishes to accompany her. He says no, apparently wishing to stay with his sisters. Teresa puts clean panties on the baby, ignoring Cirilio. Then she says to him, "Go on, run along, go buy your sweet." Instead he comes closer to Teresa. She ignores him and sits down on the floor next to the baby. She commands her brother, "Sit down, darn you."   (Romney and Romney, field observations, 1955)

Teresa is not exceptional in the differential amount of nurturance she shows to her lap-child sister versus her knee-child brother. In the subsaharan samples, the 6- to 10-year-olds who are expected to be available as child nurses are significantly more nurturant to lap children than to knee children (B. B. Whiting, 1983). In three out of four comparisons, the older children are more prosocially and egoistically dominant to knee children than to lap children. While an average of 71 percent of the interaction of 6- to 10-year-olds with lap children in the subsaharan African communities is nurturant and sociable, only 50 percent of their interaction with knee children falls in this positive interaction category. An average of 16 percent of the behavior to knee children is prosocial dominance, 19 percent egoistic dominance. Since 6- to 10-year-olds are expected to care for knee children, some prosocial dominance is considered appropriate.

Cultural Content of Prosocial Dominance

Although there are cultural differences in the socialization pressures on knee children that vary with the time schedules of the caretakers and the different expectations of normal behavior, there are universal lessons to be learned by the knee-child age group. In our samples, most of these children have been followed by an infant sibling and must learn to do without continuous close body contact and the concentrated attention of their caretakers. They must give up breast feeding and must learn bowel and bladder control. In addition, they must begin to learn the rudiments of appropriate social behavior.

Tantrums, rage, and expressions of hostility toward a new baby are considered normal. As noted earlier, jealousy is a recognized emotion in all of our samples. While expression of this emotion is expected, the child is often teased or ignored rather than given some special positive attention (the latter being a common practice of Orchard Town mothers). Individual mothers are observed using placation, distraction, ignoring, teasing, or punishment. Tairan mothers and siblings use all of these techniques. Maretzki and Maretzki summarize the behavior of eight children between the ages of 18 months and 2 years who were weaned from back and breast during the field study.

> Temper tantrums in which the child would sit down and scream his head off, hurl dirt and stones at his mother, older siblings, or adults who stopped to have a kind word with him or to ridicule him, and incessant whining were symptomatic of the repercussions of abrupt withdrawal. Sulkiness, stubbornness, and tyrannical behavior, however, are short lived. The child finds that although this kind of behavior brought immediate and rewarding responses in the past, he now faces further withdrawal and punishment as a result. The mother impatiently screams back at him to stop crying, and siblings simply leave him behind to keep up with his own pace or drag him along forcibly and

uncomfortably, with threats of punishment if he refuses to cooperate. As if to heap more abuse on deprivation, he finds the newly arrived baby the center of the household and taking his place at his mother's breast. He is encouraged and discouraged by turns. "You are an older brother or an older sister. You do not drink your mother's milk now. And see how big you are and such a good child," now encourage visitors. "Come here, hurry!" scream older siblings or mother when he fails to keep in step with them on walks. For about three months the child's bleary eyes, tear-streaked face, and woebegone expression are unquestionable evidences of the most unhappy interval of his childhood. (Maretzki and Maretzki, 1963, p. 477)

Nyansongo mothers were reported to use harsher treatments. If a displaced child cried frequently or threw temper tantrums during the period following the baby's birth, the mothers caned or threatened to cane the child because the "crying is interpreted as *okoema,* murderous jealousy" (LeVine and LeVine, 1963, p. 152)—that is, an aggressive death wish that could actually cause the baby to die.

The Orchard Town mothers tried not to be punitive of the expression of hostility toward the new baby; rather, they attempted to placate the older child. As Fischer and Fischer stated (1963, p. 966): "Jealousy is thought to be the natural thing between siblings of close age if one receives some attention from parents that the other does not. Parents try not to give one something without doing the same for the other." However, modern American culture is much more demanding than the rural Kenyan cultures in expecting knee children to use words to negotiate disputes or label their emotions. American adults attempt to discourage all grabbing, pushing, and hitting at an early age—behaviors that are expected of knee children in the other sample communities. In most of our non-Western samples, adults are less apt to interfere in children's squabbles. When observing in Ngeca, Beatrice Whiting often felt tempted to intervene in children's fights. Most often some adult could also hear the quarrel but chose to ignore it. When the dispute was between siblings who were old enough to protect themselves, the mothers did not run to see why the younger child was whining in frustration or even screaming in rage; they evidently assumed that the older child would not actually hurt the younger. In fact, the aggressive encounters usually did stop without anyone being really hurt. As a consequence of this strategy of nonintervention, there are fewer attempts in these non-Western communities by knee children or their older siblings to seek the help of adults in settling disputes, and little tattletailing and complaining by knee children to adults. The mothers do monitor the older siblings' behavior, however; if a child nurse is too rough and her charge is continually whining and complaining, mothers eventually punish the nurse.

Our observations suggest, furthermore, that there are many more disputes to be negotiated in societies where children own many things. With the exception of Orchard Town, Bhubaneswar (the middle- and upper-class families), and some of the wealthier and more "modern" families in the other communities, children do not own toys in our sample communities. Announcements of "mine" are infrequent. The children do take things away from one another, but justifications based on ownership rather than first possession are comparatively rare. There is also less verbal negotiation than in societies like Orchard Town; children receive less practice in "presenting their case," less training in a legal style of dispute settlement.

The manner in which socializers handle children's disputes is one of the ways in which the former transmit their values concerning the legitimate power ascribed to gender and age. For example, the tendency for Kenyan parents to ignore children's squabbles unless they disturb adults' work or social interaction implicitly sanctions the authority of older over younger siblings, since the former can successfully use coercive techniques to get their way. In all the Kenyan communities seniority gives one the right to command juniors, and Kenyan parents allow older siblings to punish younger ones physically. However, in subsaharan African communities girls lose their seniority rights to their brothers as the latter approach the time (initiation) when they are recognized as "male."

In contrast, American middle-class parents believe that relative age does not legitimate dominance by older children. When they intervene, these parents "hold court" and require children to present accusations and defenses. Parents play the role of judges, attempting to justify their decisions with discussions of fairness and morality. Because this strategy goes against the universal tendency for older and bigger children to dominate younger and smaller children, parents must be continually on the alert for power struggles when their children are young.

Knee children in the majority of our samples receive far less maternal attention after weaning than in American middle-class families, but they are seldom if ever alone, day or night. Rather, they are always in the company of siblings, aunts, grandparents, and occasionally fathers, all of whom are expected to look out for the child. The knee children seek the company of their older siblings and are allowed to tag along after them. This is particularly true of the children in polygynous and extended family compounds. Although their 4- and 5-year-old brothers and sisters may prefer the companionship of older siblings, when these brothers and sisters are not present or not interested in interaction the knee children are considered good playmates.

Knee children spend much more time alone in Orchard Town than in our other samples. As Fischer and Fischer state in their description of Orchard Town, too much attention is believed to "spoil" babies. From the time they are 2 to 3 months old, Orchard Town babies may sleep alone in their room, and "most of them spend a good part of each day alone in a crib or playpen or in a fenced-in yard. Children learn early in Orchard Town that interaction with others is spaced, separated by periods of withdrawal" (1963, p. 947). The 2- and 3-year-olds spend many hours playing by themselves while their mothers do housework. Since there were no kindergarten classes in Orchard Town when the observations were made, a 4- or 5-year-old sibling might also be at home, but in general mothers encouraged each child to have his own project. Many mothers reported that they tried to protect the older child from being disturbed by the younger one, a consideration that appears to be relatively infrequent in our other sample communities.

Table 5.4 presents the proportion of interaction of 4- to 5-year-olds and 6- to 10-year-olds with knee children in the subsaharan African sample. (Data for the Six Culture communities are not available because 2-year-olds were classified with infants.) It can be seen that for the 4- to 5-year-olds an average of 36 percent of the interaction of girls and 31 percent of the interaction of boys is with knee children; for the 6- to 10-year-olds, an average of 23 percent of the girls' and 26 percent of the boys' interaction is with knee children. The gender differences are not consistent.

Spending time with these younger children gives older children a chance to practice legitimate prosocial dominance. In some cases, however, it is clear that the older children take advantage of their power position and justify egoistic dominance by reference to rules or responsibilities.

Table 5.4. Percentage of interaction of 4- to 5-year-old and 6- to 10-year-old children that is to knee children

	4–5 years		6–10 years	
Community	Girls (%)	Boys (%)	Girls (%)	Boys (%)
Kien-taa	33	31	18	38
Kokwet	42	23	31	36
Kisa-Kariobangi[a]	21	34	19	7
Ngeca	47	36	22	21
Average	36	31	23	26

a. Data for Kisa and Kariobangi are combined because of low frequencies.

Although the older children are more prosocially dominant than the younger children, we have examples of both boys and girls as young as age 5 commanding younger companions prosocially. Having recently been taught proper behavior, they are permitted to practice the role of the socializer. The following protocol is an example of the socializing role behavior of Tarong boys and girls.

Romulo (boy, age 7) and Norma (girl, age 5) are squatting opposite each other on the kitchen floor dishing out food. Romulo has dished out food for Roberto (brother, age 2), who starts to eat immediately. Romulo says, "Do not scatter food, hah, you children." He calls to Antero (boy, age 4) who is visiting. "Come here, Tero." Antero shrinks shyly behind the door. Romulo smiles at him and says, "Come on, now. Do not be ashamed." As Romulo serves himself, Antero joins the group. Romulo serves him and then they all eat. Later Norma says to Antero, "It is our rule not to have crumbs." (Nydegger and Nydegger, field observations, 1955)

In the role of caretaker, an older child can justify dominant behavior over a knee child. Because the role assigned to the older child demands that he or she monitor the younger child's behavior, dominance is appropriate. A child may imitate parental behavior and enforce the rules of good behavior that she has so recently learned. Adults who delegate the care of knee children are giving older children the opportunity of practicing prosocial dominance, since by their very nature these young explorers elicit this type of behavior.

Effects of Age, Gender, and Culture on Behavior to Knee Children

Prosocial dominance is seen to increase with age. Children who are close in age to knee children treat them as companions more than as individuals to be trained; they play with, tease, and nurture them. In contrast, children in the older age group behave more like socializers who are responsible for the safety and training of their younger siblings.

Evidence for these conclusions is presented in an analysis of the behavior profile of Kenyan girls and boys in two age groups (this sample is the only one in which the data are dense enough for the comparison). Figure 5.1 presents Optimal Scaling values for the interaction of yard and school-age children with knee children. The frequency of ten behaviors of girls and boys of the two age grades is the basis of the analysis; the scaling was performed on the intercorrelation matrix of these frequencies. In the figure, girl actors are represented by circles and boys by triangles, and the three societies are designated by a letter key. (Kisa and Kariobangi are combined because of low frequencies.) In the top part of the figure we computed and plotted the profile position of the girls and boys in interaction with knee children, and we drew boundary lines around yard children and around school-age children. In the bottom part of the figure the ten behaviors are plotted in the same space: nurturance, prosocial dominance (mands concerning chores, child care, and etiquette), reprimands, egoistic dominance, insults, assaults, dependency, verbal teasing, physical teasing (assault sociably), and sociability.

Comparing the top and bottom of Figure 5.1, the distance between a specific dyad and the particular behaviors indicates the frequency with which this behavior appears in the profile of the interaction of the plotted dyads. It can be seen in the bottom part of the figure that nurturance, prosocial dominance, reprimands, and dominance are in the upper left-hand quadrant, while verbal and physical teasing, insulting, and assaulting are in the right-hand quadrant. Sociability is the only behavior in the lower quadrants.

Boys and girls in each of the communities are very similar in behavior at both ages. The greatest differences are between the age groups themselves. For example, it can be seen in the figure that the Kisa-Kariobangi yard children (C and D) are at a distance from the Kisa-Kariobangi school-age children (I and J). At the younger age the boys and girls were observed most frequently in sociable inter-

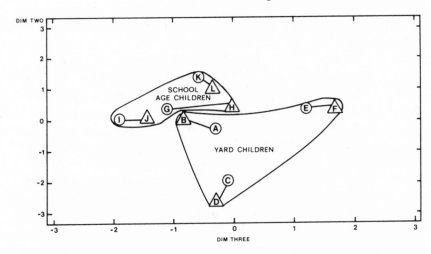

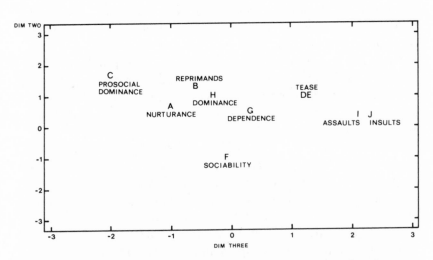

Figure 5.1. (*top*): Graph of Optimal Scaling values for behavior of yard children and school-age children to knee children in three Kenyan samples over the frequency of ten types of social behavior. The actors to knee children are as follows: Yard children: A = Kokwet girls, B = Kokwet boys, C = Kisa-Kariobangi girls, D = Kisa-Kariobangi boys, E = Ngeca girls, F = Ngeca boys. School-age children: G = Kokwet girls, H = Kokwet boys, I = Kisa-Kariobangi girls, J = Kisa-Kariobangi boys, K = Ngeca girls, L = Ngeca boys. (*bottom*): Graph showing location of ten types of behavior in the same space.

action, while the older group are in the quadrant that includes so-cializers and socializing behaviors: nurturance, prosocial dominance, and controlling behavior (egoistic dominance and reprimands). In Ngeca, the yard children (E and F) are comparatively high in teasing verbally and assaulting physically, as well as in assaulting and in-sulting, while the school-age children (K and L) are more "maternal." The change with age is least in Kokwet (A and B, G and H), where the yard children behave more like socializers than the yard children in the other samples.

We interpret the greater similarity between the communities at the school-age period as evidence that the responsibility expected of older children in Kenya increases the similarity of the dyadic profiles. Like the subsaharan African mothers, the older children are spending time training and controlling the knee children. Thus the 6- to 10-year-olds are more prosocially dominant than the 4- to 5-year-olds; they reprimand more and are more egoistically dominant. These older children are also more nurturant. The knee children are eliciting these types of behaviors from them.

There is a suggestion of a sex difference in the profile of school-age children. It can be seen by comparing the top and bottom parts of Figure 5.1 that the girls in Kokwet, Kisa-Kariobangi, and Ngeca are all closer in distance to prosocial dominance than are the boys. With age, girls more than boys use a maternal interactional style—assigning chores, advising about proper behavior, and reprimanding behavior that needs changing. The boys, on the other hand, are proportionately higher on egoistic dominance than the girls. The ratio of prosocial to total dominance (prosocial and egoistical dominance) in interaction with knee children is greater for girls than for boys at ages 4–5, 6–7, and 8–12 (B. B. Whiting, 1983). The proportion of prosocial dominance of the Ngeca and Kokwet girls in the oldest age group is similar to that of their mothers. Averaging across male and female knee children, 26 percent of Ngeca mothers' interaction is coded as prosocial dominance (see Table 3.5), as compared to 21 percent of the 8- to 12-year-old girls' behavior. In Kokwet, about 20 percent of the mothers' behavior and 26 percent of the 8- to 12-year-old girls' behavior to knee children is prosocial.

Figure 5.2 presents Optimal Scaling values of the eight most fre-quent behaviors of mothers and 8- to 12-year-old girls and boys to knee children. The mean of the profile position of mothers and that of 8- to 12-year-old girls and boys were computed and plotted for

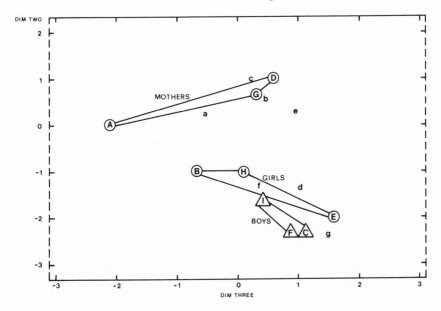

Figure 5.2. Graph of Optimal Scaling values for behavior of mothers and 8- to 12-year-old girls and boys to knee children in three Kenyan samples over the frequency of nine types of social behavior. The actors to knee children are as follows: A = Kokwet mothers, B = Kokwet girls, C = Kokwet boys, D = Kisa-Kariobangi mothers, E = Kisa-Kariobangi girls, F = Kisa-Kariobangi boys, G = Ngeca mothers, H = Ngeca girls, I = Ngeca boys. Behaviors: a = nurturance, b = reprimands, c = prosocial dominance, d = seeks attention, e = verbal teasing, f = physical teasing, g = dependence, h = seeks submission, i = assaults.

three Kenyan communities, Kokwet, Kisa-Kariobangi, and Ngeca. The figure shows the mean of the eight behaviors in the same space. It can be seen that the profiles of the mothers cluster; mothers show more prosocial dominance, nurturance, reprimands, and verbal teasing in interaction with knee children than either the girls or the boys. The girls and boys are more egoistically dominant (submission-seeking), physically teasing, and dependent (help- and attention-seeking) than are the mothers. The profile of the girls, however, is more similar to that of their mothers than is the profile of the boys.

It is undoubtedly true that both the girls and the boys are modeling their behavior on that of their mothers. Since girls are in the presence of their mothers more frequently than boys, they have more opportunity to observe maternal behavior.

Carol Ember's research among the Luo of Western Kenya presents further evidence for the importance of caring for younger children and being around the mother in increasing the proportion of prosocial dominance (coded as responsible suggestions; see Ember, 1970, 1973). She asked 56 children to list the tasks they were asked to perform and to report whether these tasks were considered women's work, men's work, or in the domain of both men and women. The social behavior of 26 of these children between the ages of 7½ and 16 was observed. The proportion of prosocial dominance of boys who performed tasks considered "feminine" was compared to the proportion of prosocial dominance of boys who did not do such tasks, and to the proportion of prosocial dominance of girls. It was found that the girls had the highest proportion of prosocial dominance, the boys who performed "feminine" chores had the next highest proportion, and the boys who did not perform such chores had the lowest proportion. The boys who did chores outside the house—for example, carrying wood and water (tasks in the domain of adult women)—were observed to be proportionately less prosocially dominant than the boys whose "feminine" chores were performed inside the house. It may be the case that these latter boys had more opportunity to observe and model the mothers' behavior.

Conclusions

In sum, interacting with lap and knee children elicits prosocial behavior. Lap children elicit positive responsiveness from adults and children of all ages. The evidence supports the idea that this responsiveness to lap children is a biologically prepared response, present in all humans. When assigned the caretaking role, child nurses have the opportunity to practice nurturance. Frustration and associated aggressive behavior occur, however, when a young child nurse is unable to keep his or her charge contented, or when the length of time of the nurse's responsibility for the lap child is prolonged. As caretakers, the 6- to 10-year-olds are more competent and more nurturant than are the knee children. Girls are assigned as caretakers of lap children more frequently than boys, interact with lap children more frequently, and thus have more opportunity to practice nurturance. Since they are more frequently in the company of their mothers than are boys, they have more access to a model of caretaking behavior. Successful nurses are able to guess the needs and desires of their preverbal charges, and in doing so, they obtain practice in empathy and intuition.

Older siblings entrusted with the supervision of knee children are also nurturant, but the task of protecting and controlling these mobile children requires prosocially dominant behavior. Although there is a consistent pattern across cultures for girls and boys to dominate younger children, in the role of protector the older children also learn responsibility for others, and they practice a style of dominance that is legitimated by a role that assumes that the actor knows how the younger child should behave. Girls interact with younger children more frequently than boys do, and girls also use a more prosocial style of dominance.

Chapter 6

Yard Children: Entering Middle Childhood

Four-year-old children no longer elicit the type of behavior that is directed to lap and knee children. Whereas young children have many qualities that elicit nurturance and affectionate sociability, 4-year-olds definitely think, behave, and interact in ways that class them with older children. They have boundless energy, an energy that elicits certain responses from others. Furthermore, for the first time they have younger as well as older child companions and become involved in establishing their position in the pecking order. Perhaps most important, they are conscious of their gender, and this influences their behavior and others' behavior toward them. Thus, their awareness of their relative age, size, and gender influences their interaction with others and the responses of their companions.

The Autonomy of Yard Children

As we have seen, lap and knee children by their very nature demand specific behaviors of their caretakers. The imperatives of caretaking directed toward survival (LeVine, 1977) leave little leeway for the cultural diversity that emerges in middle and late childhood. In the yard-child period, there is a transition roughly between the ages of 4 and 6 when the physical and social conditions of adult life play a more active part in scheduling the settings and the associated activities and companions of children.

No individual has complete autonomy to choose settings and companions; rules concerning appropriate behavior limit even the lives of adults. There are private areas that only members of the family or relatives may enter, public places that are off limits to children and sometimes restricted to one sex, sacred places that only a few

designated individuals may enter. These rules concerning setting occupancy play a major role in the development of children's social
behavior because they set the stage for learning how to initiate and
maintain interaction with a variety of different individuals. Inasmuch
as the type of setting children may frequent varies from one community to another, they have different experiences and practice different types of behavior. In some of the communities, the settings
girls and boys frequent are similar; in others, girls are more restricted.

As we have seen, the settings frequented by the lap and knee
children are primarily the family house and yard, and the people
who interact with the children are primarily the people who share
the intimate space. In these early years, moreover, children have little
opportunity to explore the environment or to choose the individuals
with whom they initiate interaction. As children become more able
to explore, the nature of their settings and the individuals who are
available as companions become more important in shaping their
profile of social interaction. Parents, however, still have the ultimate
power to control setting occupany.

Five factors influence parental decisions about the settings that 4-
and 5-year-olds may frequent: beliefs about the nature of the child;
the parents' perception of the physical and social dangers of the
environment; the settlement pattern of the community, which determines who lives on adjacent land and how close the houses of neighbors are to one another; the mother's workload; and the presence of
institutions such as preschools.

Beliefs about the Nature of Children. Beliefs about the nature of
4- and 5-year-olds influence the rules about how far children may
wander from the immediate environs of the house and how much
supervision they require. In many societies around the world, parents
believe that children do not "acquire reason" until around the age
of 6 or 7 (Whiting and Whiting, 1960; Rogoff et al., 1975). For
example, the Tairan mothers agree that children under 6 years "do
not have sense" and are unteachable; serious training is postponed
until they have the capacity to "understand and know." As Maretzki
and Maretzki report, "Kindergarten children pilfer from gardens,
have temper tantrums, and attack each other physically, but very
little enforcement takes place" (1963, pp. 480–481). Similarly, the
Mixtecan mothers do not think that children in this age group have
the capacity for reason, believing rather that they are only capable
of learning by sheer repetition. As Romney and Romney state, "In

Mixtec belief, the child in this early stage is capable of learning by sheer repetition but is not thought of as having the capacity to learn by reason; nor can a child of this age recognize right from wrong, and he is not expected to be responsible for his behavior" (1963, p. 647). The Rajput mothers state that the preschool child is considered too young to learn from instruction. They expect very little of preschool boys, who spend most of their day observing the busy world around them (Minturn and Hitchcock, 1963, p. 331). Tarong mothers agree that children of this age group have little sense, but they do expect their children to be responsible and obedient, and to refrain from quarreling or fighting (Nydegger and Nydegger, 1963). The Tarong mothers are more like the mothers of Orchard Town, who believe that character training should begin during early childhood (Fischer and Fischer, 1963). The parents of Nyansongo and the other subsaharan communities expect the most from their children: they believe that children of this age group can be taught to be responsible, and that physical punishment is necessary in order to instill obedience and responsibility (LeVine and LeVine, 1963).

One intriguing theoretical problem is the relation between beliefs about the nature of the child and the mother's needs. The mothers who need the most help assign daily chores to yard children; it appears that these mothers believe that children can learn at an early age to be responsible. The Kenyan mothers, as we have seen, have the heaviest workloads, and they value the help of their children. The Ngeca mothers stated that both girls and boys could learn to perform responsible tasks from an early age, an opinion that appears to be shared by the other Kenyan mothers. The busy mothers of Tarong also assign tasks to the children of this age group. The Orchard Town mother has no adult at home during the day to help her, and when her second child is born, usually two years after the first, she must begin training the older one so that she is able to trust him not to get into trouble when she is feeding and caring for the new infant. In contrast, the mothers who need less help believe that it is useless to try to train children before the age of 6 or 7. For example, the Rajput mothers of Khalapur, who do not work outside the home, rarely assign regular chores to 4- and 5-year-olds.

It is also interesting to note that parents like the Tairan mothers, who do not consciously spend time training their young children, believe that a child is born "pure" and "innocent," a gift of the gods. Similarly, the Rajput mothers believe that fate is written on a child's brow at birth, and there is little a parent can do to influence the child's character. In contrast, the Orchard Town mothers believe that they are responsible for molding the character of their children. Similarly, the Ngeca mothers we interviewed agreed that responsibility, obedience, and respect for older individuals were behaviors that could and should be taught. Their statements are similar to those made by the other subsaharan mothers.

Parental Perception of Social and Physical Dangers. Of particular importance in influencing the amount of autonomy granted to children is the adults' perception of the safety of the environment, including both physical and social dangers. In rural environments there are bodies of water, insects and snakes, poisonous plants, and other flora and fauna whose dangerous properties the child must learn about. In some of the communities we studied, there were roads or streets with truck and automobile traffic. The busy thoroughfares in Orchard Town and Claremont were particularly dangerous.

Equally important is the parents' perception of the dangers that may result from fights between children from different households. In some of our sample communities the parents are fearful that such fights will result in feuds between families, witchcraft, and "poisoning." To prevent conflict, the parents may attempt to keep the children at home or in the homes of trusted others. This was clearly the case in Ngeca: parents disapproved of what they called "roguish behavior," defined as visiting other homesteads and standing around in the doorway of the houses, and they told their children never to eat in other people's houses.

Settlement Patterns. As described in Chapter 2, the arrangement of the houses and compounds of the sample families was found to be a major determinant of the type of companions that children have in the early years. In communities with clustered housing, children have a wider choice of companions at an earlier age than children who grow up on isolated farms. In kin-based comunities, where next-door neighbors are relatives, children may be allowed to visit neighboring homesteads at an early age.

Mothers' Workloads. As described in Chapter 3, in those societies where the mothers work outside the home, children are assigned the care of younger children and taught at a young age to begin to do work for the household. In these societies the autonomy of the children is most restricted by task assignment.

Preschools. At the time of our observations, preschools were available in Taira, Ngeca, Kariobangi, and Kisa; there were no nursery schools in the other communities.

Thus it can be seen that a number of factors influence parental decisions about how much autonomy to grant yard children. A concrete result of the decision-making process can be seen in the amount of adult supervision that children in each community receive. The presence of authority figures in sight of the child means that the child's behavior can be constantly monitored.

Table 6.1 presents the percentage of observations of the Six Culture children in which some authority figure is present. It can be seen that in Orchard Town, Khalapur, Juxtlahuaca, and Tarong, 4- and 5-year-olds are in supervised settings about 78 percent of the time. In sharp contrast are their age mates in the village of Taira: in only 45 percent of the observations of girls and 38 percent of the observations of boys was an authority figure in sight. Nyansongo falls between the two extremes; an authority figure was in sight in 66 percent of the observations of girls and 53 percent of those of boys. It should be noted that, with the exception of Orchard Town, girls are in the presence of authority figures more frequently than are boys, although in four of the communities the difference in the percentages is small.

In the Kenyan communities, the size of families' landholdings determines the amount of supervision of the yard children. In Nyansongo the pastures and water holes at the river are shared by related families. These areas are not close enough to the homesteads to allow for constant supervision of the activities of the herd boys and the younger children who accompany them. Thus, although the Nyansongo children spend their time on land owned by the family or

Table 6.1. Percentage of observations of 4- to 5-year-old children in which an authority figure was present

Community (Six Cultures)	Girls (%)	Boys (%)	Diff.
Nyansongo	66	53	+13
Juxtlahuaca	79	62	+17
Tarong	78	69	+9
Taira	45	38	+7
Khalapur	84	81	+3
Orchard Town	83	86	−3
Mean	73	65	

shared with relatives, they are away from authority figures during an average of 60 percent of the observations. In the other Kenyan communities in the New Samples, with the exception of Kokwet, the landholdings on the average are small. For example, in Ngeca the children of the yard-age group are seldom away from the household yard, and unless all adults are absent from the homestead, there is always some authority figure not far away. In 1968, when we were observing in Ngeca during the morning hours, we were often greeted by a 6- to 8-year-old child caring for a lap-child sibling and supervising a knee child while the mother worked in the garden, sometimes adjacent to the house, sometimes at a distance. In case of trouble, however, adults were not far off.

Those children who are granted permission to play in public settings away from the houses have more opportunity to interact with individuals who are not kin. We computed the percentage of observations in which yard children were found exclusively with related children. The children in Nyansongo, Juxtlahuaca, and Tarong are found to be with siblings, half-siblings, cousins, and young aunts and uncles an average of more than 86 percent of the time. In Taira, Khalapur, and Orchard Town, siblings and cousins are present in the observations of young girls an average of 60 percent of the time, and in those of young boys an average of only 43 percent of the time. The New Sample Kenyan communities are similar to Nyansongo in that the children are in private settings in the company of related children during most of the daylight hours.

Channeling the Energy of Yard Children

In examining the observations, we became interested in the strategies that authority figures use to channel the energy of yard children. It appears that, left to their own devices, healthy 4- and 5-year-olds in all cultures are constantly on the move. They are characterized by a high level of activity and by an intense interest in the physical and social environments. They also appear to shift the goal of their activities frequently and to be unable to control the outcome of their interaction. Without adult direction, their interaction in groups becomes hyperactive, with much laughter or crying. In the absence of intervention, conflicts arise between children, who at this age are prone to use physically aggressive ways of attaining their goals.

We have observed four strategies that socializers use to channel the energy of yard children: they may keep a close supervision of children's activities and distract or reprimand the children when they become obstreperous; they may assign work that the children are physically and cognitively capable of performing; they may structure the children's play, teaching them games that have rules for taking turns and simple goals; or they may set up institutions like preschools and kindergartens, where adults organize and supervise the children's activities.

Table 6.2 presents a summary of the type of activities in which yard children were engaged when the sequences of interaction were recorded. In the Six Culture samples, it can be seen that more than 80 percent of the activities were judged to be either play or casual social interaction in all of the communities except Nyansongo. The percentage scores for the Spot Observation samples confirm the fact that the Kenyan and Peruvian children are engaged in work more often than the 5- to 7-year-olds in the other cultures. In contrast, the yard children in Taira, Khalapur, Orchard Town, and Claremont were rarely seen working.

In the Six Culture study and the New Samples, Taira, Kariobangi, Kisa, and Ngeca were the only communities that had institutions to organize the 4- and 5-year-olds. (In 1955 and 1956, when the Fischers observed in Orchard Town, there were no kindergartens there.) The kindergarten in Taira, held under a banyan tree in the center of town, was informal, free, and open to all preschool-age children. In the Kenyan communities there were school fees to be paid. Theoretically the minimum age was 4 years, but 3-year-olds occasionally tagged along with their older siblings. The schools were crowded, and there were not enough teachers in each class to organize the play activities of the children.

Although all of the communities used a variety of techniques for channeling the energy of the children, each society usually favored one. It is clear that the busy mothers of Kenya favored work. Some of the mothers in Ngeca were outspoken in their preference for work over any type of play in organizing their children's time; they refused to send their 4- and 5-year-olds to the preschool because in their opinion the children spent too much of their time playing in the school yard. When leaving their children at home, mothers instructed the oldest child about the work they expected each of the younger children to perform in their absence. If the 4- and 5-year-olds were considered old enough to begin training in gardening, they were taken

Table 6.2. The activities of yard children

Percentage of observations in which children aged 4–5 years are engaged in various activities

Community (Six Cultures)	Play			Casual social interaction			Work			School learning		
	Girls (%)	Boys (%)	Diff.	Girls (%)	Boys (%)	Diff.	Girls (%)	Boys (%)	Diff.	Girls (%)	Boys (%)	Diff.
Nyansongo	17	20	−3	47	51	−4	36	29	+7	0	0	0
Juxtlahuaca	42	59	−17	54	41	+13	4	0	+4	0	0	0
Tarong	43	55	−12	38	27	+11	19	14	+5	0	4	−4
Taira	79	92	−13	14	0	+14	5	4	+1	2	4	−2
Khalapur	18	34	−16	73	63	+10	8	3	+5	0	0	0
Orchard Town	43	55	−12	54	41	+13	0	0	0	3	4	−1

Percentage of observations in which children aged 5–7 years are found playing and working

Community (Spot Observations)	Play			Work		
	Girls (%)	Boys (%)	Diff.	Girls (%)	Boys (%)	Diff.
Nyansongo	15	13	+2	38	44	−6
Vihiga	8	28	−20	53	24	+29
Ngeca	16	23	−7	55	32	+23
Conacoste/ Santo Domingo	23	31	−8	30	23	+7
Santa Barbara	15	33	−18	56	30	+26
Claremont	32	38	−6	5	6	−1

to the garden to help break the soil with hoes or to help pick vegetables. The observation of the mother and young Nyansongo boy reported in Chapter 3 illustrates the strategies for teaching work habits. In contrast to Nyansongo, where the young boys could be sent to the pastures to learn how to herd the cattle under the direction of older boys, in Ngeca there were few animals; by the early 1970s land pressure had resulted in diminishing pastures. Few families owned more than one or two cows, and these animals were often tethered or fenced. Thus, the principal work assigned to the youngest age group involved doing errands around the house and in the neighborhood, and picking and preparing vegetables.

In Nyansongo, a third of the observations of social behavior of the 4- to 5-year-old children take place in the context of work. Both boys and girls run small errands and care for lap and knee children. The herding of cattle and goats is mainly performed by boys, while girls perform household tasks. It should be noted, however, that in many situations it is possible for children to combine play with work. In the observations of Nyansongo children, a large part of the time spent in herding cattle and goats in the lineage pastures involves some play. The play is seldom organized, however, because it may be interrupted at any moment if the animals wander out of the area into the unfenced gardens that border on the pastures. The children in charge of the cattle typically range from 5 to 11 or 12 years of age. Analysis of the nature of the play indicates that about 25 percent involves roughhousing, teasing, and mock aggression, while another 10 percent involves general activity. In 60 percent of the Nyansongo observations, there are four or more children of various ages in the setting. Obviously, the combining of work and play in a group of children of different ages is not a good situation for competitive games that require matched skills or complicated rules. Only two types of play that were observed can be classified as games with rules: a game of tag played by a group of girls and a dirt-throwing competition between several young boys.

The following observation illustrates the quality of this combined work/play in a typical Nyansongo scene of a group of boys herding cattle. Present are five boys—Ogoi, his brother Lawrence, and three cousins from neighboring homesteads.

Ogoi (boy, age 4) is standing on the edge of the group holding M's (boy, age 11) slingshot. He moves over and sits down with the group of boys. M grabs the slingshot from Ogoi, who makes no protest. M is snapping the rubber band of the slingshot against A's (boy, age 6) foot, with the latter's permission. Everyone, including Ogoi, is intently watching and laughing when A gets hit. Then M stops. A spits on Ogoi. Ogoi angrily whines, "Don't spit on me like that." A ignores him.

Lawrence (boy, age 5) says to Ogoi, "Go get the cows." Ogoi does. P (boy, age 8) and A have also gone to retrieve their own cows. Ogoi is up higher on the hill but runs down to where Lawrence and M are sitting. Lawrence asks, "What's in your mouth?" Ogoi opens his mouth and they all peer in. They all tell him to stick out his tongue. He does.

Suddenly P and M start to fight. Ogoi just sits and watches. Lawrence playfully grabs at Ogoi's foot. He laughs. Lawrence pushes Ogoi over on his back. Ogoi smiles. Lawrence, looking into Ogoi's mouth says, "Oh look! Here's a tooth that is going to come out!" Ogoi is still smiling as Lawrence pushes him around on the ground some more. Then they go and join the others who are shouting from the next hill that the cows have gone into the maize field. [Note the pecking order, older to younger.]   (LeVine and LeVine, field observations, 1956)

Combining work with caring for younger siblings is a daily occurrence in the Kenyan communities. In the following observation, Agnes, a 4-year-old Nyansongo girl assigned the task of carrying her younger sister, is with a group of eight children in the pasture not far from her home. Three of the children are her sisters, Sarume, Nyamwara, and Clem. The other girl, NN, is a cousin from a neighboring homestead. The boy who is present is a cousin, accompanied by his 2-year-old brother.

Clem (girl, age 1½) is tied to the back of her sister, Agnes (girl, age 4). Agnes laughingly knocks food out of Clem's hands and tells NN (girl, age 6) to eat it. NN laughs. Agnes pushes NN, both laughing, then Agnes runs and sits down. Clem screams, and for several minutes the scene is dominated by Clem's screaming. Sarume (sister, age 8) takes the baby off her younger sister's back and holds and quiets her. (Note: She does not reprimand Agnes.) Agnes and the others sit more or less still and watch until the baby has finally been comforted.

Then Agnes starts a game of tag with NN, both laughing. In this game, Agnes constantly chases NN and never vice versa. Agnes begins to pick up sticks and throw them at NN, saying while laughing, "I'll beat you."

Finally both return to the group. Agnes goes over and talks to Clem. Then she grabs the toddler that her boy cousin is in charge of and jounces him around, making faces at him. She jounces the little boy rather harshly, then finally gives him back to the boy.

NN introduces a game of tag again, and Agnes chases her. Both laugh and Agnes pushes NN. Nyamwara (Agnes' sister, age 6) pulls Agnes from behind. Both fall to the ground and roll around. When Agnes hits the ground she looks as if she is going to get angry and tearful, but then she laughs and shouts. She crawls on all fours and tells Nyamwara to get on her back. Agnes squeaks at her, "Titi mama, titi mama" [what girls say to babies to make them hold onto their backs]. Nyamwara gets on Agnes' back and Agnes tries to crawl around supporting her. There is much laughter. [All of this takes place in five minutes.] The interaction then becomes rather wild, with all the smaller children including Agnes playing tag. Sarume (girl, age 8) who has been initiated,* does not join in.   (LeVine and LeVine, field observations, 1956)

It should be noted that there are no adults present either in this observation or in the observation of the boys. Although there are no lap or knee children or girls present with the boys who are herding the cattle, this is not always the case; mixed-sex play groups also gather in the pastures.

The Mixtecan mothers of Juxtlahuaca use both work and adult supervision to control the activities of their girls. Children are kept inside the courtyards, where there is usually an adult present and therefore little opportunity for the children to get out of hand. At any time they can expect to be called to run some errand for their parents. Since play can be interrupted at any time and involves children of varying ages, it is most frequently unstructured. The only game with rules observed in the yard-child groups was London Bridge, although there were several abortive attempts by girls of this age grade to initiate games. During one 5-minute observation, three children of ages 3–6 started four different games: a game of tag, a ball game, and two other games in which one person was "it." The children could not agree, however, on who should have the ball first, or who should be "it." In the end each of the older children left the group and went to her own house. During all this time the mother

---

*Around the age of 8 Nyansongo girls participate in a transition rite, referred to as a circumcision ceremony, in which the clitoris is excised. This ceremony marks a change in status and in the type of work required of girls. Older girls are not required to carry younger siblings or to herd cattle if there is a younger girl or boy who can be assigned the responsibility (LeVine and LeVine, 1963, p. 183).

Playing house, Juxtlahuaca (1955)

of one of the girls observed the children from the doorway but made no attempt to help the children organize a game with rules.

In none of the Mixtecan observations do boys and girls of this age play games together. The girls make houses on the floor using their *rebozas* and mats, pretend to sew, and make tortillas. The boys spend more time outside the courtyard in the street close by the house; they spin tops and tag along after their older brothers, who are far less aggressive toward them than their Nyansongo counterparts. The boys also play with toy cars, making roads and models of trucks out of mud (these toys were introduced by the field researchers' children). Their only introduction to games with rules is in top-spinning contests. These boys are never actually observed working.

As Table 6.2 shows, the families in Tarong rank second to Nyansongo in using work as a way of scheduling yard children's time, but they also depend on organized games. The children are observed working in 16 percent of the observations (less than half the percentage observed in Nyansongo). Adults are always close by, though sometimes out of sight, when these activities are in progress. The houses, perched on piles, allow adults to oversee the entire yard without being seen (see Figure 2.22); a child can escape view only by playing directly under the house.

After school, however, the adults turn the supervision of the younger children over to their school-age siblings, who organize groups of yard children in games. As described by Nydegger and Nydegger, the older children devote time and patience to teaching the young children the rules and skills required in a variety of games involving stick tossing, rock hitting, hide and seek, tag, drop the handkerchief, and other games learned at school:

> Play groups are encouraged if they are not voluntarily formed. Older children, especially those whose freedom is somewhat curtailed by a hip-baby, often organize junior versions of school games—fantastic games labeled basketball or baseball, but bearing little resemblance to the originals. As many as 20 children, ranging in age from toddlers to 10 years, were observed in such riotous games. One attempt to instill in such a group a newly learned military drill was the most hilarious travesty imaginable, and all the adults of the *sitio* came out to watch and laugh.   (Nydegger and Nydegger, 1963, p. 834)

The yard children of Orchard Town and Taira have the greatest number of formal games to occupy their time. In the case of Taira, the community hired a nursery school teacher whose main function is to organize the activities of preschool children during the morning hours when the adults of the village are working in the gardens and cutting lumber on the mountains. The observations indicate the patience with which the teacher teaches turn-taking and other behaviors that are necessary for playing games with rules. The 4- and 5-year-olds frequently have babies strapped to their backs while attending the outdoor nursery school, so even the lap children observe organized play.

In the afternoons after school, as in Tarong, the Taira parents count on the older children to take over the supervision of lap and knee children while the mothers and grandmothers prepare the evening meal and finish the daily chores. The Tairan 4- and 5-year-olds, however, are not expected to do any chores because their parents consider them senseless and irresponsible.

In the Ngeca preschool, where children are crowded onto benches in the classrooms, an attempt is made to begin literacy training. The children stand to recite in unison or sing songs. During the many recesses there is little attempt on the part of the teachers to organize play. Similarly, when the children are at home and not working, their play is unorganized.

Table 6.2 suggests that the children in Khalapur, when home, do the most standing around, talking, and engaging in casual social interaction. In part this type of behavior is a result of the crowded conditions of the courtyards, which are shared by several women and their children. The children are observed playing less frequently than children in the other communities, probably because such activities are discouraged. Moreover, 4- and 5-year-old boys are not expected to do any work, and girls do only light household chores. Both girls and boys help to entertain and supervise younger siblings while their mothers cook. When the children are outside the courtyard, they enjoy joining the older boys who take care of the cattle, accompanying them to the river to help water and wash the animals. There they can observe the older boys playing the different forms of hockey that are a favorite pastime, and they can learn by observation that there are rules to the games.

In many ways the Orchard Town mothers have the most difficult time in scheduling their 4- to 5-year-old children, especially during the winter months when it is necessary to bundle them up in snow suits, mittens, and boots every time they go out, only to have them want to return to the warm house after a short period. Unless the yard is fenced, the mothers feel they must keep an eye on the children when they are outside to see that they do not get too near the busy roads or other environmental hazards. In contrast to the other communities, there are a few adults coming and going who can keep an eye on the children. For this reason, many hours are spent by the mother and her preschool children shut up in the house. Parents invest hundreds of dollars in purchasing objects and games to entertain the children and keep them from running around in the confined space. The mothers entertain themselves and the children by exchanging information and pleasantries. They encourage the children to draw, paint, look at books, or watch educational television programs—all good preparation for school. When all else fails, the mothers prepare snacks which they offer to keep peace among the yard children and their younger siblings.

Friends watching television, Orchard Town

These, then, are the settings that yard children occupy, the individuals who share the settings, and the activities that they most frequently engage in. In all of the communities, parents appear concerned with controlling the children and with teaching them the skills and behaviors that they consider necessary for maturation. The Kenyan parents, for example, stress the socialization of work habits and the skills required of an agricultural economy, while the Orchard Town mothers emphasize the skills needed in a society where literacy and verbal facility are essential for well-being. All of the socializers attempt to channel the energy of the yard children and keep them from hurting themselves and each other.

Finding One's Place in the Dominance Hierarchy

One of the main tasks of the 4- and 5-year-olds is to learn to control their attempts to reach desired goals by using physical force, and their inclination to take out frustration by aggressive acts. With their new autonomy, the 4- and 5-year-olds are often anxious in their pursuit of egoistic goals to get others to change their behavior. Probably for this reason they elicit a high proportion of egoistic dominance from older children who refuse to comply, then countermand. Table 6.3 presents the proportion of dominance of 6- to 10-year-olds to younger children. It can be seen that, with two exceptions, 4- and 5-year-olds receive a higher proportion of dominance from 6- to 10-year-olds than do children in the other three age groups (lap children,

Table 6.3. Percentage of egoistic dominance of 6- to 10-year-olds to social partners

Community	To lap children (0–1 year old)	To knee children (2–3 years old)	To yard children (4–5 years old)	To school-age children (6–10 years old)
New Samples				
Kien-taa				
Girls	5	7	14	33
Boys	18	29	48	17
Kokwet				
Girls	19	18	28	19
Boys	13	26	31	28
Kisa-Kariobangi				
Girls	11	10	16	10
Boys	—	10	24	14
Ngeca				
Girls	5	21	26	13
Boys	0	17	29	14
Six Cultures[a]				
Juxtlahuaca				
Girls	13	—	39	20
Boys	2	—	48	9
Tarong				
Girls	11	—	58	10
Boys	6	—	46	7
Taira				
Girls	0	—	49	8
Boys	25		25	10
Orchard Town				
Girls	—	—	45	13
Boys	—	—	51	17
Average				
Girls	9	13	32	15
Boys	11	20	36	15

a. For the Six Culture samples, lap children are defined as 0–2 years old. Nyansongo and Khalapur are omitted because of the low frequency of interaction with 4- and 5-year-olds.

knee children, and 6- to 10-year-olds). The yard children's desire to participate in the activities of older children elicits direction, as well as agonistic behavior if the older children do not want them around. There is plenty of evidence in the observations that both girls and boys in the yard-child age group, but especially boys, seek the company of older same-sex children. The older children may use the eager 4- and 5-year-olds to help them with assigned tasks or in projects of their choosing.

Yard children's attraction to older children does not seem to be diminished by the dominance they experience. For instance, as recorded in the observation of Nyansongo boys presented at the beginning of this chapter, Ogoi persisted in playing with the older boys even though they ordered him around and sometimes hurt him. The Nyansongo observations demonstrate the acceptance by all the boys of the dominance hierarchy based on age: the 11-year-old hits the 6-year-old, who does not protest but displaces his irritation onto Ogoi, the 4-year-old. Ogoi is at the bottom of the heap but, we believe, accepts the position because he knows that no adult will interfere. There is evidence from this observation and others that he wants to be with the older boys even if they boss him and are sometimes rough and hurt him.

Psychologists in the United States have studied dominance hierarchies that develop in groups of children who are in face-to-face relations daily (Omark, Omark, and Edelman, 1973; Omark and Edelman, 1975; Omark, Strayer, and Freedman, 1980). In all of our samples, we have observed conflicts over dominance to arise and hierarchies to develop. The responses of parents to the dominance of older over younger siblings differ across the cultures, however. In most of our sample communities, parents and other socializers expect children to work out their own disputes and establish clear-cut dominance hierarchies. Because parents delegate the care of younger children to older ones, they accept the implicit right of older children to exercise authority over younger ones. Parents expect that children will command their younger siblings and appropriate a greater than equal share of "turns" or "resources" (food, however, is expected to be shared equally). Yet dominance hierarchies are not all to the benefit of the elders; older siblings are also expected to stand up for and protect their younger siblings when outsiders threaten or abuse them.

A dominance relationship among three Nyansongo sisters is illustrated by the following observation of a group of women and children working in a garden. A mother and her three daughters are present; the mother and the two older girls are hoeing while Nyambura, age 2, stands around. Agnes, age 4, intent on keeping up with the older girls, refuses to share her hoe with her knee-child sister. She slaps her when she asks for the hoe, kicks dirt in the child's face, and insults her by calling her an uncircumcised girl, an insult that only a much older girl can rightly use, since Agnes herself is uncircumcised. The mother, although she is obviously aware of what is going on, does not interfere until the conflict has lasted for a long time and the knee child begins to cry.

Nyambura (girl, age 2) goes over to Agnes, her 4-year-old sister, and says, "Let me use the hoe a bit." Agnes slaps Nyambura, says nothing and goes on hoeing. Nyambura goes away, then comes back to watch Agnes busily hoeing. Agnes stops and rests a minute, but doesn't offer her sister the hoe. Nyambura tries again, "Let me help you." Agnes looks up, then resumes hoeing. She says, "You go and look for your own hoe, I'm working hard with mine." Agnes goes on hoeing, then turns around and sees her little sister still standing watching her. She shouts, "What are you doing here?" and angrily kicks at the soil so that dirt flies up into Nyambura's face. Another girl Agnes' age chimes in, "Nyambura where is YOUR hoe?" Agnes continues, insultingly, "Go away, you uncircumcised girl." Nyambura stands looking sad and then goes over to stand by her mother. Then she finds a hoe dropped by a teenage girl who has stopped working. She goes over to work by Agnes. Agnes says, "Look how I do it properly." Nyambura tries to pull Agnes' hoe away from her, then begins to cry. The mother now intervenes for the first time. She says to Agnes, "Let her have it." Agnes does and then gets another hoe from her mother. The two girls hoe together. Agnes says, "You work hard. I am about to finish my row. There, I have finished my row. I am going to begin again down there." The mother commands the eldest sister, Nyamwara (age 6), "Bring your hoe." The girl brings it and exchanges it with the mother. Agnes watches them intensely for a short time, then resumes work. She says to her older sister, "I've finished mine." The older sister ignores Agnes, so Agnes confronts little Nyambura, "You work hard and finish yours." Agnes entreats her older sister, "When we finish, let's go back and begin another row together." Then in a harsh tone commands her younger sister, "Keep away! Don't dig so near me. Stop digging near me, Nyambura, you uncircumcised girl." (LeVine and LeVine, field observations, 1956)

Note the desire of all the young girls to be included in the cooperative women's work group. The fact that even the 2-year-old owns a hoe indicates how early the culture instills in girls their important role in agriculture. The members of the work group compete with each other to see who can complete hoeing a row the fastest, and even the youngest ones catch the spirit of competition. It is the desire of the younger children to do what the older children are doing that explains in part their willingness to tolerate the dominance and aggressive behavior of the older children.

The pattern of parental nonintervention serves a useful function for the mothers: it allows them to continue their work without having to stop frequently to deal with children's problems. Although the Nyansongo and many of the Ngeca mothers are at the extreme in their policy of letting the children work out their own conflicts and settle their own disputes even in early childhood, mothers in the other communities also are noninterventionists as compared with the Orchard Town sample.

That intervention requires time and patience is demonstrated in the following observation of an Orchard Town mother, home alone with her daughter, Debbie, and her son, John. It can also be seen in this and other observations that intervention is frequently ineffectual with knee children and their older siblings; often the mothers, in exasperation, give up their arbitrating.

Debbie (girl, age 4) and John (boy, age 2) are sitting on the floor eating marshmallow topping out of a jar. Debbie looks at her hands and comments, "Sticky! John, you're getting sticky hands too." John says, "Let me have some." He takes the jar. Debbie screams and tries to get the jar away from John. She calls to her mother, "He won't let me have some," and starts to cry. The mother intervenes, saying first to Debbie, "Listen here, you're getting your share. Now stop it." Then she orders John, "Now you give her some." Finally, she says to Debbie, "Oh, stop your crying . . . Oh, I give up." She throws up her hands and withdraws. Debbie now starts kicking John. The mother returns and declares, "This is a new angle [new solution]. Now here, one more spoonful [each], and we're putting the jar up." She gives out the spoonful, which the children accept. Then Debbie says, "There! [I'll] go in there [bathroom] and get my hands washed." John goes in too and climbs on the toilet to share the basin with Debbie. He tries to push her over, and she cries. She says angrily, "John, I'll put some soap on your hands." Their mother comes in. She gets John a chair and tells him to stand on it. John does, but still keeps trying to move Debbie over so that he will have more room. There is more screaming. Debbie tells John he has lots of marshmallow on his face. Then things quiet down. (Fischer and Fischer, field observations, 1955)

Even with their older children, the Orchard Town parents frequently intervene and adjudicate their children's disputes; they often stop their children's bickering and ensure that their rights, especially property rights and rights to participate in an activity, are protected. The following observation is an example of the Orchard Town pattern and illustrates the use of distraction, a common technique for stopping conflict when the parents are unable to mediate successfully. The children, three girls aged 4, 6, and 8, seem to expect and need their parents to help them resolve their disputes. This makes hard work for their mother—work that mothers in most of our other communities avoid by giving older children responsibility and allowing them authority.

The whole Smith family is outside looking at the horses in their paddock. The oldest of the three daughters, age 8, has drawn a hopscotch court with a piece of chalk. As the youngest daughter, Andy (age 4), steps on the outline, Donna reproves her, "Oh, you're making it all a big mess." Their mother tells Donna, "Let her be." Donna turns to Susan, the middle sister, and says, "Let's start over. I'm first." The children play by themselves for a few moments. The two oldest girls argue with each other about who should go first [eventually Donna goes]. Then the youngest girls begin to push and hit because Susan (age 6) dislikes the way Andy (age 4) steps on the lines and smears them. Their father now intervenes. "Gently, Sue." Andy retreats from the fighting and goes to sit on a rock and watch the two older girls play. After a while, she returns. Donna says to her mother, "Make Andy leave us alone." The mother tries to help Donna, accepting that the two older girls should be allowed to play without Andy's interference. She calls Andy to come over near her. Andy goes and spends a few moments, then later returns to the hopscotch. She tries again to get a turn by picking up a stone and going to the starting square. The two older girls both say, "No." Andy seeks her mother's aid, "Hey, they won't let me have a turn." The mother now tries to help Andy and asks the two older girls, "Have you two had turns?" Donna says, "Yes," so the mother commands them to give Andy a turn. They say, "We don't want her. She messes everything all up." The mother repeats, "Well, you give her a turn." The girls refuse and start fighting with Andy. The mother just watches helplessly saying with a laugh to the observer, "Well, one thing, she [Andy] is not afraid to stand up for herself." Finally the mother intervenes to solve the problem, using a new technique—distraction. She calls out that they all are going to go to their friends' house. The fight stops and all the girls troop off, interested in the expedition. (Fischer and Fischer, field observations, 1955)

Because the Orchard Town mothers reward their children's requests for intervention, the children constantly report the deviations of their siblings, expecting the mothers to help them get what they desire. Note the following behavior of a Nyansongo mother in contrast:

The mother and children are at home in the yard. Agnes (age 4) is standing around idly while her mother shells maize. She goes over to a visiting infant, makes some noises at it, then picks it up awkwardly. Her mother reproves her for bothering the infant, "Why do you pick up a child that is quiet?" Agnes ignores her mother and plays with the baby. Then she wanders over to her mother who is working at shelling the maize. Agnes sits on the stone used for their work and calls to her older sister, Nyamwara (age 6) who is resting against the house, "You've done this enough. Now let me do it a while." The older girl rushes back to her stone and pushes Agnes off the stone and resumes shelling the maize. Agnes calls to her mother for help, "Mama, she doesn't let me do it." However, her mother ignores her and talks to Sarume (girl, age 8) and to Nyamwara about going to the market once the work is finished. Agnes protests that she wants to go too. Sarume goes into the house and emerges with a smile and her mouth chewing. Agnes stares hard at her and suddenly begins crying to her mother, "Mama, she has candy and won't give me any." The mother ignores her. Agnes rushes over to Sarume. She screams, threatens to hit, and clutches the bigger girl's dress. Sarume then removes some of the candy from her mouth and gives it to Agnes and the other children present until finally she has given away almost all that she was eating. (LeVine and LeVine, field observations, 1955)

Orchard Town mothers who do not work are home all day with their children; they do not delegate the care of younger children to older siblings until late childhood, and they have more time to adjudicate their children's conflicts. More important, however, is the value they place on equality. They conceive of their society as egalitarian: old and young, males and females theoretically have equal rights, and if, for some reason, they do not, the differential in privilege must be explained. To the extent that mothers attempt to promote this egalitarianism that goes against the pecking order based on size and age, they are engaging in a difficult task, one that requires constant monitoring. Furthermore, the mothers' expectations require explanations and justification by reference to rules of fairness. Parents are seen to model behavior similar to that of the protagonists in a court of law.

In the process of attempting to arbitrate their children's conflicts, the Orchard Town mothers issue many commands that the children do not obey. Since they are trying to adjudicate, the mothers do not like to resort to force; as a consequence, they ignore the disobedience.

The Growing Awareness of Gender

In examining the observations of yard children, we expected to see evidence of their growing awareness of gender identity. Students of child development, psychotherapists, teachers, and parents have all reported the increased awareness of self that occurs between early and late childhood. The ages of 4 and 5 are often cited as a period during which notable changes can be observed in the cognitive processes of children. Freudians note that the resolution of the Oedipal complex occurs around this age: the little boy gives up his close attachment to his mother and begins to identify with his father. Gender becomes increasingly salient to the child, and its permanence from childhood to adulthood is accepted (Kohlberg, 1966; Slaby and Frey, 1975; Munroe, Shimmin, and Munroe, 1984). The boy, for example, who has been able since age 2 to declare his gender, is now able to identify his maleness in himself and to associate the clothes he wears, his toys or tools, and the activities he performs with his gender. The growing awareness of gender makes the child more attentive to the roles of same-sex adults and older same-sex children.

Psychologists differ in the degree to which they attribute the growing understanding of gender and sex-role identity to the general increase in cognitive ability (associated with physical maturation) as contrasted with socialization pressures exerted by parents, teachers, and peers. The child's concepts of appropriate behavior for males and females have been attributed to statements by socializers, the content of books read to children, and to other types of media. Our emphasis is on the less overt processes of transmission. It is evident that 4- and 5-year-olds are acute observers; they probably learn more by observation than they do from the statements of their teachers.

They draw conclusions from observing regularities in the behavior of men and women, the clothes they wear, the content of the activities they perform, and their styles of interpersonal behavior, including speech habits, gestures, and other physical habits (Maccoby and Jacklin, 1974; Luria, 1979; Maccoby, 1980).

Caretakers and socializers may consciously or unconsciously help children establish gender identity by treating boys and girls differently, but, as discussed in Chapter 3, we can identify only a few differences in maternal styles of social interaction with sons and daughters that are both robust and consistent across the samples. Evidently, during the lap and knee periods, the very nature of the immature child shapes the behavior of the mother. Evidence for the lack of discrimination between the sexes in the early stages of life is seen in the labeling of these age grades: in most of the world, as in our culture, there is not even a single word that identifies both the age grade and the gender of a lap or knee child.

There are ways, however, in which the members of a society transmit rules about appropriate sex-role behavior. These methods of transmission are not limited to the different types of social interaction that we have coded in the behavior observations.

Training for Appropriate Gender Role Behavior

Cultures differ in the degree to which they emphasize or deemphasize gender differences. One of the most obvious symbols of gender in all societies is the style of clothing of males and females. One of the ways in which mothers can accentuate differences is by making a distinction in the clothes, hairstyles, and adornments of girls and boys. In several of our communities a clear distinction is made in early childhood. Starting in infancy, the Mixtecan mothers in Juxtlahuaca and the Rajput and Bhubaneswar mothers of North India make it possible to identify the gender of their lap and knee children. For example, in Juxtlahuaca the ears of little girls are pierced during the first few weeks of life, and all females wear earrings. Young female knee children already have miniature *rebozas* (shawls), and little boys wear their *sombreros* with pride. In Khalapur the little girls may have a cloth braid worked into the lock of hair at the back of their head, and in addition may have glass beads or glass arm and ankle bracelets. The young girls already have head scarves that they are learning to wear as their mothers do. The little boys all wear a

Juxtlahuacan boys in sombreros (1955)

black cord around their navel, a symbol of their Rajput status, and an amulet to ensure that their penis will grow straight. Their hairstyles announce gender and age.

Gender is anatomically marked in communities where there are long periods of warm weather and the clothing of young children is minimal. With the exception of Orchard Town, the knee children in our samples wear few clothes until they have learned to control their sphincters. Boys wear a short shirt, girls a short dress. It is not until about 4 years of age that girls are expected to have learned to sit properly so as not to expose their genitals. In Tarong anyone has the right to pinch the exposed labia of young girls under age 4; after this age they are required to sit in such a way that their genitals are covered. The 3- and 4-year-olds already have quite an extensive vocabulary for body parts, some not approved by the parental generation, and girls and boys tease each other about their genitals. Less attention is paid to the covering of the male genitals; especially in many of the subsaharan African communities, the penis is considered asexual until the early teens, when the boys are circumcised in initiation ceremonies.

Some of the 4- and 5-year-olds who have earned the privilege of wearing more elaborate clothing, especially the girls, are obviously proud of their new gender-typed clothing. The Juxtlahuacan and North Indian girls seem to enjoy learning to manage *rebozas* and the miniature saris. Subsaharan girls like to try on the head scarves that women wear. The Juxtlahuacan boys constantly check the condition of their large hats, which they like to wear all the time. Tairan girls are proud of the underpants they may now wear, often exposing them with bravado to their age mates. Orchard Town girls compare notes about their Sunday School and party-going apparel. The subsaharan 4- and 5-year-olds seem the least concerned with clothing, perhaps because these societies are age-graded, and the emphasis for young children is more on size and maturity than on gender. Establishing one's gender is the concern of the initiation ceremonies that take place in late childhood or early adolescence in the subsaharan communities (Whiting, Kluckhohn, and Anthony, 1958; Munroe, Munroe, and Whiting, 1981).

The division of labor by gender in the adult world that exists in all societies is also obvious to observant children. When it is possible, some of the parents in our samples call attention to the adult division of labor by assigning different types of chores to girls and boys. As we have seen, in preindustrial societies parents ask children to perform tasks beginning as early as age 4, both because the children actually can be of help and because work helps to structure their random activities and channel their boundless energy. In channeling this energy into productive work, parents are preparing the children for the adult world. Societies differ, however, in the degree to which they are able to replicate in childhood the division of labor by gender that is the norm in the adult world. Children of ages 4 and 5 are not strong enough to perform many of the adult chores, particularly those assigned to men.

Regardless of what tasks are assigned to young girls and boys, the division of the world into male and female domains seems to be clear to the children in all the samples by the age of 4 or 5. We know from studies in the United States that, regardless of how hard parents and teachers try to discourage this behavior, children as young as 4 and 5 see work as divided into stereotyped gender categories. In earlier chapters we discussed the division of labor in our samples and the work that is assigned to children; it is useful here to review the tasks that are assigned to 4- and 5-year-olds from the point of view of the messages transmitted to children about sex roles.

Because it is the policy in most societies to keep children under 6 close to home or in settings where they can be supervised by adults and older children, inevitably most of the work in these settings is in the domain of women. Young boys are therefore preempted to help the mother. In some societies, perhaps in all, the mother is probably influenced consciously or unconsciously by what she considers to be appropriate work for males and females, but she is more likely to disregard the importance of gender stereotypes if she needs help.

Although infant care in all the societies we have studied is in the domain of women, both male and female 4- and 5-year-olds in many cultures are expected to perform child care. However, even in communities where boys may be asked to care for lap children, they are assigned such care infrequently in comparison with girls. Moreover, across the samples girls interact with lap children more frequently than do boys. For instance, in Ngeca, where we have a record of the chores that children were assigned in 1968, all 4- and 5-year-old girls with lap-child siblings were observed at some time carrying and caring for the child, and several were expected to do some child care daily. None of the 4- and 5-year-old Ngeca boys were observed caring for lap children, but in the interviews with mothers, all reported that they would expect boys to do so if called upon. In Nyansongo, a more traditional Kenyan community, both girl and boy nurses were observed in the 4- and 5-year-old age group.

We do not know how Kenyan boys who are assigned the care of lap children feel about being child nurses, but the young boys must be aware that boys 8 and over are not expected to carry babies, and that their fathers have little to do with the care of lap and knee children. The fact that they are asked to perform child care thus emphasizes their lowly status rather than their gender. One could speculate that the young boys envy their older brothers, who are not compelled to stay close to home and deal with child-care responsibilities. If one can judge by their observed desire to interact with older boys, this is indeed the case.

As we have seen, there is less distinction by gender in assigning the care of knee children to older siblings. For most of the 4- and 5-year-old girls and boys in our samples, the supervision of knee children is more frequent than responsibility for lap children. The 2- and 3-year-olds tag along after their older brothers and sisters, and even if the older children are not specifically asked to care for them, they are expected to see that their young siblings stay safe. It is only in Orchard Town where the 4- and 5-year-olds who have 2- and 3-year-old siblings are never observed alone with these 2-year-olds. In any case, in none of the societies, with the possible exception of Tarong, is the responsibility for knee children considered the work of adult males.

The question arises as to whether there are indeed any tasks that are distinctly male that parents can assign to their young sons. In many societies in the world, the care of large animals is the task that is considered masculine, and young boys can participate in this work beginning at age 4 or 5. In Tarong the care and use of the carabao (water buffalo) are considered to be in the domain of men, and all three of the 4- and 5-year-old boys in the sample were observed watering and grazing carabao. No girls were observed caring for these animals.

It is clear that the ability to manage the carabao is valued in Tarong. In one of the observations a 5-year-old boy climbed all over a carabao, mauling the animal and poking at its testicles with a stick. When William Nydegger commented on this behavior to the boy's father, he replied that it was good, that the boy and the animal would know each other and the boy would be able to control it when he was old enough to work with the animal (Nydegger and Nydegger, field observations, 1955). The young boy accompanied his father when he took the animal to be watered, and helped him change its tether during the day.

Parents who emphasize gender from early childhood may consciously or unconciously try to make distinctions in task assignment even when there is nothing appropriate for males that can be assigned. For example, although the care of pigs and chickens is in the domain of women in Juxtlahuaca, the work is assigned to boys rather than girls in the early years. None of the 4- and 5-year-old Juxtlahuacan girls in the sample were assigned tasks that involved animals, but all the boys of this age fed pigs and chickens. The care of burros, however, was the work of adult men, and the one young boy who helped corral and tie up the family burro must have felt grown up.

Throughout Kenya, the care of cattle is considered the domain of men and boys. The supervision of animals in unfenced pastures adjacent to the homestead is assigned to boys. Although, as in the care of lap children, the task may be assigned to the opposite sex if a child of the appropriate age and gender is lacking, there is a clear preference for boys. It is stated in Nyansongo that girls are not assigned the care of cattle after they are initiated, although necessity may also lead to deviation from the rule. In Khalapur the care of the buffalo is in the domain of men, and the older boys are in charge of taking the animals to the river to be watered and washed. Young boys tag along with their older brothers and sisters at the river. Few of the 4- and 5-year-olds in any of the societies we studied are observed caring for animals all by themselves; more frequently they accompany their older brothers, who order them about and instruct them in the necessary skills.

In sum, in those societies where there are no chores that are part of men's work in the adult world, parents are hard put if they wish to make distinctions. Children of busy mothers are asked to perform work that is "female," and they are undoubtedly aware that this is the case. Carol Ember (1970, 1973) documented this in her interviews of both parents and children concerning the division of labor by gender among the Luo families in Oyugis, Kenya. It was clear that the children classified tasks by gender similarly to their elders. The "female" work included tasks both inside the house and outside its immediate vicinity, since women in this community, as in the rest of the rural Kenyan samples, are farmers as well as housekeepers.

Orchard Town is certainly a society in which parents concerned about appropriate gender behavior have little choice in assigning tasks. The observations show that there seem to be three tasks that parents assign to boys rather than girls: taking out the garbage, cutting the grass, and cutting and carrying wood, perhaps reflecting the inside/outside metaphor that is popular with American sociologists for dividing the world into male and female domains. Four- and five-year-olds are not strong enough for most of these tasks.

When boys are assigned "female" tasks, they often adopt a style that is different from that of girls. For example, in Ngeca, when boys are asked to carry water from the river or the town well, they carry cans with handles or roll barrels, whereas the women and girls use round metal containers and tumplines. When boys carry wood, another "female" chore, they often have some contraption with a wheel. We never saw a boy carrying wood with the tumpline used by the women. One could argue that the different styles reflect the differential strength of boys' shoulders and arms, but in any case the style is associated with being male, not female. As noted in Chapter 5, boys also have a different style of caring for lap children. It may be that the style of behavior is in part influenced by a conscious effort to be different from their mothers and sisters.

There are many distinctions between male and female roles that can be observed by children themselves. For instance, children can draw inferences as to the relative status of men and women. It must be obvious even to a 4- or 5-year-old in some of the societies, if not in all, that men dominate women. The Juxtlahuacan children must have assessed the relative privileges granted to males and females when men and boys were served food first, waited on by the women, and given chairs to sit on while women sat on the ground. Nyansongo children observe the women preparing special baskets of food for their husbands—more than the men can possibly eat, but not to be shared until the husband has had his fill. In all of our samples women do the daily preparation of meals and serve the men.

There are countless acts witnessed by children that symbolize the differential power of men and women. All subsaharan men order their wives around, and probably most children in these societies by age 4 or 5 have witnessed their father, or some other man, beating his wife. For the Rajput child in North India, the picture may be more complicated. The power of the men is obvious when all females lower themselves to the floor and cover their heads when men enter the courtyard; on the other hand, children have also observed that the oldest woman in the courtyard dominates both her married sons and her daughters-in-law (the fathers and mothers of the sample children). The relative power of men and women is less obvious in Orchard Town, Taira, and Tarong. In these samples the fathers are around more frequently, and in the home setting they are less authoritarian in their relations to their wives. In Taira and Tarong the men and women work together in the fields. In Tarong the fathers prepare meals and take care of their children if, following the birth of a new child, there are no other women living in the house. All Orchard Town fathers occasionally help their wives with child care and some domestic work. However, even in Orchard Town the 4- and 5-year-olds may interpret the mother's change in behavior when her husband returns from work, her attending to his supper, and her turning of attention to conversation with him rather than the children as a sign of his preferred status.

Not all of the children in our samples have an equal opportunity to observe their fathers. With the exception of Tarong, few of the young boys have a chance to work with the father. In those societies where the fathers do not sleep in the same house as their young children, for example in many of the Khalapur households and in the polygynous Kenyan communities where the father may have a house of his own, 4- and 5-year-olds' knowledge of men's behavior may be limited. However, the houses in the polygynous homesteads are not isolated, so that men are usually present on a daily basis even when the father is not home. Similarly in Juxtlahuaca, although 23 percent of the fathers work outside the area, in every case there is some adult man living in the extended courtyard. In Tarong there are no men in 12 percent of the households we studied, but there are related men in the shared yards. In Taira fathers are home every night in all but one of the households, and in Orchard Town the father is home in all the households, although often he returns late and leaves early in the morning, so he seldom interacts with his children except on weekends. Judging by the percentage of children's interaction with adult males, even when the fathers are present as members of the household, 4- and 5-year-olds have limited opportunity to interact with them during the daylight hours. When the children in the Six Culture Study were observed, the father was present on average in only 9 percent of the observations (see Table 2.7). He was present most frequently in Tarong (17 percent of the observations), and least frequently in Khalapur and Taira. He was observed interacting with his 4- and 5-year-old children most frequently in Orchard Town and Tarong, the two communities with the highest percentage of nuclear households, but even in these communities only 3 percent of the children's interaction was with their fathers. In the New Samples of African communities, less than 1 percent of the knee children's recorded interaction was with their fathers. (Appendix E presents the total number of yard children's social interacts.)

Although what a child observes seems to be more important at age 4 or 5 than what he or she hears, there is also evidence in the observations that parents in some of the communities make comments about gender differences. The following quotation taken from the observations in Juxtlahuaca, where we have noted other evidence of early training for approved gender-specific behavior, is illustrative:

Gaviel (boy, age 4) did something that his aunt interpreted as bad behavior, and she hit him hard on the arm. He moved to hit her back and she caught his hands and held them as he struggled. He smiled for a while and then began to look angry. Fidencia, his friend, stepped in and started hitting the aunt. Another aunt of the boys, standing nearby, asked the observer so that the boys could hear, "Are boys so *bravo* also in the States that they hit their aunts?"   (Romney and Romney, field observations, 1955)

That being male implies extra privileges is learned early by young girls. In one observation a 4-year-old Juxtlahuacan girl was told by her mother to "fetch a chair for the man," in this case the 3-year-old male child of the ethnographers! In Kenya, when boys reach puberty it is expected that they will dominate girls. The hierarchy of dominance based on age and gender replaces the hierarchy based on age, and this new dominance pattern is legitimated in the boys' initiation rituals.

If this increased awareness of gender occurs in all societies from middle to late childhood, we would expect to see changes in the interpersonal behavior of girls and boys that reflect the new awareness. First, we would expect children to begin to discriminate according to the gender of their companion, treating male and female children differently. We would also expect differences in the interaction of cross-sex and same-sex dyads, and we would expect these differences to be greatest in those societies that emphasize gender differences. If, as we hypothesize, young boys who have attained what American psychologists label "gender permanence" perceive males as having more power than females, and if they envy the status that has power, we would expect a change in behavior that reflects this preference; that is, we would expect boys to act in ways that they consider appropriate for males and to emphasize the fact that they are not females.

We have explored several types of behavior that we can interpret as evidence of girls' and boys' new sense of self in terms of having a fixed gender: the preference for interacting with same-sex children, the preference by boys for leaving the house and avoiding the mother, boys' conflict with their mothers, and different behavior in same-sex versus cross-sex interaction.

Interaction with Same-Sex Children.   If by 4 to 5 years of age there is evidence that children have developed gender permanence—the recognition that their gender will not change—we expect indications in their behavior that mirror this growing awareness and self-consciousness of gender. One of the ways in which children can demonstrate preoccupation with gender identity is by spending the majority of their time with same-sex companions, monitoring their behavior, and through reciprocal interaction forming concrete ideas of their sex role.

There is evidence that as early as 3 years of age children are attracted to same-sex companions (see review in Hartup, 1983). Luria (1979) has argued that the critical period for the development of gender identity is between 18 and 36 months. Because our observational data in the Six Culture and Spot Observation samples do not include 2- to 3-year-olds, we have no evidence for the same-sex-only preference of these children. However, our knowledge of their daily routines would suggest that the fixed sex ratio of individuals in the home setting would make preferential choice of companions difficult.

The most detailed analysis of the companions of knee and yard children is found in the report of Martha Wenger's study in Kaloleni (1983), in Giriamaland in the Coastal Province of Kenya. The observations were made in the large polygynous homesteads where there were several families with young children, allowing for a choice of companions who were close in age. The homesteads ranged in size from 6 to 36 members, with a mean of 16; the average number of children ranged from 0 to 11, with a mean of 6. Using the methodology developed by Ruth Munroe and Robert Munroe, Wenger made random spot observations in the homesteads and the area immediately adjacent, identifying the activities and companions of 105 children between the ages of 2 and 11. Table 6.4 shows the percentage of observations in which only same-sex children, aged 2–11, were in the interactional space of four age groups of children. As Wenger summarizes:

Table 6.4. Percentage of observations in which all children within the focal child's interactional space are of the same sex as the child observed

Gender of focal child	Age of focal child (years)			
	2–3	4–5	6–7	8–11
Girls	32	33	52	48
Boys	22	41	55	70

Note: Observations in which adults are present are excluded. The children are from Kaloleni, Kenya.

Source: Adapted from Wenger (1983), fig. 4.7, p. 108.

From ages 2–3 through 6–7 both girls and boys display a linear increase in the percentage of observations in which they are in gender-exclusive groups. The greatest increase for boys was 19 points and occurred when expected, between ages 2–3 and 4–5. Subsequent increases for boys, however, are substantial, and at 8–11 years some 70% of their all-child companionship is male-only. Girls, who at 2–3 display a greater preference than boys for same-sex companions (32%), make no dramatic change at ages 4–5. Their greatest change occurs between ages 4–5 (33%) and 6–7 (52%). At the oldest age point, girls' rates of same-sex companionship drop about 6 points, so that at this age boys' percentages are substantially higher than girls'. (Wenger, 1983, pp. 108–109)

Girls in the oldest age group are restricted in their choice of companions by task assignment.*

The preference for same-sex peer companions is even more evident when one controls for both the gender and the age of companions. If the choice of companions is motivated in part by the desire for self-discovery, children who are close in age are the best mirrors. In addition, they are more apt to share the same preferences for activities. Table 6.5 presents Wenger's findings on the percentage of observations of peers that involved only members of the same sex as the child observed. (Peers were defined to include children one or two years older or younger than the focal child.) As can be seen, there is a linear increase with age. In this case the greatest increase

Table 6.5. Percentage of observations in which all children within the focal child's interactional space are of the same sex and the same age as the child observed

Age group	Females	Males
2- to 3-year-olds	43.6	31.6
4- to 5-year-olds	52.0	40.0
6- to 7-year-olds	53.3	67.9
8- to 11-year-olds	92.0	95.0

Note: Observations in which adults are present are excluded. The children are from Kaloleni, Kenya.
Source: Adapted from Wenger (1983), fig. 4.8, p. 110.

*Since the definition of the setting is different in the Six Culture samples from that in the Kaloleni sample, and since both the age groups and setting analysis are different in the Spot Observation sample, comparisons can only be made within each study.

for boys is between the ages of 4–5 and 6–7. The 6- to 7-year-olds are school-age children who are allowed or required to leave the confines of family-owned land; thus they have a greater number of potential companions who may visit the child's homestead. By ages 8–11, over 90 percent of the observations of a focal child with his or her peers are with children of the same sex. There are virtually no gender differences in the percentages (92 percent for girls, 95 percent for boys).

The Spot Observations also suggest that most same-age groups interacting or engaged in the same activity are sex-segregated (see Table 2.13). Moreover, the data on the percentages of dyadic interaction in the New Samples and the Six Culture samples indicate a preference for same-sex dyads. As Table 6.6 shows, in our samples an average of 66 percent of the interaction of 4- and 5-year-olds with children is with same-sex children (aged 3–10). The average for girls is higher than that for boys: 61 percent for the boys versus 71 percent for the girls. The range for boys is from 42 percent in Ngeca to 76 percent in Juxtlahuaca. The range for girls is greater, from 39 percent in Kokwet to 93 percent in Kisa-Kariobangi. Both girls and boys in Ngeca and Kokwet, and boys in Kisa-Kariobangi and Orchard Town, are well below the average. It seems clear that since the majority of these 4- and 5-year-old children do not range far from the house and yard, the sex ratio of these groups limits the choice of companions. Of the three communities where the percentage of same-sex interaction of the boys is over 70 percent, two are in locations with nucleated settlement patterns, Taira and Juxtlahuaca, where children play in the streets and public places. The third is Nyansongo, where boys are found together in the pastures herding the cattle.

A better measure of the preference for same-sex child companions is the percentage of interaction with same-sex children who are not siblings. When children are able to leave the immediate environs of their house and have daily companions who are not members of their immediate family, what is the likelihood that they will interact with children of the same sex? Table 6.7 presents these data. It can be seen that an average of two-thirds of yard children's interaction with non-siblings is with children of the same sex. By ages 6–10, the percentage increases to an average of 80 percent. Again the gender differences are not great, with both boys and girls favoring same-sex child companions.

In interaction with same-sex children who are close in age, a child

Table 6.6. Percentage of all social acts that are with children (aged 3–10) who are of the same sex as the actor

Community	Girls (%)	Boys (%)	Diff.
New Samples			
Kien-taa			
4–5 years	92	74	+18
6–10 years	44	68	−24
Kokwet			
4–5 years	39	51	−12
6–10 years	62	55	+7
Kisa-Kariobangi			
4–5 years	93	49	+44
6–10 years	81	89	−8
Ngeca			
4–5 years	50	42	+8
6–10 years	51	64	−13
Six Cultures[a]			
Nyansongo			
4–5 years	76	75	+1
6–10 years	75	60	+15
Juxtlahuaca			
4–5 years	60	76	−16
6–10 years	71	79	−8
Tarong			
4–5 years	62	61	+1
6–10 years	78	56	+22
Taira			
4–5 years	83	73	+10
6–10 years	73	78	−5
Orchard Town			
4–5 years	86	51	+35
6–10 years	95	71	+24

a. Khalapur was omitted because there were insufficient data for the 4- and 5-year-olds.

can compare her appearance, behavior, and likes and dislikes with those of the companion. These experiences teach understanding of the self, as well as understanding of the behavior of others who are perceived as similar in salient attributes of gender. In sum, interacting with same-sex companions can be seen as aiding a child to establish gender and sex-role identity.

Table 6.7. Percentage of all social acts of 4- to 5-year-old and 6- to 10-year-old children that are with same-sex children (aged 3–10) other than siblings

Community	Girls (%)	Boys (%)	Diff.
New Samples			
Kien-taa			
4–5 years	100	94	+6
6–10 years	81	80	+1
Kokwet			
4–5 years	79	58	+21
6–10 years	82	79	+3
Kisa-Kariobangi			
4–5 years	0	0	0
6–10 years	0	100	−100
Ngeca			
4–5 years	38	65	−27
6–10 years	83	73	+10
Six Cultures[a]			
Nyansongo			
4–5 years	56	56	0
6–10 years	71	67	+4
Juxtlahuaca			
4–5 years	42	63	−21
6–10 years	71	83	−12
Tarong			
4–5 years	61	62	−1
6–10 years	90	79	−11
Taira			
4–5 years	78	74	+4
6–10 years	73	88	+15
Orchard Town[b]			
4–5 years	65	22	+43
6–10 years	84	86	−2

a. Khalapur was not included because there were insufficient data for 4- and 5-year-olds.

b. The ethnographers' two daughters were included in many of the observations.

In communities where interaction with adult males is infrequent, young boys seek interaction with older boys. In all the communities, boys interact with older boys more frequently than girls interact with older girls. In interacting with older boys the younger boys are usually dominated, told what to do, and sometimes physically teased, as we saw in the observations of the mixed-age groups of boys in the Nyansongo pastures. The acceptance by the younger boys of what may seem to be uncomfortable situations may be motivated by a desire to observe and participate in male behavior.

The older boys in their peer groups are modeling styles of egoistic dominance. It is probable that the yard-age boys associate this style of behavior with "masculinity." In general, as we have seen, the yard-age boys have a more egoistically dominant profile in interaction with younger children than the girls have. Table 6.8 presents a comparison of the dominance of Kenyan 4- and 5-year-old girls and boys to knee children. It can be seen that boys in three of the comparisons score proportionately higher than the girls in seeking to dominate egoistically, as well as in total egoistic dominance (combined scores of attempts to dominate egoistically, assaults, and insults). The more prosocial style of dominance of the older girls, described in the previous chapter, may seem "feminine" to the gender-conscious boys.

We have no way of assessing the relative contribution of preparedness and experience in comparing the egoistic dominance scores of boys and girls. As early as ages 2 and 3, the Kenyan boys are

Table 6.8. Proportion of all social acts of yard children to knee children that are coded as egoistic dominance behavior

Community	Attempts to dominate (%)	Assaults (%)	Insults (%)	Total dominance (%)
Kien-taa				
Girls (8)	7	3	1	11
Boys (4)	19	5	10	34
Kokwet				
Girls (18)	9	2	4	15
Boys (22)	17	4	1	22
Kisa-Kariobangi				
Girls (10)	4	2	4	10
Boys (7)	3	3	4	10
Ngeca				
Girls (12)	7	2	8	17
Boys (6)	10	4	15	29
Mean				
Girls (12)	7	2	4	13
Boys (11)	12	4	8	24

proportionately more egoistically dominant than the girls are, but since this type of behavior elicits reciprocal responses, the difference at this early age may be seen as the result of interacting with dominating social partners. The older boys whose company the yard-age boys seek have had more experience in interacting with boys whose behavior involves conflict over dominance hierarchies. In any case it is clear that, in general, yard-age boys both elicit more dominance than do girls of the same age (see Table 6.2) and are more egoistically dominant than the girls.

Preference for Leaving the Home Environs and Avoiding the Mother. Since, as we theorize, the boy has to change his primary identification with his mother in order to identify with male figures, we expect that he will begin, conciously or unconsciously, to avoid interaction with his mother. As Chodorow (1974, 1978) states the theory, boys must negate their primary attachment to their mothers and withdraw from them in order to consolidate their gender identity. We have seen that, across the samples, fathers are present in the observations infrequently; thus it is conceivable that the young boy's concept of masculinity may involve being absent from the house and yard.

Table 2.5 gave the percentage of observations in which 4- and 5-year-old boys and girls in the Six Culture Study were observed in the house, yard, or homestead area. In all the communities, girls were found to be closest to home. It is not possible to assess, however, whether the girls actually chose to stay at home or whether they were more restricted by the tasks that were assigned. In the Spot Observation samples it appears that the former is probably the case, because when a distinction is made between "directed" and "undirected" activities, it is during the latter that boys are found further from home (see Table 2.6). It is likely that the majority of these undirected activities were coded as play or idle pastimes, activities that boys are observed to be engaged in more frequently than girls. It is also the case that in almost all of the samples, girls were observed working more frequently than boys.

There is no question that, in our samples, girls of ages 4 and 5 are in the presence of their mothers significantly more than are boys of a comparable age (see Tables 2.7 and 2.8). Wenger reports that in Kaloleni, in the Coastal Province in Kenya, the percentage of time when an adult female is in the interactional space with boys decreases by approximately 50 percent between the ages of 2–3 and 4–5, from

48 to 23 percent of the time, and continues in a steady but small decrease to age 11 (Wenger, 1983, p. 105). By comparison, the change in the presence of an adult female in the girls' interactional space for the same ages is small. If avoidance of the mother is an indication of 4- and 5-year-old boys' reaction to the growing sense of a masculine gender identity, this is clearly reflected in the Kaloleni data and in Wenger's interpretation of these data. She points out that girls remain relatively constant in their contact with their mothers.

Although we favor the interpretation that the 4- and 5-year-old boys are at least in part avoiding their mother as a result of their attempt to consolidate their gender identity, one can still ask whether the girls would also leave home more frequently if they were not restricted by mothers who wanted their help around the home. It is not possible to assess the degree to which the differences in the distance from home and the percentage of observations in which the girl is in the presence of the mother or an adult female can be attributed to the boys' greater desire to disassociate themselves from females, or simply to a desire to get away from authority figures who assign work, and to seek out companions who will join them in pleasurable activities. We know that boys are less often in the presence of their mothers and are assigned less work than girls, and that boys are less obedient to their mothers. We have no information, however, that tells us how often the boys are absent without the consent of their mothers, and whether they are shirking work that has been assigned.

Conflict with the Mother.   As noted in Chapter 3, there are more dominance battles between mothers and sons than between mothers and daughters (see Table 3.6). An analysis of the reciprocal behavior shown in Table 4.7 reveals that in eight of the twelve comparisons involving the dominance and aggression of 3- to 6-year-old and 4- to 5-year-old children to the mother, boys score higher than girls. The increase in the dominance battles of sons with the mother at ages 4 and 5 can also be seen in the New Samples. Where a comparison can be made between the behavior of knee and yard children, in six of the seven comparisons there is an increase between the ages of 2–3 and 4–5 in both the proportion of the mothers' attempts to dominate their sons and the boys' attempts to dominate their mothers. There is less consistent change in the dominance struggles between mothers and daughters.

As the data in Table 4.7 show, there are striking cultural differences among the communities. The percentage of attempts by boys to dominate their mothers is highest in the North Indian communities, where mothers have the highest scores in the proportion of their attempts to control the behavior of their sons. When one reads through the behavior observations for both Khalapur and Bhubaneswar, one is struck by the physical battles in the conflicts between mothers and sons. Minturn and Hitchcock describe such a scene.

> Many of the older boys were not only disobedient, but also rude to their mothers. The boys' increased awareness of the low status of women in village society probably contributes to the ineffectiveness of their mother's discipline. A rather extreme example of such a difficulty is illustrated by the following observation:
>
> Mrs. Singh is attempting to persuade her sons, Bir, aged 9, and Patram, aged 7, to leave for school. Bir is sulkily trying to push his foot into his oxford without untying the lace, which is knotted.
>
> Having failed to persuade him to untie the lace, Mrs. Singh tries to help Bir put on his shoe, but he pulls her hair. In retaliation, she hits him and they start wrestling. After considerable struggle, she pins her son to the ground and beats him with a shoe. Bir hits her back, crying loudly. He grabs a stick to continue the assault, and his mother, with some effort, tears it from him.
>
> After temporarily vanquishing her eldest son, she turns her attention to Patram. Discovering him in the bedroom, she beats him, exclaiming, "I will see how you will go to school. You sit there and do not come out of the room at all. If you just step out I will beat you. You are just like daughters-in-law, not to go out at all." (Minturn and Hitchcock, 1963, p. 347)

Both boys are reduced to loud crying, and Mrs. Singh sits down and cuddles her 2-year-old daughter. It is not surprising to read in the continuation of the observation that Patram soon teases this young sister and reduces her to tears.

An account of the interaction of a Bhubaneswar mother and her son presented in Chapter 4 describes a similar incident of a 5-year-old boy's disobedience and ensuing conflict with his mother. It is not surprising that these conflicts are particularly violent in North India, where, as the young boy becomes aware of his identity and the power of males, he tries out his relative power with his mother, who has been, along with the other adult women in the courtyard, the person who has hand-fed and bathed him since he was born. The fact that these young boys have been singled out by their mothers for preferential treatment makes the struggle for autonomy more difficult for the boys.

In Juxtlahuaca, where we would also expect boys to be increasingly aware of the dominance of males, boys tended to avoid their mothers. We have only two observations of 4- and 5-year-old boys interacting with their mothers, and only two of 6- to 8-year-olds. There is no indication of an overt dominance battle in Juxtlahuaca; neither the mother-son nor the son-mother dyads score high in dominance. Juxtlahuacan mothers, however, scored highest of the Six Culture mothers in initiated nurturance, and thus one could interpret the boys' lack of interaction with their mother as an attempt to wean themselves. It may be that the mothers are contributing to the weaning as well; by the time children reach age 7, the proportion of mothers' nurturance to boys has decreased perceptibly (see Table 3.3).

Interaction in Cross-Sex Dyads.   The percentage of interaction in cross-sex dyads decreases as children have the opportunity to choose companions. The most important finding is the relative infrequency of cross-sex social partners. Because of the small size of our cross-sex data set, we were not able to make detailed comparisons of the 4- and 5-year-olds' profile of social behavior in same-sex versus cross-sex dyads; the frequency of interaction was too low to control for the relative age and the gender of both the actor and the social partner.

Conclusions

The cultural differences in the activities and companions of children become more salient in the 4- and 5-year-old age group. The strategies that parents use to channel the energy of their yard-age sons and daughters and to teach them the skills required by the daily life of their community are determined in large part by the basic economy and settlement pattern of the communities. The communities differ in the amount of work that mothers do outside the home and the types of tasks that they can delegate. Where there is work that can be assigned, both girls and boys are asked to help. With the exception of the care of large animals, the tasks assigned are predominantly those that are considered the work of adult women. Girls are assigned and actually perform more work for the household than boys. Girls also interact with lap children more frequently than do boys. In communities where women do not work outside the home, there are fewer tasks to channel the yard child's boundless energy.

In communities with isolated homesteads, the yard children continue to interact primarily with siblings, half-siblings, and courtyard cousins and thus have limited opportunity to choose companions. In the communities with nucleated settlements, yard children are allowed out of the homestead and favor same-sex companions.

Evidence for the yard child's growing concern with gender identity can be seen in the selection of same-sex companions when a choice is possible. That boys may be more concerned with gender identity than girls is evidenced by the fact that they are observed at a greater distance from home than the girls when not involved in assigned work. In addition, the boys' increased dominance struggles with their mothers can be interpreted as attempts to wean themselves from maternal control and from the domain of women.

These findings also suggest that any interpretation of gender differences should allow for the possibility that future research will discover neurophysiological factors that set the stage for the differential development of the social behavior of girls and boys. With new technologies that make possible detailed analysis of the development of the brain and the nature and balance of hormones, we may be able in the future to add physiological data to our model of the genesis of gender differences in social behavior. We must ask whether boys elicit more dominance conflicts with their mothers and other social partners because they are genetically prepared to be more active and goal-oriented than are girls. Are boys found further from home because they take more risks in terms of physical activity than girls do? Are girls genetically prepared to be more responsive to other human beings, more interested in infants than are boys? Continuing research is essential to complete our understanding of the role of gender in shaping social behavior.

Chapter 7

The School-Age Child

The cultural determinants of patterns of social behavior become salient in late childhood. For children of the 6- to 10-year-old age group, there are significant societal differences in frequented settings and daily companions. The major contrast is between those communities that have universal education and those that do not. School settings are in sharp contrast to the settings of the lap and knee child, as well as to those of the yard child in communities that lack kindergartens and preschools or even village play areas. School children may spend half the daylight hours segregated into classes where they interact with companions of approximately the same age, the majority of whom are not close relatives. The learning is of a symbolic kind rather than that of pragmatic skills.

There are four major tasks that face school-age children. First, they must learn new motives involving the acceptance of remote goals. The motives for good performance in school relate to success at some future time. There are immediate rewards for good performance, of course, but both teachers and parents talk to the children about the future rewards they can expect if they become literate. For most children in the developing countries, the future promises made are for economic security and well-being. For the younger children, the symbols of success are possessions such as automobiles, radios, and other coveted products of the industrial world. For the older children, the promise is for a job in the modern sector.

Second, the school child must learn to perform individually. The promise of future goals, the desire for the approval of the teacher, and the rewards and privileges resulting from good performance are granted to each student as an individual. Moreover, the child must accept the constant evaluation of a non-relative in the presence of peers. This requires a self-image different from that of the child who identifies with a large extended family or a kin-based community; the work that the child has done around the home has been primarily for the family. Among our sample communities, only in the families of Orchard Town has there been a long-term emphasis on individual achievement in the manipulation of symbols.

Third, children must learn to manage competition with peers—children who are not related, who have not been constant companions since early childhood, and whose relative age is not their salient characteristic. They must accept rules or develop strategies that keep competition from resulting in aggressive encounters or in loss of self-esteem.

Finally, children in societies with social classes or mixed ethnic groups must learn to interact with children whose families have different conventions and styles of life. If they become friendly with these children with conflicting values, they must develop moral values that are acceptable to the mixed group (Edwards, 1978, 1981, 1982, 1986a).

The School Setting

In the Six Culture communities, children enter school between the ages of 6 and 8. Parents in all of these communities appear to accept this as an appropriate age. (When schools are first introduced into a community, the first grade may include children 10–11 years of age or even older.) Both folk wisdom and the findings of psychologists agree that between the ages of 5 and 7, there is a change in the intellectual capabilities of children. The Tairan mothers, for example, have an explicit belief that the child at 6 to 7 years of age becomes capable of knowing what he is doing and has "sense" (Maretzki and Maretzki, 1963, pp. 480, 496). The Mixtecan mothers believe that the child of this age develops "reason" and is most malleable and teachable (Romney and Romney, 1963, p. 663).

In most of the societies in our sample, parents have little concern for chronological age but do recognize the development of "sense." As noted earlier, the perception of the child's new capabilities is associated with an increase in the complexity of the tasks assigned by parents. Ethnographers in a large sample of preindustrial societies report the regular assignment of chores to children at this stage. Rogoff and colleagues (1975) used this fact as an index of parents' perception of the shift in cognitive ability at ages 5 to 7 and its universality across cultures.

School children have two new categories of daily companions: peers, children of roughly the same age who are not related; and teachers, adult authorities who are also non-relatives. New patterns of social interaction with these social partners must be learned and practiced.

By 6 to 7 years of age, children in all the communities have learned to discriminate in their social behavior according to the relative age of their social partners. They enter the school setting with experience in interacting with both older and younger companions. As one would expect, the older children are more nurturant, more prosocially dominant, and more controlling (reprimanding and dominating egoistically) in their interaction with younger children than they are in interaction with older children. Younger children are proportionately higher in initiating friendly interaction with older children than vice versa. The dependent behaviors—seeking help, attention, emotional support, and material goods—are, as one would predict, twice as great in younger-to-older dyads than in the older-to-younger dyads. Four of the behaviors—verbal and physical teasing, assaulting, and insulting—are reciprocal kinds of behaviors, similar in proportion in older-to-younger and in younger-to-older dyads. When a child initiates these types of behaviors, a response in kind is frequent. It will be seen that these behaviors are also characteristic of peer dyads. However, the proportion of two types of social behavior, sociable assaulting (rough-and-tumble play and wrestling) and miscellaneous aggression (including insults, threats, and competition), is greater in peer interaction than in the other two types of dyads.

We have seen that the acceptance of hierarchies of dominance based on age characterizes the age-graded societies of Kenya. The salience of relative age to children is demonstrated clearly in an analysis of the behavior of Ngeca children when a social partner refused to comply to their mands. David Lubin (Lubin and Whiting, 1977) analyzed the responses to noncompliance in three types of dyads: the noncompliance of older children, of same-age children, and of younger children. If the social partner who refused to comply was older, the child either repeated his mand, or deescalated using a less dominant or a clearly subservient style of appeal, or gave up the desired goal. It was rare for the younger child to escalate using threats, insults, or assaulting behavior to older children. In contrast, children were more apt to persist in attempting to reach their desired goal, and more apt to escalate to a more dominant or aggressive style, in response to the noncompliance of younger and lower-status social partners. Older children developed more varied strategies for attempting to gain the compliance of social partners.

The school setting introduces new dimensions of status that govern dyadic interaction: individuals are compared on their performance in the classroom and on the playing field as well as by age, size, and gender. Their achieved status, based on their performance in these settings, now enters into peer relations (Higgins and Parsons, 1983). Once a child enters school, relative age as a determinant of appropriate patterns of interaction is no longer an adequate guide.

In most school settings, the child spends from 4 to 8 hours a day with children who are classed together on the basis of age. Classmates are usually not more than one or two years apart in age and are considered to have similar cognitive and physical skills. If the classmates have grown up together, a dominance hierarchy will have been established by the time they enter school. However, newly achieved statuses may require the restructuring of previous patterns of interaction. If the social partner is a new acquaintance, the dominance hierarchy will not be clear and will have to be negotiated. Schools have rules, however, and there is apt to be more interference from the adults in charge than in the case of the play groups in the homesteads or the shared play areas in the villages and hamlets. There is also more opportunity for the formation of alliances, so that belonging to a specific group may give the child increased status.

Not all of the children in our sample communities attended school. Table 7.1 presents the percentage of 6- to 10-year-olds in each sample who were in school when the observations were made. Three of the communities observed in the mid-1950s had universal education: Orchard Town, Taira, and Tarong. Education was not universal in Juxtlahuaca and Khalapur; in 1956 only 44 percent of the girls in Juxtlahuaca and Khalapur attended school, while 56 percent of the Khalapur boys and 63 percent of the Juxtlahuacan boys attended school. Only one of the children in Nyansongo was in school, a boy 8 years of age.

Education in Kenya did not become universal until 1975. There was a school in the Nyansongo area as early as 1910, but it was not until 1940 that the parents began to perceive the material benefits of schooling (LeVine and LeVine, 1963). Of the 28 fathers in the sample

Table 7.1. Percentage of sample children aged 6–10 years who attend school

Community	Girls (%)	Boys (%)	Diff.
New Samples			
Kokwet	47	35	+12
Kisa	41	59	−18
Kariobangi	46	54	−8
Ngeca	95	90	+5
Bhubaneswar	85	93	−8
Six Cultures			
Nyansongo	0	25	−25
Juxtlahuaca	44	63	−19
Tarong	100	100	0
Taira	100	100	0
Khalapur	44	56	−12
Orchard Town	100	100	0

families studied in 1956, only 12 had attended school, and for only two years or less. None of the mothers had been to school. According to Robert LeVine, the fact that only one of the sample children attended school should not be attributed to families' inability to pay school fees but rather to the fact that the Nyansongo belonged to a powerful clan, and that up until the late 1950s the men were able to get employment through the influence of their chief.

Schools were introduced in the late 1920s in both Kisa and Ngeca, and later in the Kipsigis communities of Kokwet. In Kokwet 47 percent of the girls and 35 percent of the boys attended school in the early 1970s; in Kisa 41 percent of the girls and 59 percent of the boys attended school. In Ngeca, more than 90 percent of the children were in school in 1973.

It is clear that in all of the Kenyan samples, education was valued primarily as a means of attaining wage or salaried employment. Table 7.2 shows that Kariobangi and Ngeca, the two communities in or close to Nairobi, had the highest percentage of men and women who had completed high school. In Ngeca, which was close to the most highly urbanized area where the population density was making subsistence and cash-crop farming less and less viable, most families had become convinced that literacy and a high school or college diploma were the only way of ensuring a viable existence in the new

Table 7.2. Percentage of the parents of sample children in subsaharan Africa who had attended school

	Years of education				
	0	1–4	5–7	8–12	13+
Fathers					
Kien-taa	87	13	—	—	—
Kokwet	46	22	16	16	—
Kisa	23	59	18	—	—
Kariobangi[a]	20	40	30	5	—
Ngeca	40	20	27	4	9
Nyansongo	49	43	8	—	—
Mothers					
Kien-taa	100	—	—	—	—
Kokwet	63	21	11	5	—
Kisa	41	35	24	—	—
Kariobangi[a]	20	15	60	—	—
Ngeca	53	20	16	11	—
Nyansongo	87	13	—	—	—

a. For 5 percent of the mothers and fathers in the Kariobangi sample, it was impossible to ascertain the level of education.

economy. The table shows that 40 percent of the Ngeca fathers had five years or more of education. In the Kisa area, education was seen as essential; the increase in the population and the associated decrease in the size of the farms had forced the men early on to look for wage-earning jobs. It can be seen that 35 percent of the Kisa men who had jobs in Nairobi and lived in the housing estate of Kariobangi had 5 years or more of education.

The Liberian community of Kien-taa had the highest percentage of illiteracy. None of the mothers and only 14 percent of the fathers of the sample children had attended school. When Gerald Erchak was observing in the late 1960s, there was no government or mission school in Kien-taa; one 5-year-old boy attended a small private school in a neighboring town taught by a man from another ethnic group.

In the Indian sample families of Bhubaneswar, all of the upper- and middle-class fathers in the New Capital and an average of over a third of the mothers had some college or post–high school education. The contrast between these families and the upper- and middle-class families in the old part of town is striking: only 38 percent of the men and 28 percent of the women in the Old Town had more than seven years of schooling. The Rajput families of Khalapur were similar to the families in the Old Town. They tried to educate one or two of their sons, usually the youngest. Among the fathers in the sample, 24 percent of those over age 40 had some education, while 38 percent of the men between 20 and 40 were literate. Only four men in the sample had a high-school education. By 1956, when the field study began in Khalapur, there was a boys' high school and evidence of a dramatic increase in the value placed on education; 70 percent of the boys and young men between the ages of 6 and 20 were in school.

The school and its routine were familiar to the children of Taira and Tarong. Although the primary school was a mile outside of Taira, many young children had visited the school with older siblings. As Maretzki and Maretzki describe the school in Taira, "The informality in the classroom is . . . illustrated by the occasional presence of a teacher's young child, who is taken along by his parent if no one else can take care of him at home. Off and on, a student's younger sibling also sneaks in and sits quietly through a lesson" (1963, p. 523). The 4- and 5-year-old children had been to nursery school, where they learned some of the school routines. The Tarong school was also within walking distance of the young children, and they too had probably visited the school. In Khalapur, the boys' school was on an open platform and passersby could see the students at work.

The school setting was the least familiar for the Orchard Town and the Juxtlahuacan first graders. In the 1950s there were no nursery schools in Orchard Town, and the children spent the majority of their time at home with parents and siblings. In the home setting they had a great deal of individual attention from their mothers. The Sunday school they had attended was taught by parents. If they had school-age siblings, some of the younger children may have been corralled into playing school while their older siblings practiced the role of the teacher (often depicted in play as a dominant and autocratic figure).

Entrance into school was even more traumatic for the Juxtlahuacan children of Santo Domingo. The school was in the central, Spanish-speaking part of town. The teachers not only spoke a different language, but for the most part looked down on the children from the barrio and discriminated against them. Their prejudice was shared by the town children. The Mixtecan children were often perplexed by the treatment they received; they alternated between subservient and obsequious styles of seeking attention from the teacher. Outside of the classroom, the boys attempted to hide their feelings of inferiority with bravado. The following description reprinted from the study of Romney and Romney is a good illustration of the school experience in Juxtlahuaca and the chaotic nature of the classroom.

> The teacher is giving out parts of a poem for the children to recite. The teacher begins to read another poem. Alberto (boy, age 8) looks at the child who is sitting on his left and says to him, smiling, "This one is pretty." The other child smiles also and repeats, "This is pretty." Before the teacher finishes, Alberto stands up on his bench, waves his hand, and shouts, "Me, teacher, me." The child who is next to him stands up and cries, "Me, teacher, me." Alberto, the other boy, and several others get up and run toward the teacher, surrounding him and raising their hands so that he might give them a part of the poem. The teacher hands the poetry to one of the children of el Centro. Alberto immediately turns around and the boy who was his bench companion imitates him. As they are walking back to their seats, Alberto shrugs his shoulders, looks at the other, and says, "There are more." The other boy sits down, Alberto returns to the teacher and stands facing him and says, "Teacher, shall I take this?" (He is referring to the sheet on which the poetry is written.) The teacher does not answer and begins to read another poem. Alberto returns to his place. When the poem is finished, he runs down the aisle toward the teacher, but before he gets there, a group of children have already surrounded the teacher. In the middle of all the noise, Alberto raises his hand and says, "Me teacher, you haven't given me a single one; you're not giving me any." The teacher gives the poem to Alberto's bench companion, who returns to sit down with a broad smile on his face and the paper in his hand. When Alberto sees the other child with the poem, he again runs to the teacher, who is still surrounded by a group of children. Alberto tries to push apart two of them, sticking his head between the shoulders of the two, and looks over the teacher's arm. The teacher hands the last poem to another child from el Centro and says, "Now, there are no more." Alberto, not getting any, goes back to his seat. Seriously, he looks at the other boy and says, "It's all finished." The child laughingly shows him the poem he has in his hand. Alberto again returns to the teacher and asks him, "Are they all finished? Isn't there anything for me?" The teacher does not answer him. Alberto returns to his bench and sits with his head between his hands. He stands up and shouts, "Teacher." When he doesn't answer, he sits down again. He looks at his bench companion and says to him, "Don't bother me." His bench

companion laughs and stands up and then sits down again. Alberto hits him, giving him a punch in the stomach. The boys stand up. Alberto raises his foot under the table and gives him a kick at the same time. The other boy leaves, running. He stops a few feet away and looks back at Alberto with a smile. Alberto looks at him seriously. The other child moves away, and when he is a few steps farther away he looks back and says, "You'll see," and then he goes and sits in another place. Alberto remains looking at the front of the room.   (Romney and Romney, 1963, pp. 675–676)

The Mixtecan girls have less bravado. The following description of 10-year-old Rosa's behavior in school shows her interaction with her teacher. Even though this teacher was thought by Romney and Romney to be less prejudiced than the other teachers against barrio children, Rosa finds it difficult to communicate with her. The class is over and the teacher is standing in front of the class correcting notebooks.

Rosa crosses through two empty benches and walks down the aisle toward the teacher. When she gets to her the teacher is talking to another boy. In silence Rosa raises the notebook in her hand, and puts it in front of the teacher's face in order to have her attention. The teacher takes the notebook. Rosa, standing next to her, leans her head against the teacher's body with her look fastened upon the teacher. The teacher distractedly returns the notebook. The little girl takes it, remains looking for a moment and then turns around and returns, walking slowly to her bench. She sits down. She puts her notebook away.   (Romney and Romney, field observations, 1955)

Note Rosa's silent way of communicating: she leans against the teacher and watches her face, waiting for eye contact or the teacher's attention to her book. This motoric and visual style of communication is typical of girls' and young boys' communication in Juxtlahuaca (see Chapter 5).

The Mixtecan children were not the only ones who entered a school where the language of instruction was unfamiliar. With the exception of India, the schools in all of the communities were introduced by missions and colonial governments and were taught in the colonial language. In the mission schools in Kenya, the language of instruction was English. After 1963, when the country became independent and the schools were taken over by the government, an attempt was made to use Swahili instead of English. English is now the language of instruction, but there is a greater effort to make the transition from the local language to English and Swahili more gradual.

The language of instruction in Tarong is English. However, in contrast to the Juxtlahuacan parents, who do not speak the language of instruction at home, most parents in Tarong are bilingual, and thus the transition to English is not difficult. Japanese is the language of instruction in the Tairan school, and most of the children learn to speak Japanese as knee children.

For many of the children the teacher is the first non-relative who is an authority figure to be obeyed even if the reason for her mands cannot be understood. Prior to entrance into primary school, only the Tairan children have actually interacted with a teacher in a formal way. In both Tarong and Taira, however, the teachers are from neighboring communities and interaction is friendly and nonthreatening.

Classrooms in Taira are informal. The following description by Maretzki and Maretzki captures the relaxed atmosphere:

> The male teacher is going through some new expressions from their reading material with the class (4th grade). Children have their notebooks open and, as the teacher explains, take notes. Boys interrupt by shouting something, a suggestion, an answer, a question. The teacher hardly disciplines at all. He does not object to interruptions. K. (10-year-old boy), who apparently tries to show off as observers enter, shouts as crowded streetcars are discussed by the teacher, "What would happen if somebody beats you in a streetcar?" Teacher seems to disregard this question. A little later K. interrupts two more times. Boys and girls sit apart; about one-third of the students are girls. The girls hardly speak up during the session. In discussing the word "insensitive" one boy shouts as an example, "I am insensitive to teacher's scoldings." This is accepted as an example. There are three boys who have taken their shirts off on this warm morning. Two put them on as observers enter. After a while the teacher says, "Let's close this now." Somebody shouts, "Arithmetic," and the teacher concurs. (Maretzki and Maretzki, 1963, p. 523)

The Rajput children of Khalapur have had some exposure to the role behavior of teachers. The Brahmin who visits the courtyard on frequent occasions instructs the members of the household in procedures for ceremonies, and in some families he may be called upon to help with writing and other tasks that require literacy.

The greatest social distance between teacher and student exists in the Kenyan schools and in Juxtlahuaca for the barrio children. The first Kenyan teachers are men, who, like the children's fathers, are seen as remote and strict disciplinarians. The teachers also use physical punishment to maintain order in the classroom. The students are required to work in the teacher's garden and to run errands for him, as well as maintaining the school grounds. The parents expect the teachers to require obedience. It should be noted, however, that the Ngeca parents (and perhaps others) do not require as immediate obedience in the home as is frequently called for in the classroom. For example, there are many instances in the Kenyan observations in which mothers assign tasks to children who do not immediately comply, and the mother does not repeat her mand.

As illustrated in the observations given above, the situation in classrooms in both the Juxtlahuacan and Tairan schools often verges on chaos. An interesting addendum to the observation of Rosa in the Juxtlahuacan school describes her while she is preparing to leave for home: she gets under her table and unties her *reboza*, which was tied to another *reboza* two chairs away. The observer comments that she thinks the girls had been playing house under the table.

The discipline in the Khalapur boys' school is also lax. Minturn and Hitchcock report that "the fourth and fifth grade boys spend most of their school time at least looking at their books or reciting, but the younger boys spend most of their time in minor horseplay. Their work is continually interrupted by frequent borrowing of books, pens, inkpots, and so on, usually accompanied by a good deal of bickering about who owns what" (1963, p. 357). The older boys sometimes take it upon themselves to stop the horseplay of their younger schoolmates. Indeed, some of the older boys act as official monitors and, like the older brothers and cousins, sometimes discharge their duties with a sharp blow. The following is a fairly typical example of the "study habits" of the beginning students and the attempts of a self-styled monitor to control them.

> Pralard, Puran, Jaipal, and Bharat (all 6 or 7 years old) are sitting side by side; opposite them is Rup, an older and stronger boy. They all have their slates and bags in front of them. The boy next to Bharat is attempting to write on his slate but is prevented by Bharat, who is twisting his hand. The boy keeps calling for the master (teacher) in a plaintive voice. Jaipal gets up, moves to the opposite row and then moves back. Puran follows him on both moves. Pralard is singing to

himself. Bharat twists the boy's hand again. He calls for the master. Jaipal gets up again. He pushes the boy sitting opposite him. Then he backs away, returns to his seat and makes faces at the boy. Rup looks at Jaipal severely and says, "Why aren't you writing?" Meanwhile Puran and Bharat are having a tussle. Seeing them, Rup comes over and shakes his fist at Pralard. Finally the master comes over and Rup, seeing him, returns to his seat. (Minturn, field observations, 1955)

Although the school settings differ in the various sample communities, they also share important similarities. One of the most important of these is the tacit assumption that the children are roughly equivalent in their knowledge and capabilities; the work assigned to children in the same class is essentially the same for all students even though some may be older than others. However, it is recognized that some children learn faster than others, and it is impossible for children not to be aware of how their performance compares with that of their classmates. School systems and classrooms differ in the emphasis placed on individual achievement, but the evaluation of an individual's performance is always part of the learning process.

Jomo Kenyatta (1965), in his famous description of Kikuyu culture, *Facing Mount Kenya*, sounded a note of warning about the consequences of introducing Western-type schools in Kenya (pp. 95–124). He described the European system of education as one that rewarded individualism, in contrast to the traditional Kikuyu system that taught proper interpersonal behavior—the importance of respecting elders, obeying parents, working for the family, and being generous and goodhearted. In Ngeca the mothers were aware of the conflict in the values taught at home and in the school. In those families that valued education most highly, the mothers had resigned themselves to training their children in ways that they thought would help them be successful in school; they allowed their children to ask questions, to interrupt adults, to be brave about speaking up (B. B. Whiting and Marshall, n.d.).

Although competition between individuals of the same age is inevitable, teachers in the sample communities vary in the degree to which they use competition to motivate learning. In Orchard Town some of the classrooms are divided into two teams, and various accomplishments by the members of the teams are scored and a running total tallied and posted. In contrast, individual competitiveness is downplayed in Tarong. Judging from the remarks of the teachers, competitiveness is between hamlets rather than between individuals. One teacher commented that children from the same and adjacent yard groups help one another with their work, and grades are often similar for children in these groups. There did not seem to be any criticism in the remark. (An interesting comparison of two contrasting ways of managing competitiveness in American and Soviet schools can be found in Bronfenbrenner, 1970.)

Unlike the home settings, all schools have explicit rules of deportment and routine that undoubtedly seem arbitrary to the first grader. A comparison of the school observations with those made in the homes and neighborhood settings where children work and play shows that more commands per minute are given by the teachers, instructing children about proper academic and social performance. Even in play there are rules.

In all schools children must be told when their work is correct. The teaching of symbolic systems requires continual evaluation and feedback by the instructor; the child cannot tell whether he has read, pronounced, or written a word correctly unless someone identifies the performance as correct (see Cole and Scribner, 1974; Dweck and Leggett, n.d.). In contrast, when learning to do chores around the house, children can see for themselves whether the task has been accomplished. A child is a competent caretaker if the lap child is protected from danger and is contented. A child can observe and compare the result of sweeping, hoeing, weeding, and so on, with that of the model. Teachers attempt to use the same strategy when, as in Khalapur, they write words on a child's slate and the child traces over the letters. In the long run, however, the teaching of academic skills requires more feedback than for household chores; it is necessary that children be told that their performance is correct.

For many children this constant evaluation constitutes a novel experience. It appears from the observations that children receive qualitatively different kinds of feedback in the home and in the school setting. At school, evaluation is (ideally) clear and explicit: the rules or standards must be clearly stated and explained because many of the children have had little experience with written communication. The child's performance is labeled "right" or "wrong" in terms of these standards. Teachers frequently remind children of the rules and standards and try to give rationales for them so that they make sense to children. Classroom rules, especially those of "proper behavior," may seem external and arbitrary to children—imposed by the teacher and not in any way natural or necessary.

In contrast, at home children receive a much less rationalized form of feedback and information about rules. The rules and standards are conveyed to children less by explicit instruction and more by the implicit moral messages that children can and must abstract from what happens in everyday social interaction. The consequences of interaction include especially the frequent prosocial commands and suggestions and the occasional reprimands, threats, and punishment that children receive from adults and older children. From this feedback, children appear to construct a working knowledge of the complex conditions surrounding the "do's" and "don'ts" of interpersonal aggression, the distribution of resources, social roles, task assignment, damage to property, etiquette, hygiene, and other matters of proper social behavior.

This point can best be made through illustration. The moral discourse recorded in Carol Ember's observation of Luo children living in Oyugis, a rural community in Western Kenya, was analyzed to discover the ways in which Oyugis children were socialized to respect different kinds of moral and social rules (Edwards, 1986b, 1987). It was found that when children neglected or behaved aggressively toward small children or infants (and also animals), they often elicited commands, threats, or actual sanctions, with little or no discussion, from adults and older children. Oyugis adults and older children rarely engaged in reasoning with the offenders (for example, pointing out the victim's pain or evaluating the act as hurtful or unfair). The following observations illustrate such situations.

Simeon Okelo (boy, age 2½) hits baby.
Elizabeth (sister, 8): "Stop hitting the infant." Simeon hits infant again . . .
A few days later, James Odhiambo (brother, 6) hits Simeon, and Simeon cries. Now sister Elizabeth intervenes to protect Simeon. She says to James, "Stop beating the boy." He stops.

Beatrice Adoyo (girl, 6) hits Gideon Magak (cousin, 3) on the head for no apparent reason. He cries.
Martin Otieno (Beatrice's brother, 8) smacks Beatrice as punishment. Beatrice suppresses a tear. (Ember, field observations, 1968)

It might seem from this illustration that subsaharan children are constantly beating one another, but in fact there are surprisingly few incidents of "assaulting" interactions, coded as attempts to harm another child intentionally. On the contrary, there is much evidence of children's genuine concern about hurting others. Reviewing the observations from all the samples, one finds that when children get hurt the aggressor seldom shows pleasure but more often exhibits anxiety and concern.

In many of the incidents, when a child gets hurt there is no reference to rules—at most a gentle reprimand. Frequently these incidents occur in sequences of roughhousing. The shift from what we have coded as sociable aggression or horseplay to anger and the intent to injure may take place very rapidly, with no appeal to fair play or rules. The following observation of rough-and-tumble play illustrates such a sequence; the incident took place in the school playground in the central part of town in Juxtlahuaca.

> Juvenal and several boys are running around the school playground engaging each other in wrestling. There is much laughter in the wrestling match with the first boy. In spite of the fact that they are both showing strength, it is easy to see that they are not trying to harm each other. It is a game. In one of the movements they fall to the ground intertwined. They go rolling around the ground until Juvenal remains on top and stops. While he looks at his opponent, laughing and breathing heavily, he pulls up his pants which have fallen down, adjusting his belt with both hands, which seems to signal that he hopes that the other boy will stop wrestling also. The other boy stands up and begins to run looking at Juvenal. Juvenal cries: "Ayyyy!" and runs after him. He catches him and again embraces him around the waist. The two run gripped in this fashion while all the children who have been watching run behind them.
>
> Another child who is with them joins in the battle. The three run together. Juvenal lets go and leaves the boys locked together, wrestling.
>
> Another boy comes running from the courtyard and grabs Juvenal from behind as if he wants to fight. Juvenal loosens himself, and with a push almost throws him to the ground. He laughs. The two again lock in a struggle, trying to intertwine their legs so that they will both fall to the ground. They groan as they struggle. Juvenal grabs the other boy by the shirt and pulls at it as if he wants to take it off. While he does this the other takes Juvenal's leg and throws him to the ground. Juvenal gets up. The other boy remains laughing in an expectant attitude. They grab each other again. This time Juvenal throws the other to the ground. The boy hits quite hard upon falling. He gets up, no longer laughing. He grabs Juvenal by the arms and twists them. Juvenal laughs but immediately begins to try to free himself, becoming rather serious. He seems to realize that the other boy is no longer "playing"

but is now angry. The other boy throws him to the ground. From the ground where Juvenal is sitting he says to the boy: "What are you doing?" The boy pulls him from the ground by the arms and shakes him. Juvenal laughs again. The boy lets him go and runs through the courtyard. Juvenal runs after him and the roughhousing continues.

In the end Juvenal is thrown and hits the ground hard. With tears in his eyes he cries and laughs at the same time. (There is no reprimanding or verbal complaint.) (Romney and Romney, field observations, 1955)

Roughhousing is probably one of the best manifestations of the competitiveness that exists when male peers are thrown together in classrooms and playgrounds. The societies where horseplay is most frequent among school-age boys are Taira, Tarong, and Juxtlahuaca. There appear to be substantial differences among the sample communities in the degree to which horseplay is regulated by explicitly stated rules of which the children make use in reprimanding others. In some of the communities, notably Taira and Orchard Town, there is evidence of greater concern for and more explicit use of these rules. In Taira there are formalized wrestling bouts. In the observations of the Orchard Town boys' roughhousing, there are often calls for "times" or "time out" which are respected by the protagonists. A child may call for "times" to tie a shoe, or when he is out of breath or in an awkward position. If someone gets hurt there are often apologies and statements that there was no intention to do damage. One Orchard Town mother was observed encouraging the boys to imitate the rules of professional boxers; she had purchased boxing gloves so that the children would have the proper equipment for "fights" with rules. Some of the Orchard Town children seem preoccupied with rules. One of the sample children constantly took over the teacher's role and advised his peers as to appropriate behavior. Others seem more interested in testing the rules, sometimes obeying and at other times seeing how far they can go in breaking the rules.

Rules are salient in the school playground as well as the classroom. The rules of soccer, basketball, baseball, and many other games must be learned. In our sample communities, no team sports were observed that were not learned in school and made possible by the availability of an adequate number of children with relatively the same amount of skill, as well as the availability of a large, level playground.

In Nyansongo, the community with the fewest school children, boys and girls are never observed playing team sports in the home-steads or pastures; it is difficult to mobilize a sufficient number of children with comparable skills to form teams. The only games with rules played in the Mixtecan barrio are marble shooting and top spinning contests, and the rules are rudimentary. In the other sample communities, aside from chasing games, jacks, and penny pitching, few games with rules are ever observed that are not learned at school.

In the communities where children do play games with rules, there are also discussions about whether or not each player has abided by the rules. These kinds of discussions were not heard in Oyugis, nor in the other societies that have few, if any, formal games.

The Peer Dyad

Given that school children have more opportunity to interact with peers, our focus in this age group is on the profile of behavior in peer dyads. We have defined peers as children who are not siblings but who are in the same age grade (the school-age group, 6 to 10 years old) and within one or two years of age. How different are the social behaviors that characterize the peer dyads from other dyads? Are there gender differences that replicate across the samples? Are there differences in the profile of the behaviors in the peer dyads that can be attributed to identifiable cultural differences in the environment in which the children live? What evidence is there for the transfer of previous or current behaviors learned in interaction with family members to social behavior with peers?

The analysis that follows is limited to the children of the Six Culture communities. Since the observations in the new Kenyan samples were made in the home setting where non-siblings were rarely present, and since there were no observations of children aged 7 to 10 in the Liberian sample, the interaction in peer dyads in these communities is too infrequent for analysis. (Appendix G presents the total number of social acts to all partners for each sample.)

Table 7.3 presents the percentage of interaction in each of the six societies that is with same-sex and cross-sex peers. The most dramatic finding is the extremely low frequency of cross-sex peer interaction, consistent across the entire sample of communities. It is clear that at this age, when children can seek interaction with companions who are not siblings and are close in age, there is an avoidance of children of the opposite sex and a preference for interaction with children of

Table 7.3. Percentage of the social acts of children aged 6–10 years, to other children aged 3–10, that are with peers[a]

Community (Six Cultures)	With any peers			With same-sex peers			With cross-sex peers		
	Girls (%)	Boys (%)	Diff.	Girls (%)	Boys (%)	Diff.	Girls (%)	Boys (%)	Diff.
Nyansongo	3	8	−5	3	7	−4	0	1	−1
Juxtlahuaca	9	22	−13	9	21	−12	0	1	−1
Tarong	26	14	+12	23	12	+11	3	2	+1
Taira[b]	21	20	+1	17	18	−1	4	2	+2
Khalapur	10	37	−27	5	28	−23	5	9	−4
Orchard Town	37	37	0	31	29	+2	6	8	−2
Average	18	23	−5	15	19	−4	3	4	−1

a. Peers are defined as children who are in the school-age group (ages 6–10) *and* within one or two years of age of each other.
b. In Taira there is frequent behavior directed to more than one child. The play groups are generally larger than in the other communities.

the same sex. This finding is borne out in the observations of class-rooms and playgrounds, and it is similar to the findings of studies of schools in the United States and Europe (see Chapter 2).

The table shows that when sexes are pooled, there is a higher proportion of interaction with same-sex peers in those societies where there is universal education. Thus in Orchard Town, Taira, and Tarong, an average of 22 percent of the observed interaction of school-age children is with same-sex peers, compared to an average of 16 percent in Juxtlahuaca and Khalapur, the societies where more boys than girls attend school. The percentage of interaction with peers is lowest in Nyansongo, where only one boy in our sample attended school and where both boys and girls spend most of their early years on family land. In Khalapur and Juxtlahuaca, the girls are more restricted in the settings they are allowed to frequent than the girls of Orchard Town, Taira, and Tarong.

Previous research (Whiting and Whiting, 1975, p. 158) suggested that peer dyads are characterized by a high proportion of both so-ciability and aggression. That study was based on a pooled sample of same-sex and cross-sex dyads and male and female actors; the present analysis will be limited to same-sex peer interaction because the amount of cross-sex interaction is too infrequent to allow for the comparison of girl and boy actors in the communities. For girls across the samples in same-sex interaction, sociability is the most frequent behavior. In three of the cultures, helpful and supportive behavior is the second most frequent behavior. For boys sociability ranks first in four of the societies, and dominance, rough-and-tumble play, or miscellaneous aggression are next most frequent. Competitive games are popular, especially among boys. In both work and play activities, there is evidence that decisions must be made about who should lead in selecting and organizing peer activities, and whose suggestions should be accepted. Competition and jockeying for dominance are inevitable. (See Appendix F.)

Reviewing the observations of same-sex peer interaction leads us to conclude that labeling the competitive behavior (for example, sociable assaults, rough-and-tumble play, and miscellaneous aggres-sion) "aggressive" is misleading. A detailed analysis of the summary category "miscellaneous aggression" used in the earlier analysis sug-gests that a better label would be "challenges." The summary cate-gory included seeking competition, threatening, warning, and insult-ing.

As already noted, interacting with peers is a new experience for many children. In family groups, where relative age is salient, dominance hierarchies have long been established and are relatively stable. In encounters with new, non-family children who are about the same age, dominance struggles are to be expected. It appears that these struggles can take several forms: in some the conflict is carried out in straightforward attempts to control (to dominate egoistically) the behavior of the social partner; in others the conflict takes the form of various types of challenges, coded as insulting, threatening, warning, and seeking competition. For the purpose of analysis we developed two summary scores: *control*, defined so as to include both dominance mands and reprimands; and *challenges*, defined to include both miscellaneous aggression (insulting, threatening, warning, and seeking competition) and sociable assaulting (rough-and-tumble bouts, wrestling).

It can be seen in Table 7.4 that, with the exception of Orchard Town and Tarong, boys have a higher proportion of challenging behavior than girls. The boys in Taira, Tarong, and Juxtlahuaca score above the mean. The gender differences in controlling behavior (dominance mands and reprimands) are less consistent. However, with the exception of Orchard Town, boys score higher than girls on the summary score of egoistic conflict, which combines challenging and controlling behavior.

Assaulting behavior is rare, especially among girls (see Appendix F). Such behavior was not observed at all in female peer dyads in Nyansongo, Taira, and Orchard Town. The extraordinarily high score of the Khalapur girls is based on only 12 interacts; however, it is consistent with the high use of physical punishment by Khalapur mothers (Minturn and Lambert, 1964). Assaulting behavior in boys varies between 2 and 6 percent of their coded social acts (Appendix F). The three groups of boys that score the lowest are in Taira, Tarong, and Orchard Town, the more egalitarian of the Six Culture communities; the three high scorers are Juxtlahuaca, Nyansongo, and Khalapur, cultures where the high status of adult males is most salient. In an earlier analysis of physical violence of males in Khalapur and Nyansongo, Beatrice Whiting advanced the hypothesis, following the work of Burton and J. Whiting (1961) and R. L. Munroe, R. H. Munroe, and J. Whiting (summarized in 1981), that violent behavior was an index of latent cross-sex identity associated with the salience of the mother in early childhood and the tradition of warriorhood in adult

Table 7.4. Percentage of interaction of 6- to 10-year-old children with same-sex peers that is coded as controlling or challenging

Community (Six Cultures)	Seeks to control			Challenges			Sum of egoistic conflicts		
	Girls (%)	Boys (%)	Diff.	Girls (%)	Boys (%)	Diff.	Girls (%)	Boys (%)	Diff.
Nyansongo	7	8	−1	7	15	−8	14	23	−9
Juxtlahuaca	21	11	+10	3	22	−19	24	33	−9
Tarong	3	6	−3	36	36	0	39	42	−3
Taira	14	27	−13	16	40	−24	30	67	−37
Khalapur	33	41	−8	0	10	−10	33	51	−18
Orchard Town	26	24	+2	15	15	0	41	39	+2

life (B. B. Whiting, 1965). The Rajput men in 1954 still thought of themselves as a warrior caste (Minturn and Hitchcock, 1963), and the Nyansongo men served their turn as warriors who protected the property and families of their lineage and tribe from the raids of other groups. The high proportion of male aggression was interpreted as evidence of defensive behavior in the service of proving masculinity.

In studying the assaulting behavior of peer children, it is clear that Juxtlahuaca should be added to the above group with a relatively high proportion of physical violence. In Juxtlahuaca, the girls and boys in the 6- to 10-year-old age group have comparatively high proportions of assaulting behavior. In the previous chapter we advanced the hypothesis that the boys in Juxtlahuaca, like the boys in Nyansongo and Khalapur, belong to societies that consciously stress the differential status of adult men and women, and the boys have a particularly strong need to prove that they are not women and not like their sisters. The higher scores of the assaulting behavior of peer boys in these three communities may be related to this need. The hypothesis, however, does not explain why the Juxtlahuacan and Khalapur girls score higher than the girls in the other cultural groups.

It is interesting to note that Romney and Romney stress the atmosphere of control and the absence of evidence of adult aggression within the Mixtecan barrio (1963, p. 608). It may well be that the pressure for control is higher within this community because of the fear of the consequences of hostility between families. In communities where the welfare of the group depends on cooperation against outsiders, in this case the Ladinos of the central part of town, the need for control of intragroup hostilities is important. The Juxtlahuacan mothers, when interviewed about their treatment of child aggression, were the most consistent of all the mothers in the Six Culture communities in their statements that they punished such behavior (Minturn and Lambert, 1964, pp. 152–163). It may also be true that the Juxtlahuacan mothers discouraged wrestling and horseplay because of their fear that this would end in injury, or it may be that the children themselves found this to be the case.

If there are no explicit rules governing roughhousing, and if roughhousing more frequently ends in aggression, it may indeed threaten the relationships between kin and neighbors in the community. We reported earlier on the parents' fear of children's aggression in Nyansongo and other subsaharan African communities where the support

of members of the sublineage group is important. In these communities, parents attempted to keep the children in the home setting
where peer interaction was rare. The Juxtlahuaca and Khalapur
mothers reported that they were severe in the punishment of child-
directed aggression (Minturn and Lambert, 1964, p. 151). Their
children, as we observed, had the highest proportion of assaulting
behavior, so there is no doubt that the mothers had difficulty sup-
pressing this type of behavior.

To explore the interaction of gender and culture in influencing
behavior in same-sex peer dyads, we determined optimal scaling
values using the frequencies of the 9 most frequent behaviors in the
12 dyads. Figure 7.1 gives a spatial representation of the location of
both the dyads and the behaviors. Female same-sex dyads are shown

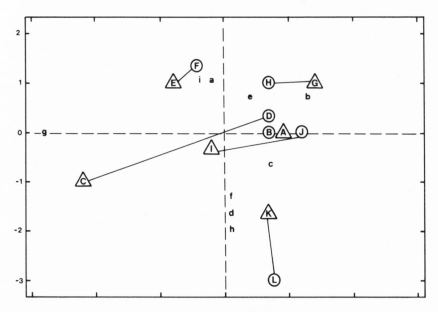

Figure 7.1. Graph of Optimal Scaling values for behavior of children 6 to 10
years of age in the Six Culture samples to same-sex peers over the frequency
of nine types of behavior. Same-sex peer dyads: A = Orchard Town boys, B =
Orchard Town girls; C = Taira boys, D = Taira girls; E = Tarong boys, F =
Tarong girls; G = Nyansongo boys, H = Nyansongo girls; I = Juxtlahuacan
boys, J = Juxtlahuacan girls; K = Khalapur boys, L = Khalapur girls.
Behaviors: a = nurturance, b = prosocial dominance, c = reprimands, d =
egoistic dominance, e = sociability, f = succorance, g = challenges physically,
h = assaults, i = challenges verbally.

in circles, male same-sex dyads in triangles, and the behaviors are represented by small letters.

It can be seen that gender differences in the profile of social behavior, as estimated by the distance between circles and triangles, are negligible in Orchard Town, Tarong, and Nyansongo. Before they are initiated, girls and boys in Nyansongo frequent many of the same settings and perform many of the same activities; they serve as child nurses and frequently work with their mothers. Their interaction with non-relatives is restricted because assigned work keeps them on the family homestead. When the observations were made in the 1950s, only one of the children of the 6–10 age group attended school. If one assumes that this restriction to the home environment influences both the behavior of children and their sense of identity, the function of initiation ceremonies becomes more meaningful. According to native belief, circumcision makes a man out of a boy (who previous to initiation was classified with women and children), and clitoridectomy makes a woman out of a girl.

In Tarong and Orchard Town, the similarity in the behavior of girls and boys can be attributed in part to the egalitarian ethos of the two societies. Comparatively speaking, girls and boys are accorded equal status. In both cultures men may be called upon to help in child care, a rare occurrence in the other cultures. Since Taira is also more egalitarian than Juxtlahuaca or Khalapur, the gender difference in behavior between the peer dyads was not expected; we conclude that it is the result of the Tairan boys' predilection for wrestling, a type of competition rarely engaged in by the older girls. Wrestling is a form of dominance battle encouraged by Tairan parents as a way of channeling competitiveness between boys, who from a young age have the run of the village and interact with a variety of children who are not relatives. The wrestling competitions have some accepted rules and may take place in prepared areas where there is less danger that the protagonists will be physically hurt. (This is similar to the importance of sumo wrestling in Japanese culture.)

The gender difference in Juxtlahuaca is not surprising. We have noted that from infancy, parents dress male and female children differently and grant young boys special privileges. The boys' comparatively high score on challenging behavior, substantially higher than that of the girls, as well as their high score on assaulting, can be attributed to their struggles with the discrimination they encounter in the school setting in the ladino section of town. For both boys and girls in Juxtlahuaca there is the perception that they are members of a ghetto, a depressed Indian barrio in a Spanish-speaking town. The boys' bravado, noted in the observation given in the previous chapter, may also be encouraged by their mothers' preferential treatment, as well as by the boys' desire to prove themselves male and separate from their mothers and sisters.

Figure 7.1 shows that girls in Tarong, Nyansongo, and Juxtlahuaca and boys in Tarong rank comparatively high in nurturance. These children are above the mean of this age group in the percentage of interaction with lap children (Table 7.5), suggesting the transfer of behavior practiced in interaction with lap children to same-sex peers.

A different type of transfer may explain the scores in the controlling behavior of Khalapur girls and boys. In Orchard Town and Khalapur, over 25 percent of the interaction in same-sex peer dyads is controlling behavior, that is, dominant mands and reprimands (see Table 7.4). These are the societies where there is frequent interaction with mothers who are comparatively high in controlling behavior, and this style learned in interaction with the mother appears to be transferred to the peer dyad. The style of dominance in the two samples of mothers and children is different, however. The Orchard Town children are below the mean in the use of physical techniques of persuasion (assaults; assaults sociably). We have noted that Orchard Town mothers encourage both male and female children as young

Table 7.5. Interaction of 6- to 10-year-old girls and boys with lap children (0–24 months) and proportion of nurturance to same-sex peers

Interaction with lap children		Proportion of nurturance to same-sex peers	
Group	Percentage	Group	Percentage
Nyansongo girls	37	Tarong girls	26
Juxtlahuaca girls	34	Nyansongo girls	20
Tarong boys	28	Juxtlahuaca girls	17
Juxtlahuaca boys	26	Tarong boys	13
Khalapur girls	20	Nyansongo boys	11
Tarong girls	18	Juxtlahuaca boys	10
Taira girls	7	Khalapur boys	10
Khalapur boys	6	Orchard Town girls	9
Nyansongo boys	6	Orchard Town boys	9
Orchard Town girls	5	Khalapur girls	8
Taira boys	4	Taira boys	8
Orchard Town boys	0	Taira girls	5
Mean	16		12

as the knee-child age group to settle their disputes verbally rather than physically. In contrast, Khalapur girls are above the mean in the use of physical techniques of persuasion, as are their mothers.

Finally, the Khalapur and Juxtlahuacan boys are above the mean in dependence. These are two of the cultures that single out boys for preferential treatment. Khalapur mothers are comparatively late in teaching their sons to care for themselves. The culture of the Rajputs accepts dependence in males; in old age men may give up their worldly possessions and live as beggars, a role that is honored.

Conclusions

In sum, same-sex peers elicit a high proportion of both sociability and egoistic conflict behavior. There are clear gender and cultural differences in the percentages of egoistic behavior. Those children who have been exposed to peers more than others have more opportunity to practice egoistic conflict behavior and challenging styles. Here the difference in the environments that children frequent is important. Both schools and nucleated settlements provide more interaction with peers. Boys, who have had more chance to play with peers than girls, score higher in egoistic behaviors than the girls.

In some of the societies, namely, Nyansongo, Tarong, and Orchard Town, there is little difference in the profile of the social behavior of girls and boys in same-sex peer dyads. When there are differences, the behavior of boys is more divergent from the norm of the pooled sample than is the behavior of girls.

The effect of previous experience can be noted in the interaction of 6- to 10-year-olds with non-relatives who are the same sex and close in age. In some cases there appears to be a direct transfer of social behaviors learned and practiced in one dyad type to behavior in a different dyad type. Thus, with one exception (Khalapur girls), children who interact frequently with lap children are above the mean in nurturance to same-sex peers; boys who are above the mean in dependent behavior to their mothers are above the mean for the pooled sample in dependence to same-sex peers. There is also evidence of reciprocal role learning. Children in communities where mothers are proportionately high on controlling behavior are above the mean on attempts to control same-sex peers. Finally, in the communities where boys have been given preferential treatment by their mothers, the boys are above the mean for the group on physical aggression.

Chapter 8

Conclusion

Children born in diverse cultures appear to enter the world with similar endowments. Both as elicitors and actors, they share panhuman characteristics that equip them for survival. We are convinced that generic, transcultural behaviors can be identified in dyadic interaction and discussed in terms of the distinctive eliciting power of certain categories of individuals who are the companions of children. The responses that these individuals elicit appear to be easily learned and to resist modification. Yet cultural forces do modulate social development and lead to increasing differences in the kinds of behavior which adults expect in children, which they give children the most opportunity to practice, and which they make meaningful to them in terms of central cultural goals and values. Furthermore, although both boys and girls appear to be equipped with behavioral predispositions to respond nurturantly to lap children, dependently to adults, and playfully and challengingly to child companions, cultural scripts in many communities set boys and girls on different courses by allowing them differential amounts of autonomy, giving them different responsibilities, and constraining the company they keep.

We began this volume with a focus on maternal behavior because mothers are responsible for children's well-being in all of the communities we studied, even those in which they delegate part of the care. The behavior of mothers shows transcultural similarities to each age group of children, especially to the three youngest groups (lap, knee, and yard children). These similarities derive from universalities in the nurturing role and from the eliciting power of children. Mothers everywhere must meet predictable needs and wants when caring for children of a given age, and they must teach them socially approved behaviors and train them in age-appropriate skills. As a result, mothers tend to direct relatively large amounts of nurturing acts toward lap and knee children, control toward yard children, and training toward school-age children. However, cultural differences are also seen, related to the company women keep and the activities they perform—more specifically, to work requirements, household and settlement patterns, and opportunities for adult female sociability.

The surrounding complex of social supports and daily routines influences which of three general patterns or styles characterize maternal behavior. The "training mothers" of subsaharan Africa, for whom prosocial commanding is the most frequent form of social acts to children, bear the heaviest workloads in our study and early on recruit their own children, especially their daughters, as their main assistants in economic and household work and child care. The "controlling mothers" of Bhubaneswar and Khalapur (North India), Tarong (the Philippines), and Juxtlahuaca (Mexico), for whom reprimanding and egoistic commanding are the most frequent acts to children, bear relatively lighter workloads. They seem to use reprimands, dominating acts, and threats, rather than prosocial commands and task assignments, in order to reduce children's annoying behaviors and their attempts to interfere with sociability between adult women. The "sociable mothers" of Orchard Town (United States), for whom sociability ranks highest in maternal behavior, have the lightest workloads and the least opportunity for adult social contact during the day.* These mothers encourage types of play and information exchange with their young children that are more egalitarian in style than in the other sample communities.

Children's behavior to mothers can be seen to be the reciprocal of maternal behavior. The universalities observed in children's behavior—particularly the high proportion of dependent or "seeking" behavior—can be attributed to the fact that children are born genetically prepared to develop behavioral systems that ensure, first, their proximity to caregivers and, second, their interaction with experienced members of society who guide their entry into culturally meaningful situations and scaffold their learning. Thus there are strong consistencies across all of the samples in the profile of children's acts

*It should be noted that these mothers were observed in 1955 and 1956. The dual-career mothers of the 1980s have a heavy workload and, we expect, a different style.

toward mothers, based on the way in which children everywhere see mothers as a primary source of resources and knowledge. Yet cultural differences also exist, and these appear to increase with age as children display behaviors toward mothers that are the reciprocal of their mothers' style toward them. For example, mothers elicit dependent or seeking behavior in all of our sample communities, but they channel or modulate the style of dependency in accordance with their theories of natural or expectable behavior. Mothers in the North Indian communities, for example, demonstrate a pattern of inconsistent nurturance that encourages an active, insistent, almost aggressive style of dependency in their young children and dominance in their older ones. Mothers in the subsaharan African communities, where infants sleep with their mothers and are usually carried by the mother or a child nurse during the daytime hours, have a style of nurturance centered on physical closeness and sensitivity to the child's bodily movements and kinesthetic cues. Children in these communities score high in physical contact seeking through the knee-child and even the yard-child age grades, rather than shifting early to the more distal and verbal modalities that are described in the American psychological literature as "mature dependency." Furthermore, maternal styles in areas of behavior other than nurturance appear to be mirrored by the reciprocal style of children. For example, the training mothers of subsaharan Africa have children who score relatively high in compliance. These children are not simply passively compliant to their prosocially commanding mothers; rather, the subsaharan children, especially the girls, seem to develop at younger ages than children in other communities into empathic and responsible assistants who can work with their mothers in a choreography of smooth cooperation.

Although mothers are important figures to children in all of our sample communities, child companions are surely as significant in terms of their formative role in children's development. Major differences exist in terms of how much time children spend with different categories of child companions; children's culture, developmental age, and sex strongly determine the company they keep. Nevertheless, when children of a given age are in the presence of a particular kind of company—a particular class of child companion—there are transcultural consistencies in their profile of interaction, a fact that leads us to speak of "generic" or "genotypic" responses as a key to understanding behavior in comparative perspective.

The influence of generic behaviors is most evident in the early years of children's lives, when there are many similarities in the profile of social behavior across societies. These similar patterns of social behavior also result from the shared physical and cognitive capacities of young children and shared dimensions of the scripts for the daily lives of young children. However, as children mature and gain new capacities based on transformation and reorganization of their cognitive skills, they acquire new motives or intentions for social behavior. These new motives diminish the power of generic responses in determining children's behavior with social partners. The new motives, which are cognitively more complex and based on new kinds of strivings for competence, lead children to construct new meanings for social situations and thus to approach them differently from the way they did before. The new motives are less readily inferred from observable behavior than are intentions to secure instrumental help, attention, comfort, social play, and the other goals of young children's social interaction. For example, major goals of yard and school-age children's behavior are establishing their gender identity, practicing sex-role behaviors, and acquiring knowledge of culturally important skills. The 5-year-old who once saw his aunt as a source of comfort and someone to be approached may now see her as a "woman" and someone to be avoided. The boy of 7 who once saw both his older and younger brothers as good playmates may now see the older one as an "authority" on important skills, while he tries to avoid playing with the younger one.

Another factor leading to differences between children's behavior is the fact that with age, the experiences of children in different communities (and of boys and girls within some communities) become more divergent as the ecological and cultural rules present varied scripts for daily life. For instance, the presence or absence of schooling is one of the experiences that most distinguishes the lives of 6- to 10-year-old children.

In earlier studies we explored evidence concerning stereotypes of masculine and feminine behavior (Edwards and Whiting, 1974; Whiting and Edwards, 1973; Whiting and Whiting, 1975) based on scores generalized across four categories of actors, 3- to 6- versus 7- to 10-year-old girls and boys. We found that interaction with different classes of social partners was characterized by different profiles of social behavior, leading us to construct categories of dyads (where the sex and age of both actor and interactant are considered) as the units of analysis in the present study.

Of the five major categories of interpersonal behavior explored in this book—nurturance, dependency, prosocial dominance, egoistic dominance, and sociability—two emerge as associated with sex differences. Across the three older age groups (knee, yard, and school-age children), girls on average are more nurturant than boys in all dyad types (see Edwards and Whiting, 1980), while boys are more egoistically dominant than girls. These findings, however, do not demand an explanation in terms of biologically prepared sex differences; the differences between boys and girls in amount of interaction with different social partners can account for the findings. Positive behavior predominates in interaction with lap children: nurturance is higher in interaction with lap children than with any other social partners. Egoistic and prosocial dominance rank high in interaction with younger children, and egoistic dominance ranks second to sociability in interaction with peers (companions within one or two years of the actor). In many of our sample communities, girls and boys spend different amounts of time interacting with these classes of individuals: girls interact proportionately more with lap and younger children, while boys interact proportionately more with other child companions. Children thereby develop different interpersonal habits and skills that extend to their interaction with other categories of partners.

We find that there is similarity across cultures in the way in which children and adults respond to lap children, and conclude that lap children have the power to elicit positive responsiveness and nurturance even from children as young as 2 years of age, and from both girls and boys. The universality of this pattern of responsiveness suggests that infants are born equipped with physical features and behavioral systems that evoke positive behavior and nurturance from both adults and children. It is obvious that children take pleasure in interacting with lap children, and that lap children respond reciprocally. Competent baby tenders enjoy their charges and demonstrate pride in their competence.

There are limits to the power of this generic responsiveness, however. The evidence indicates that young children get carried away in the excitement of interacting with lap children and tend to overstimulate them, causing the babies to cry. The children appear to be distressed by the babies' unhappiness, and when they cannot comfort them they may become impatient and strike out, increasing the babies' distress. Such experiences, along with the advice of adults, gradually teach children to modulate their playfulness, particularly when they are acting as child nurses. In the role of assigned caretakers, children must learn how to intuit lap children's needs because guessing their needs and desires correctly makes the caretaking responsibility less arduous.

There is no definitive evidence in our data that girls are more nurturant than boys to lap children, if we control for the amount of time that girls versus boys spend with lap children and the amount of responsibility that they assume. However, there is clear evidence that sex differences exist in the frequency with which girls versus boys are in the presence of lap children. Girls also engage in interaction with lap children more frequently than do boys, and they more often act as caretakers. We have speculated about the cause of these sex differences. Are they evidence of a biologically based sex difference—for example, an intrinsically greater capacity for nurturance in girls? Are they simply a reflection of the fact that girls are assigned child-care tasks more frequently than boys? Or are they the result of a learned desire of girls to interact with lap children because of having been assigned their care and having developed skills in nurturing? We favor the last hypothesis. It is not incompatible with the notion that girls' own preferences—perhaps an attraction to infants and an identification with the maternal role—play a part in their spending more time with infants. Since girls serve as designated child nurses more frequently than do boys, and interact with lap children more frequently, they receive more practice in responding to lap children. When the lap children show signs of distress, girls have more practice in intuiting and meeting their needs. They have confidence in their ability to understand what the lap children want, and they are rewarded for their skill by the lap children's obvious delight in their presence. As a result of the girls' pleasurable experience with caregiving, nurturance becomes a style of interaction that is both familiar and enjoyable to them.

Our experience with our Kenyan research assistants further convinces us of the strength of these conclusions. In looking for research assistants, we visited graduating classes in the secondary schools and as part of the application form asked the students to write a short autobiography. We were impressed by the young women's descriptions of their experiences as caretakers for their siblings; they spoke of their brothers and sisters in a maternal way. When we began our observations of child nurses, we realized that they were attached to their younger brothers and sisters in much the same way that mothers in the United States are attached to their children. The young Kenyan women whom we hired had a thorough knowledge of what mothering involves and a respect for and understanding of their own mothers. Because they had worked side by side with their mothers and cooperated with them in the care of the children, their relationship with their mothers appeared to be one of mutuality. These young women also proved to be impressive naive psychologists, with a keen awareness of developmental and individual differences in children's behavior. Having grown up in extended polygynous compounds, they had observed and interacted with numerous siblings, half-siblings, and courtyard cousins. That they did not consider the maternal role, as defined by Kenyan culture, to be burdensome was evidenced by their happy anticipation of having babies of their own; they voiced none of the ambivalence reported for groups of American middle-class women of the same age. They expected to receive help from other children and adults in caring for their children.

It is important to note, however, that the experiences of these young women as child nurses dated back to a period before adolescence. The preferred age for child nurses in many of our sample communities is between 6 and 10 years. We have speculated about why mothers prefer children of this age; our conclusion is that during middle childhood, girls are acquiring sex-role knowledge and preferences and are very interested in their mothers and other adult women as models. At the onset of adolescence they will become less interested in the world of their family and more interested in sex, the future, and their own children. Thus we believe that middle childhood is a period when learning nurturance by caring for lap children is especially easy. The overt positive responsiveness of babies to those who successfully care for them is more salient than the milder forms of appreciation expressed by older companions whom one might nurture. Furthermore, later in childhood new motives emerge that direct girls' and boys' behavior and diminish the effect of the eliciting power of lap children. That mothers in cultures in many parts of the world prefer 6- to 10-year-olds as nurses may reflect their desire to assign adolescent girls to other kinds of tasks, but it must also be at least partly a result of the children's own interest in babies and their eagerness to model their behavior after that of their mothers.

As we have seen, in many societies boys are also expected to act as child nurses, and in this role they too behave nurturantly. Across all the societies, however, boys rarely are observed carrying infants after the age of 7. It is probable that by this age the boys are treated differently from girls. Furthermore, the boys demand new roles for themselves because their behavior is now directed by powerful motives to establish their gender identity and practice sex-role behaviors. Even at ages 5 and 6, boys appear in the observations as competent but more reluctant nurses than girls.

Given that caregiving involves practice in nurturing others, what are the general implications of this experience for personality development? Does the nurturance that children, especially girls, acquire in those communities that delegate care affect their behavior with companions other than lap children? Moreover, does it create a lasting capacity for nurturance—for example, a preference to spend time in the company of people who might need or benefit from one's help? There is evidence in our data of the transfer of behavior learned and practiced in one dyad to interaction with different social partners—namely, the evidence cited in Chapter 7 that the experience of caring for lap children correlates with higher nurturance to same-sex peers. With few exceptions, both boys and girls who interact frequently with lap children score higher on nurturance to peers. Of course, these children may also have interacted more with lap children in previous years. Further evidence for our hypothesis of the importance of child care as a source of a permanent or continuing interest in nurturing others must come from future longitudinal studies.

Another important consequence of serving as a child nurse is the opportunity it provides to be part of the family work force and to assume responsibility for other members of the family. This rewarding experience of helping others and serving the family may serve to mitigate egoistic motives learned outside the home in settings such as schools that encourage individualism and competition. Schools provide little practice in nurturance, and children who do not have the opportunity to learn nurturance in the home setting may learn to regard and treat their peers primarily as competitors. Later in life, these highly competitive individuals may find it difficult to nurture others; they may give help most easily to people with whom they have no direct contact, for example, starving people far away or other strangers believed to be in great need (Whiting and Whiting, 1975).

Generic behaviors are seen not only in children's interaction with lap children but also in their interaction with other child companions. When children interact with other children who are clearly older (by 3 or more years), dependency behavior is proportionately high. For instance, Edwards and Whiting (1976a, 1976b) found that when the behavior of 2- to 3-year-old Ngeca children to their mothers was compared with that to their next older siblings (usually aged 4 to 5), dependency was high in both categories. Certain dependency behaviors ("sitting with, following after," "exchanging information, inquiring," and "watching") were about as high with the older siblings as with the mothers. In the present study, the observational materials from many of the subsaharan African communities contain instances in which the knee children approach older siblings rather than adults for help and other resources. This is not a surprising finding in communities where the older children are often designated as caretakers.

Knee children are also great observers and imitators in all of the communities we studied; they are highly motivated to copy the behavior of their older siblings. In contrast to middle-class America, where children are segregated by age during most of the daylight hours, in most of our sample communities the knee and yard children spend many hours a day together. It is clear that the knee children learn much from their next older siblings; when the older children are around, the younger children tag along, watch, seek attention, and even offer help in the hope of being included in their activities.

Dominance is another major form of generic social behavior. There appears to be a universal tendency for children to respond to the relative size of their social companions. When older children are interacting with younger, smaller children, there is a comparatively higher proportion of attempts to dominate than in interaction with older children or adults. As with other generic behaviors, dominance is difficult to suppress or prevent.

We have identified two types of dominance—prosocial and egoistic. In societies where the parents expect older siblings to care for their younger brothers and sisters, the older children take on the training and prosocial aspects of dominance, and this type of dominance is considered legitimate. In these societies a high proportion of the dominance is coded as training mands, which includes assigning work and suggesting socially appropriate behavior. Sometimes the older children may use prosocial forms of dominance to meet egoistic goals. For instance, older children who are working may direct the younger children to assume some of the work, and if they are playing, the older children may try to control or direct the play activity. At other times their dominance is overtly egoistic: the older children may give the younger children commands that are obviously intended to suit their own needs—for example, to get them something they want or to go away and break the interaction.

By 6 to 10 years of age, when children have more freedom to leave the family compound, girls spend more time with younger children and with their mothers than boys do. Girls' interaction with younger brothers and sisters comes to have an increasingly higher proportion of prosocial dominance than does that of the boys. The girls' style of dominance more closely resembles their mothers' behavior than does the boys'; the latter show more egoistically dominant behavior.

Teaching children not to dominate younger and smaller children is difficult. Cultures differ in their acceptance of generic dominance: some cultures attempt to suppress it, while others only circumscribe it. In all societies older children are prohibited from physically damaging younger children, but in many cultures, especially those with age grading, people expect that older children will dominate younger ones. In the age-graded societies of Africa, for example, the criterion of relative age is accepted as defining appropriate authority. In sharp contrast is the community of Orchard Town, where the mothers believe that children should not have dominance over others based on physical power. These mothers appear to have great trouble in teaching their children to "use words," "take turns," and "work things out fairly" without regard to relative age and size.

Dominance conflicts also occur when children come in contact with those who are their same age but are not kin. Social behavior between these nonrelated peers is characterized by a high proportion of sociability but also by frequent dominance struggles. In contrast to life within the homestead, the pecking order among peers has not yet been established. The school setting in particular increases the potential for dominance conflict. Children spend time in the company of social partners who, by definition, are approximately their same size and age and have similar physical and cognitive competencies; in this setting, relative size and age cannot serve as criteria for reducing conflict by establishing a hierarchy. Thus, in societies with schools where children spend extended periods of time segregated into age groups, there is a high proportion of dominance struggles and competitiveness. The institution of school even has a script that calls for competition in both work and play; the quality of each individual's performance is constantly being evaluated. Even when teachers attempt to downplay competition between children, they find it very difficult. There is no doubt that the management of competitiveness remains a major problem in societies like ours with age-segregated schools, and that a sense of failure undermines the self-esteem of many young people.

To regulate dominance conflicts in the school settings, rules are established by teachers, parents, and the children themselves. Informal wrestling (rough-and-tumble play) and formal competitive games are regulated in those societies with schools. Rough-and-tumble play is not necessarily aggressive; in our analyses it appears more as competitive and sociable behavior. This type of play can quickly become hostile and aggressive, however, when one of the actors is hurt. Children attempt to establish rules and strategies, such as calling "time out," that make it possible to terminate rough-and-tumble play before it becomes hostile. Boys engage in more of both informal, rough-and-tumble play and competitive games with rules than do girls. The competitive behavior of girls is more difficult to observe; it is more often expressed in insulting behavior.

A new generic motive emerges around the age of 4 or 5: the desire to behave in a way that announces one's gender and shows one's mastery of behaviors defined as appropriate to one's sex role. Young children have doubts about their gender identity and lack the cognitive maturity to understand gender permanence. Their knowledge of sex-role behavior is rigid and stereotyped—more so than it will be in later years. They seek to act in such a way as to announce to others, and assure themselves, of their gender identity and sex-role knowledge.

Concern for gender identity and appropriate sex-role behavior appears to motivate children to choose same-sex companions who are close in age. Isolating themselves in these segregated groups helps to support their identity. The motive is so strong that attempts by adults to change the pattern of same-sex association are usually unsuccessful.

It is probable that boys have more anxiety about gender and sex roles than do girls. It is difficult for boys to form a realistic image of appropriate male behavior. Since they have limited contact with adult males, and since they are assigned work primarily in the domain of adult women, their models tend to be female rather than male. The fact that boys generally distance themselves further from home than do girls may be an indication of their greater anxiety: although both boys and girls take advantage of permission to leave the immediate environment of the house and yard (dominated by women during the daylight hours), boys tend to be found further from home. They also engage in more dominance struggles with their mothers than girls do. Girls are seen to make more overtures to boys than boys make to girls.

The cultural scripts for the daily life of young children determine which aspects of adult behavior are salient to children as they develop their concepts of sex-role behavior. Children probably develop their earliest stereotypes based on their own observation of what seems important: the eating and sleeping arrangements of males and females, the sexual division of labor, sex differences in clothing, and any behaviors indicative of deference and authority associated with gender in their society.

In those societies where men are obviously of higher status than women, and where young boys have been able to observe the inequality of men and women from a young age and have themselves experienced preferential treatment from their mothers, the struggle of the young boys to disassociate themselves from women is most active and obvious to the outside observer; the boys try to avoid settings where their mother is present more than do boys in egalitarian societies. Thus in Juxtlahuaca and Khalapur, two communities where there is most evidence of the differential status of men and women, a dramatic increase in the relative distance of boys from home is seen between the ages of 4–5 and 6–10, as boys distance themselves from their mothers and from the type of work their mothers assign.

Some societies have rituals that help young people to establish sex-role identity and reassure them that there is no doubt as to their gender. For example, in Kenya a clear dichotomy is found between the scripts for the daily lives of adult males and those of adult females, but similar scripts for young girls and boys. Initiation ceremonies during middle childhood or adolescence serve to aid children in learning sex-role knowledge and affirming gender identity.

In all societies the generic social behaviors are increasingly modulated by culture as children grow older. Values concerning how responsive and nurturant a man, woman, or child should be, and which category of social partners one may express nurturance to, assume a directive force. Similarly, values about dominance and dependency modulate behavior and circumscribe those social partners to whom these behaviors are permitted or proscribed. In many societies the rules concerning these behaviors are different for males and females. For example, women in middle-class American society have in previous decades been expected to be more prosocial—responsive to the needs of others, nurturant, and responsible—while dominance battles have been considered more appropriate for males. An instrumental style of dependency was allowable in women, whereas attention seeking and boasting were considered more appropriate in men. We have no evidence indicating sex differences in the original generic behaviors: responsiveness, nurturance, prosocial and egoistic dominance, and dependency are elicited by distinctive categories of individuals from both males and females. On the other hand, we also have no evidence proving the equal strength of these prepared responses in males and females. The exploration of possible biologically determined sex differences remains an important research task. In particular, research should focus on the possibility that there are biologically determined differences in the strength of motives for physical activity, goal-oriented egoistic dominance, and responsiveness to human beings.

There is no doubt that, across cultures, girls get more practice in nurturance and prosocial dominance, boys in egoistic dominance and challenge. Our data do not tell us, however, the degree to which the choice of social partners who elicit these generic behaviors is based on children's own choices versus their assignment to settings by adults. It may be that individual or sex differences between children influence the kinds of social partners who most attract them. Research is needed on what factors influence the kinds of social environments that children like, seek, attend to, and learn from. Yet no matter what factors influence children's initial choice of preferred companions, their experiences with people surely shape their long-term views of what categories of people are rewarding and enjoyable company. One may, for example, seek companions who respond favorably to nurturance as opposed to companions who enjoy competition because one has had the opportunity to develop strategies for feeling successful as a helper. Through experience, we develop propensities for certain generic behaviors. There is some evidence for the transfer of behavior learned and practiced in frequent interaction with one category of social partner to a different category of social partners. Girls and boys who care for lap children, for example, are more nurturant to same-sex peers, and girls and boys who take care of siblings are proportionately more prosocial in their dominance to same-sex peers. Research on the transfer of behavioral propensities is an area that should be pursued.

The similarity in the dyadic interaction of categories of children across the cultures is impressive. Although the observations in our study were made by many different individuals in a variety of cultures, the profiles of social behavior are similar within dyad types. This convinces us that we can construct a cross-cultural science of human behavior. There are also differences in the profiles of behavior between geographic regions separated by space, history, and ecology—differences related to the typical learning environments of the children. Within geographic regions, however, we find the strongest similarities in the proportion scores of dyads. For example, the Kenyan children of Kokwet, Kisa, Kariobangi, Ngeca, and Nyansongo were studied by different teams of researchers, yet they show similar patterns of interaction. There is also a similarity in the two North Indian communities, which were studied a generation apart. These similarities are reassuring in terms of the objectivity of the observations and both the reliability and validity of the data.

In sum, our contextual model of social behavior allows for the explanation of individual as well as gender and cultural differences on the basis of setting occupancy. It also allows for the explanation of changes in patterns of social behavior with age as individuals enter new settings and interact with different types of social partners. Our model identifies types of experiences that may account for some of the developmental changes that have been observed by psychologists, because the company that individuals keep changes over the life course. Motives and goals, of course, also change over the life course. Social behavior is intentional: culturally transmitted value orientations, as well as maturationally related strivings for competence, lead to the emergence of new, coveted resources and the ascription of new meanings to particular kinds of social interaction, thus causing continuous modulation of the generic responses.

Appendixes
References
Index

Appendix A   The Sample Communities

Part One: The New Sample Communities

KIEN-TAA, LIBERIA
Researcher: Gerald Erchak
Fieldwork: 1970–1971; 15 households; 20 children aged 1 to 6 years; 360 minutes of observation per child.
Bibliography: Erchak (1974, 1975, 1976a, 1976b, 1977, 1979, 1980, 1985); Gibbs (1965).

The families in Erchak's sample lived in the community of Kien-taa (population 200), in Kpelleland in southeastern Liberia. They spoke Mande, a Niger-Congo language related to Bantu. These Kpelle families lived in the tropical rain forest and practiced slash and burn (swidden) agriculture, raising rice and cassava as staple crops. The families owned a small number of goats, sheep, and chickens but no cattle.

Unlike the Kenyan communities, where most of the houses were located on farmland, the Kien-taa houses were clustered in villages with little land surrounding them. The gardens were at a distance, sometimes as far as 10 miles from the village. Reaching the nearest town involved an hour's walk, crossing a river in a dugout canoe, and driving one hour to the highway. This town had two small stores, three bars, and a Lutheran church, but no school or clinic.

Although the village was isolated, all but one of the men had been away, to work in iron mines or on a rubber plantation. Some of the men had been gone for as many as 18 years, but the median number of years of wage labor for the sample fathers was 6 years. Additional contact with the outside world took place at the weekly market that brought people from the surrounding area into the town. All of the women worked on their farms to raise food for their families. Only two of the fathers had attended school, neither for more than 4 years. None of the mothers had any formal schooling.

Erchak chose a sample of young fathers. Only 5 of the 15 men were polygynously married, although it was the preferred form of marriage. Theoretically, residence was patrilocal, but 5 of the 15 households included parents or relatives of the mother of the sample children, reflecting an alternate pattern of uxorilocal residence associated with bride service in cases where the husband was not able to pay the bride's parents the required bridewealth. Five of the households were nuclear; the rest included co-wives or other adult relatives (the mean number of adults per household was 3.7). Unlike the Kenyan sample, where few polygynously married women shared the same house, co-wives in Kien-taa customarily lived together in one house.

Although theoretically the village households were divided into sections, each consisting of households related through the male line, in actuality the census data indicated that relatives of both the husbands and wives lived in the sections. Because the houses were closely spaced, children from an early age had playmates who were not siblings or half-siblings.

Fewer than half of the Kien-taa families claimed to be Christians. This represented a sharp contrast to the Kenyan samples, where, with the exception of the Kipsigis families, an average of 94 percent of the families claimed to belong to a Christian church. Perhaps the fact that the Lutherans (the church in the Kien-taa area) did not establish a mission school accounts for this low percentage; it also explains the low percentage of men and women who had any schooling.

Although most of the families were subsistence farmers cultivating the upland rice that was the staple food in every household, about 40 percent of the men also worked for wages on a local plantation tapping rubber. Twenty percent of the men worked further away and were only home part of the time.

The Kenyan Communities

The four Kenyan communities lie in the Central and Western Provinces. Their contact with the industrialized world dates from the last quarter of the nineteenth and first quarter of the twentieth centuries, when the British infiltrated the region, established a colonial government, and built the great East African railroad. The railroad was laid down primarily by the labor of workers imported from India and Pakistan, and it crossed Kenya to connect the Indian Ocean with

Lake Victoria. The railroad was one colonial institution that made possible the participation of East Africa in the international economy. Communities with closer access to the railroad became most involved in the cash economy.

Another set of colonial institutions that laid the foundation for a modern Kenya were related to Christianity. The British colonial government invited missionaries into the area, and in some cases the missionaries set up schools and clinics as well as churches. Anglican, Lutheran, Roman Catholic, Quaker, and Church of Scotland missionaries settled in different locations decided upon by a council of churches. These missions were quite different in their work, some more dedicated to educating the local populace than others, some more concerned with furnishing health facilities and improving agricultural technology. In the communities with good mission schools, families often joined the church in order to gain education for their children.

In 1963 Kenya won its independence from Great Britain. Jomo Kenyatta of the Kikuyu tribal group served as president until 1975, and Daniel Arap Moi of the Kalenjin-speaking tribal group succeeded him. Like other African nations, Kenya was characterized by rivalries between tribal groups, but it has managed to keep these rivalries under control. Since independence it has made a rapid entry into the world economy, has had an extremely high population growth, and has instituted universal primary education.

The Kenyan sample communities differed one from another in terms of their degree of participation in the modern cash economy and their mean level of education. They also differed in the extent to which they had departed from traditional East African social institutions such as polygyny (marriage of one man to two or more wives). These differences resulted largely from each community's history, for instance, the type of Christian mission found in the area and the degree of isolation from the railroad, highways, and urban centers. The Kenyan communities also vary in their language, history, and the size and fertility of their land holdings.

KOKWET, KENYA
Researchers: Sara Harkness and Charles Super
Fieldwork: 1972–1975; 64 children aged 3 to 10 years; 120 minutes of observation per child.
Bibliography: Harkness (1975, 1977); Harkness and Super (1982,

1983, 1985); Harkness, Edwards, and Super (1981); Super (1981, 1984); Super and Harkness (1982).

The people of the Kokwet area, in the South Nyanza District of the Western Province of Kenya, are Kipsigis speakers. The Kipsigis language belongs to the Kalenjin subgroup of the Eastern Nilotic language family. The Kipsigis people were originally seminomadic cattle herders closely related to the Samburu and Masai of the Rift Valley; they emerged as an identifiable group around the end of the seventeenth century and migrated southward from Mount Elgon, arriving in Western Kenya about 1000 A.D. Today the Kipsigis are primarily farmers but show substantial participation in all areas of national life, including business, academia, government, and the military. The Kipsigis may be best known in the United States for their famed Olympic runner, Kip Keino, and the president of Kenya, Daniel Arap Moi.

The sample referred to as "Kokwet" throughout this book actually consists of people from two neighboring communities, called Kokwet and Oli by Harkness and Super. Because the data on the children in the two communities seemed similar, we followed the ethnographers' recommendation to combine them and refer to the combined sample as Kokwet. Seventy-five percent of the observations were done in Kokwet, and additional cases were added from Oli to increase the sample. In the following summary the two communities will be described separately.

Kokwet (population 447 in 1974) was a model settlement scheme, a former European farm taken over by the government after independence. The land was divided into 20-acre lots and sold to owners who agreed to use improved agricultural technology and limit their herds to grade dairy cattle.

Oli (estimated population 1,468) was a former native reserve. Its people were reasonably prosperous because they were fortunate enough at the time of British colonialization and the Pax Britannica to control relatively large tracts of land. At the time of the study, farmers in Oli still had reasonably large herds of native (*zebu*) cattle, valued as a status symbol and as currency for paying bridewealth.

Traditionally, the houses throughout Kenya were made of mud and wattle with thatched roofs. One of the signs of cultural change has been the gradual increase in tin roofs, wood frames, and cement floors. In Kokwet and Oli most of the houses were of mud and wattle.

The Kipsigis were one of the first groups in Kenya to adopt the plow from Europeans. Their large, flat, fertile plots of land made its use practical. The Kipsigis men, in contrast to some of the other Kenyan men, became highly involved in their family farms. All of the men in Kokwet and Oli were farmers. At the time of the study, 84 percent of the Kokwet men were cash crop farmers only (the main cash crops being tea and pyrethrum); 8 percent of the men were also wage earners (laborers on the tea plantations around Kericho); another 8 percent were also entrepreneurs or salaried employees (for example, school teachers). Most of the women continued their traditional role of subsistence farming and worked the household gardens to raise food for their families.

In Kokwet and Oli, as in the other Kenyan communities, kinship and inheritance were traditionally patrilineal, with affiliation, land, and cattle passing through the male line. A man and his children belonged to the kinship group of the man's father, who owned the family land. A man and his brothers inherited the land upon the death of the father. Residence at marriage was patrilocal; a man was expected to bring his wife to live on his father's homestead, build her a house, and clear the land his father gave her for her garden. Households were large: in Kokwet, there were 64 households (on 52 homesteads) in 1972, with an average of 1.5 female adults (over age 16), 1.6 male adults (over age 18), and 4.2 children (under age 16) each. The household generally consisted of a man, his wives, their children, possibly children from other (non-Kokwet-resident) wives, the man's parents, siblings of the man or his wife, hired help, and so on.

The preferred form of marriage was polygyny, although not all men could afford more than one wife. In Kokwet 24 percent of the women were polygynously married, compared to 32 percent in Oli. The family of the husband traditionally paid bridewealth in the form of cattle to the woman's family at marriage to compensate them for raising the woman and for her future economic and reproductive work. Each wife was assigned a garden by her father-in-law so that she could raise food for herself and her children. Although the model farms in the Kokwet settlement scheme were sold to individual men, by 1972 some of their sons had married and moved onto the family land. Seventeen percent of the Kokwet homesteads included married sons.

Education came relatively late to the Kipsigis communities because the Christian missionaries who settled there in the colonial era were relatively uninterested in establishing schools. At the time of the study, 46 percent of the fathers in Kokwet had no schooling, 22 percent had 1–4 years, 16 percent had 5–7 years, and 16 percent had 8 or more years of schooling. Of the Kokwet mothers, 63 percent had no schooling, 21 percent had 1–4 years, 11 percent had 5–7 years, and 5 percent had 8 or more years. In Oli, the figures were comparable (but somewhat lower in terms of total years of schooling) for fathers and mothers. In 1972 only 47 percent of the boys and 37 percent of the girls aged 6–10 were in school.

KISA and KARIOBANGI, KENYA
Researcher: Thomas Weisner
Fieldwork: 1970–1972; 24 urban and 24 rural families; 68 children aged 2 to 8 years; approximately 120 minutes of observation per child.
Bibliography: Weisner (1973a, 1973b, 1976a, 1976b, 1976c, 1976d, 1979; Ross and Weisner, 1977; Weisner and Abbott,1977).

Kisa and Kariobangi are the names used by Thomas Weisner to refer to two Abaluyia communities: a rural group in Western Kenya, about 230 miles from Nairobi, and a group of men and their families living in an urban housing project in Nairobi. The language, Luluyia, is a member of the Bantoid language family, related to Gusii and Gikuyu.

Weisner was interested in rural-urban migration. He picked a sample of closely related families who lived within a 3-square-mile area of the Kisa Location in the Western Province. The Kariobangi sample consisted of the families of 24 men from the Kisa location who worked in Nairobi and lived for most of the year in Kariobangi, a housing estate with a population of 30,000. These 24 families were matched (on the basis of the age and education of the fathers of the sample children) to 24 related families who were full-time residents of the Kisa location, known as the Kisa sample.

The Kariobangi men worked as drivers, clerks, machine operators, laborers, and artisans. Several were unemployed. Their wives and children commuted back and forth between their farms and the city rooms. The wives maintained the family farm and periodically, when there was a slack period, took their younger children with them to visit their husbands. Older children occasionally went too, but more often they stayed home in Kisa to help with chores and attend school.

Forty-three percent of the matched Kisa fathers were full-time subsistence farmers; the remainder mixed subsistence farming with occasional wage work, shopkeeping, or seasonal migratory farm work.

Kisa is a fertile, rolling farm area settled mainly by the Abalshisa, Abakamhuli, Abalakai, and Abachero subclans of the Abaluyia sub-tribe, which probably arrived in Western Kenya about 1000 A.D. Kisa is about 25 miles from the city of Kisumu, and the region was settled early by Quaker missionaries who established excellent mission schools in the area. The adults in Weisner's sample were relatively well educated: 35 percent of the Kariobangi men and 60 percent of their wives had received 5 to 12 years of education. For the group of families who lived entirely in Kisa, 24 percent of the men and 18 percent of the women had received 5 to 12 years of education.

Kisa has become a densely populated area, and at the time of the study the families' landholdings were among the smallest of the Kenyan farm communities in our samples, averaging only 3 acres each. The community had the lowest rate of polygyny of our Kenyan samples, 6 to 7 percent. Two factors were probably responsible for the high percentage of monogamy: the early importance of Christianity in the area and the paucity of farm land. There was little room for married sons to both live and farm on the family homesteads.

Although the Kisa and Kariobangi communities were closely associated in terms of kinship ties and cultural values, the people in the city experienced living conditions quite different from those in the country. The town rooms were small, often shared by several men. Each house had two apartments that shared a tap and outhouse. The front yards, 12 by 24 feet, bordered on a drainage ditch and road. The houses were close together, and neighbors not only were strangers but often came from different parts of Kenya and spoke different languages.

NGECA, KENYA
Researcher: Beatrice Whiting
Fieldwork: 1968–1970 and 1973; 42 homesteads; 104 children aged

2 to 10 years; at least 45 minutes of observation per child (range 45–480 minutes).
Bibliography: Kenyatta (1965); Mariuki (1974); B. B. Whiting (1973, 1977); J. W. M. Whiting (1981b); Worthman and Whiting (1986).

Ngeca, a community of Kikuyu speakers in the Central Province of Kenya, is 20 miles north of the capital city, Nairobi. Originally a native reserve in what was known as the White Highlands, the land is on the edge of the Rift Valley (altitude 7,000 feet). The fertile soil and cool temperature made it an inviting location for British settlers, who came and took up residence at the turn of the century as the railroad connecting the coast and Uganda was constructed. The native reserve, in the center of these early British farms and tea plantations, was 5 miles from the railroad line. Missions were established in the area as early as 1898.

Kikuyu is a member of the Bantoid language family. The Bantu people probably arrived in Kenya about 1000 A.D. and settled in Ngeca around 1885. The Bantu were primarily horticulturalists (farmers with hoes but no plows or draft animals). They had small herds of sheep, goats, and cattle.

The Kikuyu speakers are the largest linguistic group in Kenya and have dominated the one-party political system ever since independence in 1963. Because the British settled in their midst, they early became involved in the labor economy and the fight for national independence. Furthermore, the Church of Scotland Mission early established excellent secondary schools in neighboring areas, the most famous being the Alliance School for boys and its counterpart for girls. In the early years of independence most of the members of Parliament were graduates of Alliance.

By 1968 there were relatively few families in Ngeca who did not believe that education was essential for survival in the new nation. The 40 percent of the fathers in our sample who had no education were the older men; the 40 percent who had finished elementary school and the 13 percent who had further training were born after 1939. Similarly, the 53 percent of the nonschooled mothers were mostly older women, whereas the younger women were relatively well educated. The Ngeca sample had the highest percentage of women with postsecondary training (11 percent) in the Kenyan samples.

The Ngeca sample was drawn from three areas of the location: two farm areas populated by families related through the male line (sublineages), and the town part of Ngeca, a former Emergency Village set up by the British during the Mau Mau Rebellion. The town houses were situated on quarter-acre lots. Most of the farm homesteads included some married sons and their wives and children. Even in the town section, there were grandparents living with their married sons. Twenty-seven percent of the 42 households were extended to include grandparents, married sons, or both.

Although land holdings in the sample averaged only around 4 acres per family for Ngeca as a whole, 31 percent of the men had more than one wife. However, most of these men were older and had larger farms. The few younger men who were polygynously married had well-paid salaried jobs that allowed them to support two sets of children.

As would be expected from their proximity to the capital, the people of Ngeca were heavily involved in wage work and business. Some of the men worked in the town of Limuru, 5 miles from the village, in the post office, retail stores, the Bata shoe factory, and the pork factory. Others worked in Nairobi as drivers, clerks, or salaried men in the post office and electric light company. Sixty percent of the men were small entrepreneurs, store owners in the Ngeca area, or truckers, wage earners, or salaried employees. Before the road into the village was improved, permitting a year-round busline to operate, many of the men came home only on weekends or once or twice a month.

The sample of Ngeca women also included more wage earners, entrepreneurs, and salaried women than the other samples, reflecting not only educational level but also job opportunities in periurban Nairobi. Eighteen percent had paid jobs. Most of the women worked on European or large African farms 2 or 3 miles from the village; others worked in Ngeca stores and in the hotel. An additional 8 percent were entrepreneurs, selling vegetable products in the local markets. One of the sample mothers taught in the elementary school, two in the nursery school. All the mothers also had gardens, and some sold surplus crops in local markets.

John Herzog worked with Beatrice Whiting to collect data during the first phase of the fieldwork. The observations were made by four Kenyan students: Jane Geteria Chesiana, Wanjiku Kagia, Grace Gyru, Irene Kamau, and Rose Maiena.

BHUBANESWAR, INDIA

Researcher: Susan Seymour

Fieldwork: 1965–1967; 24 households (8 lower-caste/class households and 16 middle- and upper-caste/class households, located in the Old Town and New Capital parts of town; 103 children aged 0 to 10 years; 16 hours of observation per household, focused on the interaction of mothers (and mother surrogates) and children.

Bibliography: Seymour (1971, 1974, 1975, 1976a, 1976b, 1980, 1981, 1983, 1985).

Bhubaneswar (population 50,000), located in the state of Orissa in North India, is an ancient Hindu temple town and pilgrimage center. In 1947 a site adjacent to the old temple town was selected to be the capital of the newly created state of Orissa. Susan Seymour spent two years studying families in both parts of the city.

The samples of families in Bhubaneswar differ from the other samples in that Seymour was interested in studying the effect of caste and class, as well as modernization, on patterns of mother-child (and mother surrogate-to-child) interaction. She selected families in both parts of the city. Within each, she chose four families from three socioeconomic groups, thus making a total sample of 24 families. On Seymour's recommendation, we have analyzed the observational data by social status/class groups, combining middle- and upper-class families from both parts of town and comparing them with lower-class families from both parts.

The upper-status families included high-ranking civil servants in the New Capital and Brahmin priests in the Old Town. The middle-status groups included middle-level civil servants and businessmen in the New Capital and ritually "clean" Shudra castes (such as carpenters, cow herders, and barbers) in the Old Town. The lower-class group, at the bottom of the social hierarchy, included a variety of "polluting" castes such as washermen, sweepers, and Bauris (an untouchable group of agricultural laborers and construction workers).

Household size in the lower-class group varied from 5 to 16 members, with a mean of 9.6. Household size in the middle- and upper-class group varied from 5 to 24, with a mean of 10.2. The largest households were in the Old Town, where lineal and collateral joint households were found (composed of the sample child's paternal grandparents and/or paternal uncles and aunts and their children, in addition to the sample child's parents and siblings). The largest of the Old Town households was composed of 24 people whose living quarters included six small rooms, two small courtyards, and a small enclosed yard. All marriages were monogamous. The houses, built of mud in the old style, were similar in construction to those in Khalapur. Men slept in the same houses as their wives, though usually in separate rooms. The New Capital households tended to be smaller because all were nuclear. The houses, built by the government, were designed for single-family occupancy; they varied in size and were assigned to families on the basis of the household head's position in the government hierarchy.

Most of the fathers (60 percent) in the lower-class group had between 1 and 7 years of education; the remainder had no formal schooling. In the middle- and upper-class group, 38 percent of fathers had 12 or more years of education, 19 percent had 8–11 years, 23 percent had 1–7 years, and 19 percent had no education. None of the lower-class mothers had any formal education, while in the middle- and upper-class group, 15 percent had 12 or more years of education, 12 percent had 8–11 years, 19 percent had 1–7 years, and 53 percent had no formal schooling.

Part Two: The Six Culture Communities

NYANSONGO, KENYA

Researchers: Robert LeVine and Barbara LeVine Lloyd
Fieldwork: 1955–1956; 18 households; 16 children aged 3 to 10 years; 75 minutes of observation per child.
Bibliography: LeVine and LeVine (1963).

The community known as Nyansongo is a Gusii community in Western Kenya, situated in the Kisii Highlands in the South Nyanza District, 30 miles east of Kavirondo Gulf in Lake Victoria. A main road connects Nyansongo with Kokwet to the southeast and Oyugis to the northwest. The Gusii language (like Kikuyu and Luluyia) is a member of the Bantoid family, the largest linguistic group in Kenya.

Nyansongo is located in the old native African reserve known as the Kisii Highlands, a cool, fertile ridge ranging fom 5,000 to 7,000 feet in altitude. At the time of the original study, the sample included 18 neighboring households (population 208) who were members of a large work group. The group included three neighborhoods (members of smaller work groups) whose members were related and belonged to the same subpatrilineage. The community was actually part of a larger community of continuous settlements in the administrative unit called Nyaribari Location (population 42,670 in 1948).

Already by the 1950s Nyansongo was densely populated and feeling the growing shortage of land. The average size of the farms was 7 acres, larger than the Kisa and most Ngeca homesteads but smaller than in previous decades. Traditionally the Gusii combined subsistence agriculture and animal husbandry, though cattle herding overshadowed cultivation in prestige and social significance. By the late 1960s, when further study was made of the community (see the Spot Observation communities), land shortage and the growing cash economy had brought about a shift in focus to cash cropping, with the farmers raising maize, eleusine, sweet potatoes, bananas, legumes, tomatoes, and coffee for the market. Eighty-one percent of the men were cash farmers; the rest were wage earners working as agricultural laborers.

The level of schooling among the adults was not high in Nyansongo, either in the 1950s or the 1960s. Among the Kenyan communities studied, this was the one with the highest percentage of nonschooled adults and the lowest percentage of adults who had received 5 or more years of education.

As in the other Kenyan communities, polygyny was the ideal form of marriage in Nyansongo at the time of the original study. In 1956, 37 percent of the sample fathers were polygynously married. However, by the time of the second study in 1967, only 27 percent of the fathers had two or more wives. The change was undoubtedly due in part to land pressure.

TARONG, THE PHILIPPINES

Researchers: William Nydegger and Corinne Nydegger
Fieldwork: 1954–55; 24 children aged 3 to 10 years; 135 minutes of observation per child.
Bibliography: Nydegger and Nydegger (1963).

Spanish contact in Tarong, on Luzon Island, dates from the last quarter of the sixteenth century. The first Catholic church was built around 1660; it was located in the municipal center of Poblacion, 6 miles from the barrio of Tarong. The United States colonial government took over Luzon Island from the Spanish in the first quarter of the twentieth century and introduced inoculation and health programs, a school system, and improved roads. At this time also a land title system was inaugurated and large tracts of land were taken over by families with power and wealth, forcing many of the Tarongans to become tenant farmers. In 1946 the Philippines became independent, and a strong national government was established.

The 24 families studied by the Nydeggers in 1955 lived in three hamlets (*sitios*) that formed a barrio; the houses were built along the ridges of the foothills of an inland chain of mountains in the northwestern area of the island of Luzon. The foothills sloped steeply into narrow valleys, which made travel difficult. At the time of the study, the one road into the barrio was unpaved and traveled only by the heavy lumber trucks on their way to the mountains.

The barrio, a 2-mile-square area, had a population of 259 people belonging to 61 families, most of whom were the descendants of the 7 families who had settled the area in 1860. The three *sitios* varied in size, the smallest having 3 houses, the largest 17. Within the *sitios* were clusters of houses usually owned by close relatives. Marriages were monogamous, with the preferred spouse being a second cousin. There was no restriction on marriage within the barrio. It was customary for the father of the groom to provide a house for the married couple, but in some cases the new house was built in the yard of the bride's parents. Thus, although 19 of the 24 households were nuclear, 18 of these shared a yard with grandparents of either the husband or wife, and, in one case, with both. The average number of children in the sample families was three, but there was an average of six children per shared yard, and six of the families had yards with ten or more children.

The small areas of flat land on the ridges were reached by climbing steep slopes that were terraced for rice paddies. The families produced most of their own food; some worked on their own land, some as tenants on land owned by the residents of the municipal center. Wet and dry rice, bananas and other fruits, and vegetables were raised. Eggplant grew well in the area and was sold in the municipal market. Sugar cane and tobacco were grown as cash crops. In addition to carabao, used as draft animals, most families had chickens. Most also had one or two goats, and some families had cows and pigs.

Three barrios shared the elementary school that was built in 1916.

All of the children finished four grades, and two-thirds of them completed the sixth grade. In order to attend high school, the children had to live in Poblacion and pay for room and board as well as tuition. Twenty-five percent of the families sent at least one child to high school, and eight of the barrio families had sent a child to college.

All of the sample families were Roman Catholic. However, they rarely attended the church in Poblacion except for baptisms, marriages, and funerals. Christianity was blended with the indigenous belief system, which included numerous malevolent and ancestor spirits.

JUXTLAHUACA, MEXICO
Researchers: A. Kimball Romney and Romaine Romney
Fieldwork: 1954–1955, 1956; 22 households; 22 children aged 3 to 10 years; 79 minutes of observation per child.
Bibliography: Romney and Romney (1963).

Juxtlahuaca is one of the most isolated of the communities studied in this book. The town is located in the state of Oaxaca in a narrow valley 6,500 feet above sea level and is surrounded by mountains over 10,000 feet in altitude. In 1954 the access was by truck over a very poor road 65 miles long, which was impassable during the rainy season between May and September. The trip took an average of 14 hours. The road joined the Pan American Highway at Huajuapan. Planes at the small airport in this town could be hired to fly government officials into Juxtlahuaca; the landing strip was a corn field outside of town. Of the 3,600 inhabitants in the town, 600 were Mixtecan Indians who lived in the barrio of Santo Domingo. The barrio was located on the site of a pre-Columbian Mixtecan town. Although Spanish families moved into the area in 1620 and built a Catholic church, barrio life retained many elements of the precolonial period.

The barrio families lived in adobe houses clustered along unpaved streets, their courtyards separated by fields of corn and alfalfa and small gardens with vegetables and fruit trees. Houses were built along the street with windowless *adobe* walls, or else set back in the courtyard. All marriages were monogamous. Each family had its own one-room house and a cook shack. Courtyards were often shared by a group of families. Nineteen of the twenty-two households were nuclear, but half of them had one or more grandparents sharing the same courtyard. Ideally, a young couple moved into the courtyard of the husband's family, but in actual practice a man would move into his wife's courtyard if there was more room. After the birth of the first one or two children, the family moved into a separate dwelling. Since relatives settled close to each other and interacted with each other daily, family life focused around the extended family even when relatives did not share the same courtyard. Some families had small gardens and fields adjacent to their houses, but because much of the land in the barrio was owned by the townspeople, the main crops were grown on communal barrio property on the hillsides outside the settlement. Maize, beans, and chile were grown, as well as other vegetables, fruit, and alfalfa. Plows had been introduced and were pulled by oxen rented from the owners. Some families owned burros, which were used to transport crops and firewood.

The barrio was separated from the center of the Ladino (Spanish-speaking, non-Indian) town both physically and culturally. A deep gully and stream ran along the boundary. Mixtecan was spoken in the barrio homes, and when Romney and Romney worked in the village, many of the older inhabitants could not speak Spanish. Although the Indians were similar to the Ladino townspeople in physical type, they wore distinctive dress and were looked down upon by the townspeople. The barrio children who attended the school in the center of town were often badly treated by both the teachers and the Ladino children.

It does not appear from the ethnographers' reports that any of the parents of the sample children had attended school. Knowledge of the outside world came from visiting and traveling outside Juxtlahuaca. Most of the men had visited Oaxaca; some had worked in the mines in Tlaxiaco or at the sugar refinery at Pueblo, and a few men had worked briefly in the United States.

Although all of the barrio men in the sample were primarily farmers (working on their own or communal land or as tenant farmers), there were some specialized occupations that furnished cash for purchases in the town. One man was a baker, one a butcher, one a wood carver, and one a trader of maize that he took to a neighboring town. Several of the young men did leather work. Some of the younger men made adobe tile, while others worked as carpenters in town.

The women had less contact with the world outside of Juxtlahuaca, although at the time of the study several younger Santo Domingan girls had migrated to Oaxaca and Mexico City to work as servants. The barrio women did spend time in the town, however, selling tortillas, eggs, pork, prepared chocolate, and surplus vegetables. Some women embroidered blouses for sale in the market, and one or two who had sewing machines made clothes to order. Some of the younger girls worked as servants in town.

All of the families were Roman Catholic, but their beliefs and ceremonies were a mixture of the precontact culture and the tenets of the Catholic Church.

TAIRA, OKINAWA

Researchers: Thomas Maretzki and Hatsumi Maretzki
Fieldwork: 1954–1955; 24 children aged 3 to 10 years; 74 minutes of observation per child.
Bibliography: Maretzki and Maretzki (1963).

Taira is a village on the northwest coast of Okinawa, the largest of the Ryukyuan chain of islands southwest of Japan. At the time of the study, the 700 inhabitants lived in a clustered settlement bounded on one side by a sandy beach and bay and on the other by sloping fields dotted with rice paddies and by mountains beyond. The village is said to have been established around 1550 by two noble families who fled the Hokuzan Kingdom when it was conquered by the southern Okinawan Kingdom of Chuzan. Historical records indicate that Okinawa has had contact with China, Japan, and Korea since the seventh century, but its ties with Japan and mainland Southeast Asia date from prehistoric times. Japan annexed Okinawa in 1872 and deposed the last king of the Ryukyuan islands in 1879.

During World War II, Taira was destroyed and many of the inhabitants were killed. The population of the rebuilt village was augmented by refugees from other parts of the island. Although the United States took over the government of the island in 1945, Japanese remained the language of instruction in the schools at the time of the study. All of the young were bilingual.

At the time of the study, many Okinawans had visited Japan, and some had worked in factories there for extended periods. Some people had spent time in the Pacific Islands and Brazil.

The village houses in Taira were clustered along lanes that were roughly parallel. The sliding doors, kept open during the day, and the small yards made for easy communication between houses. The area chosen for study was centrally located: it was close to a store, two tanks that supplied water to the village, and an open area next to a large banyan tree where a teacher ran a kindergarten for pre-school-age children during the morning hours. Children played in this area and in the area adjacent to the beach.

The families in the sample raised most of their own food—rice, sweet potatoes, wheat, beans, and vegetables. Men and women worked together in the gardens and rice paddies and in the mountains where they cut firewood and lumber to sell for cash. Pigs were raised for sale, and a few families owned horses used to pull plows.

Marriages in Taira were monogamous, and descent was reckoned in the male line. Households were nuclear or stem, the latter type consisting of a couple and one of their married sons who stayed on to care for his parents and inherited the house and land of his father. Twelve of the 24 houses were nuclear, while the others were stem or extended to include other relatives. Most of the families in the sample could trace a kin relationship to one another. Since marriage within the community was permitted and about half of the wives had kin in the community, children were surrounded by relatives. The community thought of itself as a large kin group.

Traditionally all land was communally owned, and although private ownership had subsequently become the rule, the ethos of co-operation remained. The store, for example, was owned by an all-village cooperative.

At the time of the study, neither Buddhism, Christianity, nor any of the other great religions had taken the place of ancestor worship and the belief in animistic deities.

Education was highly valued. A small school had been built in Taira in 1891, and adolescents and adults as well as children attended it during its early years. By 1955, 97 percent of the population was bilingual and literate. All children attended the local schools. Every child finished junior high school, and some continued to high school and college.

KHALAPUR, INDIA
Researcher: Leigh Minturn
Fieldwork: 1954–1955; 24 households; 24 children aged 3 to 10 years; 95 minutes of observation per child.
Community restudied 1974–1975.

Bibliography: Minturn and Hitchcock (1963); Minturn, Boyd, and Kapoor (1978); Minturn (1984).

Khalapur (population 5,000) is situated on the alluvial plain between the Jumna and Ganges rivers in Uttar Pradesh, North India. The village is 90 miles north of Delhi and 4 miles from Bhudana, a town of 25,000, the provincial capital during the period when the Islamic dynasty ruled North India. This period lasted from the sixteenth century until 1858, when British colonial rule was established in the area. The 24 sample families were members of a patrilineal clan of the Rajput *jati,* a hereditary group that claimed descent from the ancient Hindu warrior rulers, the Ksatriya caste. The founding members of the clan probably moved into Khalapur in the fifteenth century.

The Rajputs were the wealthiest group in town and owned most of the land. Most families had hired help who plowed the fields and worked throughout the year. The Rajput families were enmeshed in interdependent relations with nine other traditional occupational groups (castes), including the priests or Brahmins, water carriers, sweepers, carpenters, blacksmiths, barbers, potters, washermen, and leatherworkers. The services of these people were paid for by allotments of grain at the time of the biannual harvests.

Cash cropping had become the predominant occupation of the Rajput families. An irrigation system from the Ganges River ensured good harvests. Wheat, sugar cane, maize, rice, millet, oats, barley, and cotton were grown in the fields located on the outskirts of the town. A branch of the railroad made it possible to sell sugar cane and grain to the central markets. The farmers were dependent on the products of the industrial world and bought chaff cutters, kerosene lanterns, water pumps, and many other manufactured items. At the time of the research, the plows were still pulled by bullocks. Milk from the cattle, who were housed adjacent to the courtyard, was an essential item in the diet.

All of the sample families were Hindu. A few Rajputs in the village, however, were Muslim, and there was a Muslim saint's tomb in the village. This saint was regarded as the village protector, and his shrine was visited by both Hindus and Moslems. The culture of the Islamic conquerors, who ruled the area for 300 years, persisted at the time of the study through the custom of *purdah,* a practice prescribing the seclusion of women of childbearing age. These women were confined to the courtyard, which they shared with their mother-in-law and sisters-in-law. In these extended family courtyards, there might be three or even four generations of women. With the exception of a few newly married men who slept with their wives, the husbands slept in separate quarters, sometimes but not always adjacent to the courtyard. The courtyard was surrounded by windowless mud walls, with the houses adjoining one another in rows along the narrow, winding streets. The women visited each other over the rooftops. Men ate in the courtyard and visited their wives at night. All but one of the marriages were monogamous (there was one polygynous marriage of a man whose first wife was barren; under the circumstances men sometimes take a second wife with the permission of the first wife). Six of the 24 sample households were nuclear, the rest extended. The typical household included a senior man, his wife, and his married sons; others were extended further to include the senior man's brothers, their wives, and their married sons and families.

Most of the adults in the same families were illiterate, but every family tried to have at least one member who could read and write. There were both a boys' and a girls' school in Khalapur. The latter had only six grades, and at the time of the study most of the girls did not attend. Those who did not finish usually dropped out after fourth grade. The boys more frequently finished eight grades.

ORCHARD TOWN, U.S.A.
Researchers: John Fischer and Ann Fischer
Fieldwork: 1954–1955; 24 children aged 3 to 10 years; 82 minutes of observation per child.
Bibliography: Fischer and Fischer (1963).

Orchard Town is a section of a New England town whose inhabitants numbered about 5,000 at the time of the study. The 24 families selected for study were either members of the Baptist Church or associated with members of the church. The men were wage earners, either salaried or self-employed; 12 men held blue-collar jobs and 12 had white-collar jobs. Almost all of the fathers commuted to work and were away from early morning until 5:00 to 7:00 in the evening. A few of the women had part-time jobs, but most were homemakers.

All but two of the families lived in single-family houses surrounded by large yards where the children could play during the daylight hours when the weather was clement. The houses had many rooms and the conveniences of American middle-class culture. Two of the families lived in apartment houses.

All the children of ages 6 and over attended school, but there were no kindergarten or preschools. Young children were home all day with their mothers. Television, games, books, and pencil and paper or crayon projects helped to keep them busy when it was too cold for them to play outdoors. Preschool-age neighborhood children could play with one another if they lived on the same side of the highway that ran through the area. For the most part, however, their parents had to arrange for the children to visit each other. Sunday School, Girl Scouts, and Boy Scouts were formal settings outside of school where children could meet and join in activities with peers.

Although several of the parents had relatives living in town or within commuting distance, even those grandparents living with or adjacent to their grandchildren did not appear to play an important role in the family's daily life. The only help that the sample mothers received on a regular basis was from hired baby sitters.

Part Three: The Spot Observation Communities

NYANSONGO, KENYA
Researchers: Sara Nerlove, Ruth Munroe, and Robert Munroe
Data collection: 1967; 22 children aged 5 to 7 years; 20 observations per child.
Bibliography: Nerlove, Munroe, and Munroe (1971).

For description of the community see the earlier section on Nyansongo under the Six Culture communities.

VIHIGA, KENYA
Researchers: Ruth Monroe and Robert Munroe
Data collection: 1967; 16 children aged 5 to 7 years; 16 observations per child.

Bibliography: R. H. Munroe and R. L. Munroe (1978); R. H. Munroe et al. (1983); R. L. Munroe and R. H. Munroe (1971).

The Logoli of Western Kenya, like the other two East African members of the sample, are a Bantu-speaking people. Because of population and land pressures in their rural habitat, the Logoli of Vihiga had lost most of their grazing land, which had resulted in a great decline in herding activities. For the same reason, most married males in the 25–45 age bracket were engaged in outside employment. Horticultural activities, the mainstay of the subsistence economy, were mostly in the hands of adult females, who received some help from both boys and girls. Farming was carried out on homestead fields adjacent to or near the houses.

The settlement pattern of Vihiga was one of scattered houses, without village nucleation. The primary domestic group was the patrilineally extended family homestead, although this grouping had become more attenuated as land scarcity increased. Polygyny occurred much less frequently than among the Kikuyu and Gusii. The mean household size of the sample families was 9.1 persons.

NGECA, KENYA
Researchers: Ruth Monroe and Robert Monroe
Data collection: 1970–1971; 21 children aged 5 to 7 years; 18 observations per child.
Bibliography: R. H. Munroe et al. (1983).

For description of the community see the earlier section on Ngeca under the New Sample communities.

CONACOSTE/SANTO DOMINGO, GUATEMALA
Researcher: Sara Nerlove
Data collection: 1971; 53 children aged 5 to 7 years; 20 observations per child.
Bibliography: Nerlove et al. (1974).

The Guatemalans are Spanish-speaking Ladino villagers. Their subsistence economy, which was horticulturally based, involved maize and bean staples; cash crops such as tomatoes and chiles were also grown. Cultivated land lay on the edge or outside of the communities.

Two villages, Conacoste and Santo Domingo, were studied and

the data pooled. They were located 27.5 kilometers from each other in an area of poor soil and scrub vegetation. The settlement pattern was the typical Guatemalan grid, with the plaza, national tree, and church in the village center. The basic social unit was the neolocal, nuclear, monogamous family.

SANTA BARBARA, PERU

Researchers: Charlene Bolton, Ralph Bolton, and Carol Michelson
Data collection: 1974; 11 children aged 5 to 7 years; 14 observations per child.
Bibliography: Bolton et al. (1976); R. H. Munroe et al. (1983).

The Canchitos of Santa Barbara, Peru, are a Quechua-speaking people with a mixed horticultural and herding economy. Both male and female adults participated in horticultural activities, and they received subsantial help from children of both sexes. Fields of tubers and grains were located outside the village. Herding—of sheep and of relatively docile alpacas and llamas—was carried out extensively by both male and female adults and by children. Animals were taken to pastures outside the village.

The settlement pattern consisted of a central hamlet with outlying pastures and fields and many dispersed households in the surrounding countryside. The fundamental social unit was the neolocal, nuclear, monogamous family. The mean household size was 4.1 persons.

CLAREMONT, U.S.A.

Researcher: Amy Koel
Data collection: 1975; 17 children aged 5 to 7 years; 8 observations per child.
Bibliography: Koel (1975); R. H. Munroe et al. (1983).

The Claremonters of the state of California, U.S.A., participated in an urban-industrial economy. All sample families were dependent upon wage labor for their livelihood.

The sample was taken from a primarily upper-middle-class suburban community of 30,000 in Los Angeles County. The settlement pattern was the familiar American grid block alignment, with detached houses facing toward the street. The basic social unit was the neolocal, nuclear, monogamous family. Mean household size was 4.6 persons.

Appendix B Total Number of Social Acts
Received by Children of Each
Sex and Age Group from Their
Mothers

Community	Age 2–3 years		Age 4–5 years		Age 6–8 years	
	Girls	Boys	Girls	Boys	Girls	Boys
New Samples						
Kien-taa, Liberia	123 (3)	81 (3)	180 (4)	129 (4)	49 (1)	50 (2)
Kokwet, Kenya	203 (12)	130 (8)	94 (9)	89 (10)	127 (12)	79 (8)
Kisa, Kenya	46 (4)	54 (3)	32 (4)	41 (3)	36 (5)	63 (6)
Kariobangi, Kenya	239 (13)	51 (4)	108 (7)	121 (6)	98 (6)	35 (2)
Ngeca, Kenya (combined)	232 (16)	332 (18)	287 (17)	241 (16)	314 (18)	292 (17)
Bhubaneswar, India (lower class)	108 (4)	113 (4)	1 (1)	59 (2)	24 (2)	58 (6)
Bhubaneswar, India (middle and upper class)	224 (4)	477 (8)	110 (4)	352 (10)	214 (8)	155 (10)

	Age 3–6 years		Age 7–10 years	
	Girls	Boys	Girls	Boys
Six Cultures				
Taira, Okinawa	13 (3)	7 (4)	6 (5)	5 (1)
Tarong, Philippines	173 (6)	145 (6)	56 (6)	72 (6)
Khalapur, India	73 (6)	29 (5)	28 (5)	31 (6)
Juxtlahuaca, Mexico	80 (6)	35 (5)	39 (6)	24 (5)
Orchard Town, U.S.A.	160 (6)	149 (6)	14 (5)	2 (1)
Nyansongo, Kenya	34 (4)	61 (4)	73 (4)	65 (4)

Note: The number of mother/child dyads is given in parentheses after the number of acts. The data were analyzed as follows. The acts from each individual mother to child were separated. In the New Samples only individual mothers who had at least 5 acts to her child were included; in the Six Culture samples all mother-to-child dyads were included. The number of mothers fitting these criteria are given in parentheses. Then, for statistical analysis, the acts of all these mothers were aggregated into a summed score for each sex/age group of child. For example, for Kien-taa, Liberia, there were 3 mothers with at least 5 acts to daughters aged 2–3 years. The acts of these 3 mothers were aggregated into a sum of 123 acts. Tables 3.3 to 3.7 are based on percentage scores using the aggregated sums as the denominators for the proportion scores.

Appendix C   Total Number of Social Acts Directed by Children of Each Sex and Age Group to Their Mothers

Community	Age 2–3 years		Age 4–5 years		Age 6–8 years	
	Girls	Boys	Girls	Boys	Girls	Boys
New Samples						
Kien-taa, Liberia	78 (3)	60 (2)	134 (4)	91 (4)	23 (1)	30 (1)
Kokwet, Kenya	209 (9)	124 (6)	53 (6)	52 (5)	57 (6)	28 (3)
Kisa, Kenya	66 (6)	52 (5)	29 (4)	33 (4)	56 (6)	36 (4)
Kariobangi, Kenya	155 (12)	50 (4)	56 (6)	59 (4)	61 (6)	22 (2)
Ngeca, Kenya (combined)	133 (12)	259 (15)	123 (11)	141 (11)	153 (11)	91 (11)
Bhubaneswar, India (lower class)	71 (4)	159 (6)	18 (2)	46 (3)	11 (3)	24 (4)
Bhubaneswar, India (middle and upper class)	120 (4)	234 (7)	43 (3)	115 (9)	62 (6)	75 (8)

	Age 3–6 years		Age 7–10 years	
	Girls	Boys	Girls	Boys
Six Cultures				
Taira, Okinawa	7 (4)	5 (2)	9 (2)	4 (3)
Tarong, Philippines	132 (6)	85 (6)	32 (5)	32 (5)
Khalapur, India	77 (4)	14 (5)	13 (6)	21 (6)
Juxtlahuaca, Mexico	72 (6)	30 (6)	30 (5)	9 (2)
Orchard Town, U.S.A.	153 (5)	126 (6)	15 (4)	4 (1)
Nyansongo, Kenya	22 (3)	18 (4)	39 (4)	28 (4)

Note: The number of mother/child dyads is given in parentheses after the number of acts. The data were analyzed as follows. The acts from each individual child to the mother were separated; in parentheses are given the number of individual children of a given sex and age who interacted with the mother. In the New Samples we excluded individual dyads with fewer than 5 interacts. In the Six Culture samples all individual dyads were included regardless of the number of interacts. For statistical analysis the acts of all children of a given sex and age group were aggregated or pooled into a summed score. For example, for Kien-taa, Liberia, there were 3 girls in the age group 2–3 years who each directed at least 5 acts to her mother. The acts of these 3 children were aggregated or pooled into a sum of 78 acts. The tables in Chapter 4 are based on percentage scores using the aggregated sums as the base or denominator of the proportion. For example, for Kien-taa girls aged 2–3 years, if of the 78 social acts, 48 were dependent, the group received a 61.5 percent score for total dependency (see Table 4.2).

Appendix D   Proportion of Nurturant Behavior by 4- to 10-Year-Old Children to Infants

New Samples

Girls				Boys			
Identification of child and community	Age	No. of acts	Propor-tion	Identification of child and community	Age	No. of acts	Propor-tion
Ng-a	8	12	100				
				Ng-A	6	12	.75
Ng-b	4	11	.73				
Kis-a	6	6	.66				
Kien-a	7	21	.66	Kok-A	7	6	.66
Kis-b	7	9	.66				
Kar-a	5	22	.64				
Ng-c	5	11	.55				
Kar-b	7	20	.55				
Ng-d	8	12	.50				
Kar-c	7	6	.50				
Ng-e	8	13	.46				
Kok-a	8	9	.44				
				Kien-A	6	40	.43
				Ng-B	10	12	.42
Kar-d	8	5	.40				
Kien-b	10	15	.40				
Kar-e	5	15	.40				
Kok-b	8	33	.39				
Kien-c	5	26	.38				
Ng-f	6	13	.38	Kok-B	7	8	.38
Kok-c	4	9	.38				
Kien-d	9	38	.34				
Kok-d	5	5	.33	Kar-A	5	15	.33
Ng-g	4	9	.33	Kar-B	4	12	.33
Kar-f	5	19	.32				
Ng-h	10	10	.30	Kok-C	11	10	.30
Ng-i	8	7	.29				
Kok-e	3	11	.27				
Kar-g	5	20	.25				
				Kok-D	6	5	.20
Kok-f	5	10	.20	Kok-E	5	10	.20
				Kar-C	8	5	.20
				Kien-B	10	10	.20

Appendix D (*continued*)

Girls				Boys			
Identification of child and community	Age	No. of acts	Propor-tion	Identification of child and community	Age	No. of acts	Propor-tion
Ng-j	6	11	.18				
Kok-g	9	7	.14				
Kis-c	6	1	.14				
Kien-e	4	8	.13				
				Kok-F	6	9	.11
				Kien-C	5	19	.11
Kar-h	4	24	.04				
				Kis-A	4	5	.00
Kok-h	6	5	.00	Ng-C	9	5	.00
				Ng-D	5	7	.00

Mean:	No. of children	Propor-tion	Mean:	No. of children	Propor-tion
Kien-taa	5	.38	Kien-taa	3	.25
Kokwet	8	.27	Kokwet	6	.31
Kisa	3	.49	Kisa	1	.00
Kariobangi	8	.39	Kariobangi	3	.29
Ngeca	10	.47	Ngeca	4	.29
Pooled sample		.39	Pooled sample		.27

Appendix D: Individual scores for Nyansongo, Juxtlahuaca, and Tarong[a]

Girls				Boys			
Identification of child and community	Age	No. of acts	Propor- tion	Identification of child and community	Age	No. of acts	Propor- tion
Jux 435	6	10	.80				
				Tar 223	7	53	.79
				Nya 612	5	19	.74
Nya 634	6	24	.71				
Jux 432	6	7	.71				
Tar 234	5	10	.70				
Jux 442	8	32	.69				
				Nya 623	8	9	.66
				Jux 421	7	6	.66
Tar 246	10	49	.63				
Nya 644	8	54	.57				
Jux 443	8	9	.56				
				Tar 222	7	29	.52
Tar 231	3	38	.47				
Nya 642	5	25	.44				
Nya 633	6	36	.44				
Tar 242	7	27	.41				
				Jux 415	6	5	.40
Tar 235	5	49	.39				
Jux 440	8	14	.36				
Nya 641	8	26	.31				
				Tar 214	4	65	.26
Nya 632	4	9	.22				
				Jux 422	7	16	.19
				Jux 410	6	6	.17
				Nya 614	6	7	.14
				Tar 213	3	39	.08

Mean:	No. of children	Propor- tion	Mean:	No. of children	Propor- tion
Nyansongo	5	.45	Nyansongo	3	.51
Tarong	5	.52	Tarong	4	.41
Juxtlahuaca	5	.62	Juxtlahuaca	4	.36
Pooled sample		.53	Pooled sample		.42

Note: Jux = Juxtlahuaca; Kar = Kariobangi; Kien = Kien-taa; Kis = Kisa; Kok = Kokwet; Ng = Ngeca; Nya = Nyansongo; Tar = Tarong.

a. No score was included for a child if the number of interacts was less than 5.

Appendix E   Total Number of Social Acts of 4- to 5-Year-Old Children of Each Sex to All Social Partners

	New Samples			
	Kien-taa	Kokwet	Kisa-Kariobangi	Ngeca
Girls	338 (18)	414 (43)	581 (39)	853 (58)
Boys	347 (21)	441 (45)	493 (31)	787 (53)

	Six Cultures					
	Taira	Tarong	Khalapur	Juxtlahuaca	Orchard Town	Nyansongo
Girls	99 (35)	423 (32)	87 (16)	123 (23)	243 (27)	130 (24)
Boys	124 (35)	226 (22)	35 (16)	76 (21)	295 (39)	147 (25)

Note: The number of 4- to 5-year-old dyads is given in parentheses after the number of acts.

Appendix F   Proportion of Ten Types of Social Behavior by 6- to 10-Year-Old Children to Same-Sex Peers

Behavior[a]	NYA[b]	JUX	TAR	TAI	KHA	OT
Nurt.						
Girls	20	18	26	5	[8]	10
Boys	11	16	13	8	10	9
Proc. soc.						
Girls	7	6	6	10	[0]	2
Boys	19	5	2	0	6	9
Repr.						
Girls	7	12	3	3	[8]	8
Boys	4	5	3	6	15	12
Dom.						
Girls	0	9	0	11	[25]	18
Boys	4	6	3	21	27	12
Soc.						
Girls	53	44	26	39	[17]	41
Boys	37	32	39	13	6	28
Sk. att.						
Girls	7	0	0	10	[8]	0
Boys	7	7	0	2	4	11
Sk. help						
Girls	0	6	2	5	[0]	7
Boys	0	11	2	6	17	3
Ass. soc.						
Girls	7	0	11	5	[0]	2
Boys	0	13	17	34	2	4
Ass.						
Girls	0	3	1	0	[33]	0
Boys	4	6	2	3	4	2
Misc. agg.						
Girls	0	3	25	11	[0]	13
Boys	15	9	19	6	8	11

Note: Numbers in brackets are based on extremely low frequency.

a. Nurt. = nurturance; Pro. soc. = prosocial dominance; Repr. = reprimands; Dom. = egoistic dominance; Soc. = sociability; Sk. att. = seeks attention; sk. help = seeks help; Ass. soc. = assaults sociably (rough-and-tumble play); Ass. = assaults; Misc. agg. = seeks competition, threatens, warns, insults.

b. NYA = Nyansongo; JUX = Juxtlahuaca; TAR = Tarong; TAI = Taira; KHA = Khalapur; OT = Orchard Town.

Appendix G   Total Number of Social Acts of 6- to 10-Year-Old Children of Each Sex to All Social Partners

| | New Samples | | | | |
	Kien-taa	Kokwet	Kisa	Kariobangi	Ngeca
Girls	333 (17)	705 (74)	370 (30)	185 (22)	1402 (114)
Boys	294 (17)	632 (56)	58 (6)	331 (31)	1141 (84)

| | Six Cultures | | | | | |
	Taira	Tarong	Khalapur	Juxtlahuaca	Orchard Town	Nyansongo
Girls	362 (42)	549 (57)	220 (62)	373 (55)	206 (46)	357 (41)
Boys	348 (45)	614 (59)	176 (58)	399 (64)	203 (37)	362 (43)

Note: The number of 6- to 10-year-old dyads is given in parentheses after the number of acts.

References

Allaman, J. D., C. S. Joyce, and V. C. Crandall. 1972. The antecedents of social desirability response tendencies of children and young adults. *Child Development* 43:1135–1160.

Barker, R. G. 1968. *Ecological Psychology: Concepts and Methods for Studying the Environment of Human Behavior.* Stanford, Calif.: Stanford University Press.

Barry, H., III, M. K. Bacon, and I. L. Child. 1957. A cross-cultural survey of some sex differences in socialization. *Journal of Abnormal and Social Psychology* 55:327–332.

——— 1967. Definitions, ratings and bibliographic sources of child-training practices of 110 cultures. In *Cross-Cultural Approaches,* ed. C. S. Ford. New Haven, Conn.: Human Relations Area Files Press, pp. 293–331.

Barry, H., III, I. L. Child, and M. K. Bacon. 1959. Relations of child training to subsistence economy. *American Anthropologist* 61:51–63.

Barry, H., III, and L. Paxson. 1971. Infancy and early childhood: Cross-cultural codes 2. *Ethnology* 10:466–508.

Baumrind, D. 1971. Current patterns of parental authority. *Developmental Psychology Monographs* 4 (1, part 2).

Baumrind, D., and A. E. Black. 1967. Socialization practices associated with dimensions of competence in preschool boys and girls. *Child Development* 38:291–327.

Bee, H. L., L. F. Van Egeren, A. P. Streissguth, B. A. Nyman, and M. S. Leckie. 1969. Social class differences in maternal teaching strategies and speech patterns. *Developmental Psychology* 1:726–734.

Bell, R. Q., G. M. Weller, and M. F. Waldrop. 1971. Newborn and preschooler: Organization of behavior and relations between periods. *Monographs of the Society of Research in Child Development* 36, Serial no. 142.

Berman, P. W. 1980. Are women more responsive than men to the young? A review of developmental and situational variables. *Psychological Bulletin* 88:668–695.

——— 1986. Young children's responses to babies: Do they foreshadow differences between maternal and paternal styles? In *Origins of Nurturance: Developmental, Biological and Cultural Perspectives on Caregiving,* ed. A. Fogel and G. F. Melson. Hillsdale, N.J.: Lawrence Erlbaum, pp. 25–51.

Berman, P. W., L. C. Monda, and R. P. Myerscough. 1977. Sex differences in young children's responses to an infant; An observation within a day care setting. *Child Development* 48:711–715.

Birns, B. 1976. The emergence and socialization of sex differences in the earliest years. *Merrill-Palmer Quarterly* 22:229–254.

Bloch, J. H. 1976. Issues, problems, and pitfalls in assessing sex differences: A critical review of *The Psychology of Sex Differences*. *Merrill-Palmer Quarterly* 22:283–308.

Bloch, M. N. 1987. The development of sex differences in young children's activities at home: The effect of the social context. *Sex Roles* 16 (5–6):279–301.

——— In press. Young children's play at home and in the community: A cultural ecological framework. In *The Ecological Context of Children's Play*, ed. M. N. Bloch and A. Pellegrini. Norwood, N.J.: Ablex.

Bloch, M. N., and D. J. Walsh. 1985. Young children's activities at home: Age and sex differences in activity, location, and social context. *Children's Environments Quarterly* 2 (2):34–43.

Bolton, C., R. Bolton, L. Gross, A. Koehl, C. Michelson, R. L. Munroe, and R. H. Munroe. 1976. Pastoralism and personality: An Andean replication. *Ethos* 4:463–481.

Bookman, A., and C. Ember. In press. *Luo Child and Family Life*. New Haven, Conn.: Human Relations Area Files.

Bowlby, J. 1969. *Attachment and Loss,* Vol. 1, *Attachment.* New York: Basic Books.

Brazelton, T. B., B. Koslowski, and H. Main. 1974. The origins of reciprocity: The early infant-mother interaction. In *The Effect of the Infant on Its Caregiver*, ed. M. Lewis and L. A. Rosenblum. New York: Wiley-Interscience.

Brazelton, T. B., E. Tronick, L. Adamson, H. Als, and S. Wise. 1975. Early mother-infant reciprocity. In *Parent-Infant Interaction*, ed. M. A. Hofer. Amsterdam: Elsevier.

Bronfenbrenner, U. 1970. *Two Worlds of Childhood: U.S. and U.S.S.R.* New York: Russell Sage Foundation.

Bronson, M. 1971. Social behavior of two-year-olds in two societies: A comparison between samples of U.S. urban and rural Kikuyu children. Manuscript, Harvard Graduate School of Education, Cambridge, Massachusetts.

Brooks-Gunn, J., and W. S. Matthews. 1979. *He and She: How Children Develop Their Sex-Role Identity.* Englewood Cliffs, N.J.: Prentice-Hall.

Burton, R., and J. W. M. Whiting. 1961. The absent father and cross-sex identity. *Merrill-Palmer Quarterly* 7:85–95.

Buss, D. M. 1981. Predicting parent-child interactions from children's activity level. *Developmental Psychology* 17:59–65.

Chodorow, N. 1974. Family structure and feminine personality. In *Woman, Culture and Society*, ed. M. Rosaldo and L. Lamphere. Stanford, Calif.: Stanford University Press.

——— 1978. *The Reproduction of Mothering: Psychoanalysis and the Sociology of Gender.* Berkeley, Calif.: University of California Press.

Clarke-Stewart, K. A. 1973. Interactions between mothers and their young children: Characteristics and consequences. *Monographs of the Society for Research in Child Development* 38 (153).

Cole, M., and S. Scribner. 1974. *Culture and Thought: A Psychological Introduction.* New York: John Wiley.

Cox, H. 1970. Intra-family comparison of loving-rejecting child-rearing practices. *Child Development* 41:437–438.

D'Andrade, R. G. 1966. Sex differences and cultural institutions. In *The Development of Sex Differences,* ed. E. E. Maccoby. Stanford, Calif.: Stanford University Press, pp. 173–204.

Dixon, S., E. Tronick, C. Keefer, and T. B. Brazelton. 1981. Mother-infant interaction among the Gusii of Kenya. In *Culture and Early Interactions,* ed. T. Field et al. Hillsdale, N.J.: Lawrence Erlbaum, pp. 149–168.

Dweck, C. S., and E. L. Leggett. n.d. A theory of personality and motivation. Unpublished paper, University of Illinois, Department of Psychology.

Edwards, C. P. 1975. Societal complexity and moral development: A Kenya study. *Ethos* 3:505—527.

——— 1978. Social experience and moral judgment in Kenyan young adults. *Journal of Genetic Psychology* 133:19–29.

——— 1981. The comparative study of the development of moral judgment and reasoning. In *Handbook of Cross-Cultural Human Development,* ed. R. H. Munroe, R. L. Munroe, and B. B. Whiting. New York: Garland, pp. 501–527.

——— 1982. Moral development in comparative cultural perspectives. In *Cultural Perspectives on Child Development,* ed. D. Wagner and H. W. Stevenson. San Francisco: Freeman, pp. 248–279.

——— 1984. The age group labels and categories of preschool children. *Child Development* 55:440–452.

——— 1985. Rationality, culture, and the construction of "ethical discourse": A comparative perspective. *Ethos* 13:318–339.

——— 1986a. Cross-cultural research on Kohlberg's stages: The basis for consensus. In *Lawrence Kohlberg: Consensus and Controversy,* ed. S. Modgil and C. Modgil. Barcombe Lewes, Sussex, England: Falmer Press, pp. 419–430.

——— 1986b. Another style of competence: The caregiving child. In *The Origins of Nurturance,* ed. A. Fogel and G. Melson. Hillsdale, N.J.: Lawrence Erlbaum, pp. 95–121.

——— 1986c. *Promoting Social and Moral Development in Young Children: Creative Approaches for the Classroom.* New York: Teachers College Press.

——— 1987. Culture and the construction of moral values: A comparative ethnography of moral encounters in two cultural settings. In *The Emergence of Moral Concepts,* ed. J. Kagan and S. Lamb. Chicago: University of Chicago Press.

Edwards, C. P., and M. Lewis. 1979. Young children's concepts of social relations: Social functions and social objects. In *The Child and Its Family,* ed. M. Lewis and L. Rosenblum. New York: Plenum, pp. 245–266.

Edwards, C. P., M. E. Logue, S. Loehr, and S. Roth. 1986. The influence of model infant group care on parent/child interaction at home. *Early Childhood Research Quarterly* 1(4):317–332.

——— 1987. The effects of day care participation on parent/infant interaction at home. *American Journal of Orthopsychiatry* 57(1):116–119.

Edwards, C. P., and B. B. Whiting. 1974. Women and dependency. *Politics and Society* 4:343–355.

——— 1976a. Dependency in dyadic context: New meaning for an old construct. Paper presented at the annual meeting of the Eastern Psychological Association, New York.

——— 1976b. Sibling companions: The interaction of 2- to 3-year-old children with their next older siblings in an East African community. Paper presented at the annual meeting of the American Anthropological Association, Washington, D.C.

——— 1980. Differential socialization of girls and boys in light of cross-cultural research. In *Anthropological Perspectives on Child Development*, ed. C. Super and S. Harkness. San Francisco: Jossey-Bass, pp. 45–58.

Ellis, S., B. Rogoff, and C. C. Cromer. 1981. Age segregation in children's social interactions. *Developmental Psychology* 17(4):399–407.

Ember, C. 1970. Effects of feminine task assignment on the social behavior of boys. Ph.D. diss., Harvard University.

——— 1973. Feminine task assignment and the social behavior of boys. *Ethos* 1:424–439.

——— 1981. A cross-cultural perspective on sex differences. In *Handbook of Cross-Cultural Human Development*, ed. R. R. Munroe, R. L. Munroe, and B. B. Whiting. New York: Garland Press, pp. 531–580.

Erchak, G. M. 1974. The position of women in Kpelle society. *American Anthropologist* 76:344–345.

——— 1975. The nonsocial behavior of young Liberian Kpelle children and its social context. In *Socialization and Communication in Primary Groups*, ed. T. R. Williams. The Hague, Netherlands: Mouton, pp. 27–39.

——— 1976a. The nonsocial behavior of young Kpelle children and the acquisition of sex roles. *Journal of Cross-Cultural Psychology* 7(2):223–234.

——— 1976b. The nonsocial behavior of young Liberian Kpelle children and its social context. In *Socialization and Communication in Primary Groups*, ed. T. R. Williams. The Hague: Mouton.

——— 1977. *Full Respect: Kpelle Children in Adaptation.* New Haven, Conn.: Human Relations Area Files Press.

——— 1979. Socialization and subsistence, symbol, and surgery: Women in a West African society. *Sociologus* 29(1):84–96.

——— 1980. The acquisition of cultural rules by Kpelle children. *Ethos* 8(1):40–48.

——— 1985. The transmission of Kpelle culture: An adaptational model. Paper presented at the annual meeting of the American Anthropological Association, Washington, D.C.

Feldman, S., and S. Nash. 1979. Sex differences in responsiveness to babies among mature adults. *Developmental Psychology* 15:430–436.

Feldman, S. S., Nash, S. C., and Cutrona, C. 1977. The influence of age and sex on responsiveness to babies. *Developmental Psychology* 13:675–676.

Field, T., A. Sostek, P. Vietze, and P. H. Leiderman. 1981. *Culture and Early Interactions*. Hillsdale, N.J.: Lawrence Erlbaum Associates.

Fischer, J. L., and A. Fischer. 1963. *The New Englanders of Orchard Town, U.S.A*. In *Six Cultures: Studies of Child Rearing*, ed. B. B. Whiting. New York: John Wiley. (Reprinted as a separate volume, 1966.)

Fogel, A., G. F. Melson, and J. Mistry. 1986. Conceptualizing the determinants of nurturance; A reassessment of sex differences. In *Origins of Nurturance: Developmental, Biological and Cultural Perspectives on Caregiving*, ed. A. Fogel and G. F. Melson. Hillsdale, N.J.: Lawrence Erlbaum, pp. 53–67.

Frankel, D. G., and D. Roer-Bornstein. 1982. Traditional and modern contributions to changing infant-rearing ideologies of two ethnic communities. *Monographs of the Society for Research in Child Development*, Serial no. 196, no. 4.

Friedl, E. 1975. *Women and Men: An Anthropologist's View*. New York: Holt, Rinehart and Winston.

Gibbs, J. 1965. The Kpelle of Liberia. In *Peoples of Africa*, ed. J. L. Gibbs. New York: Holt, Rinehart and Winston.

Harkness, S. 1975. Child language socialization in a Kipsigis community of Kenya. Ph.D. diss., Harvard University.

——— 1977. Aspects of social environment and first language acquisition in rural Africa. In *Talking to Children: Language Input and Acquisition*, ed. C. Snow and C. Ferguson. Cambridge: Cambridge University Press.

Harkness, S., C. P. Edwards, and C. M. Super. 1981. Social roles and moral reasoning: A case study in a rural African community. *Developmental Psychology* 17:595–603.

Harkness, S., and C. M. Super. 1982. Why African children are so hard to test. In *Cross-Cultural Research at Issue*, ed. L. L. Adler. New York: Academic Press, pp. 145–152.

——— 1983. The cultural construction of child development: A framework for the socialization of affect. *Ethos* 11:221–232.

——— 1985. The cultural context of gender segregation in children's peer groups. *Child Development* 56:219–224.

Hartup, W. W. 1983. Peer relations. In *Handbook of Child Psychology*, Vol. 4, *Socialization, Personality, and Social Development*, ed. P. H. Mussen. New York: John Wiley, pp. 103–196.

Hatfield, J. S., L. R. Ferguson, and R. Alpert. 1967. Mother-child interaction and the socialization process. *Child Development* 38:365–414.

Hetherington, E. M., M. Cox, and R. Cox. 1982. Effects of divorce on parents and children. In *Nontraditional Families: Parenting and Child Development*, ed. M. L. Lamb. Hillsdale, N.J.: Erlbaum, pp. 233–288.

Higgings, E. T., and J. E. Parsons. 1983 Social cognition and the social life of the child: Stages as subcultures. In *Social Cognition and Social Development*, ed. E. T. Higgins, E. N. Ruble, and W. W. Hartup. New York: Cambridge University Press.

Hoffman, L. W. 1974. Effects of maternal employment on the child: A review of the research. *Developmental Psychology* 10:204–228.

——— 1977. Changes in family roles, socialization, and sex differences. *American Psychologist* 32:644–657.

Hoffman, M. L., and H. D. Saltzstein. 1967. Parent discipline and the child's moral development. *Journal of Personality and Social Psychology* 5:45–57.

Hrdy, S. B. 1981. *The Woman That Never Evolved.* Cambridge, Mass.: Harvard University Press.

Jacklin, C. N., and E. E. Maccoby. 1978. Social behavior at thirty-three months in same-sex and mixed-sex dyads. *Child Development* 49:557–569.

Johnson, O. R. 1981. The socioeconomic context of child abuse and neglect in native South America. In *Child Abuse and Neglect: Cross Cultural Perspectives,* ed. J. E. Korbin. Berkeley, Calif.: University of California Press, pp. 56–70.

Kagan, J. 1971. *Change and Continuity in Infancy.* New York: John Wiley.

Katz, M. M., and M. J. Konner. 1981. The role of the father: An anthropological perspective. In *The Role of the Father in Child Development,* 2nd ed., ed. M. E. Lamb. New York: John Wiley, pp. 155–186.

Kendall, M. G., and A. Stuart. 1961. *The Advanced Theory of Statistics,* vol. 2. London: Griffin, pp. 568–578.

Kenyatta, J. 1965. *Facing Mount Kenya: The Tribal Life of the Gikuyu.* New York: Random House.

Koel, A. 1975. Some personality differences between Peruvian and U.S. children. Honors thesis, Pitzer College, Claremont, California.

Kohlberg, L. 1966. A cognitive-developmental analysis of children's sex-role concepts and attitudes. In *The Development of Sex Differences,* ed. E. E. Maccoby. Stanford, Calif.: Stanford University Press, pp. 82–173.

Konner, M. 1982. *The Tangled Web: Biological Constraints on the Human Spirit.* New York: Holt, Rinehart and Winston.

Korbin, J. E. 1981. "Very few cases": Child abuse and neglect in the People's Republic of China. In *Child Abuse and Neglect: Cross Cultural Perspectives,* ed. J. E. Korbin. Berkeley, Calif.: University of California Press, pp. 156–185.

Lamb, M. E. 1978. Influence of the child on marital quality and family interaction during the prenatal, perinatal and infancy periods. In *Child Influences on Marital and Family Interaction: A Life Span Perspective,* ed. R. M. Lerner and G. B. Spanier. New York: Academic Press.

LeVine, R. A. 1973. Patterns of personality in Africa. *Ethos* 1:123–152.

——— 1974. Parental goals: A cross-cultural view. *Teacher's College Record* 76:226–239.

——— 1977. Child rearing as cultural adaptation. In *Culture and Infancy: Variations in the Human Experience,* ed. P. H. Leiderman, S. R. Tulkin, and A. Rosenfeld. New York: Academic Press, pp. 15–27.

——— 1980. A cross-cultural perspective on parenting. In *Parenting in a Multicultural Society,* ed. M. D. Fantini and R. Cardenas. New York: Longman, pp. 17–26.

—— 1983. Fertility and child development: An anthropological approach. In *Child Development and International Development: Research-Policy Interfaces,* ed. D. A. Wagner. San Francisco: Jossey-Bass, pp. 45–56.

LeVine, R. A., and B. B. LeVine. 1963. *Nyansongo: A Gusii Community in Kenya.* In *Six Cultures: Studies of Child Rearing,* ed. B. B. Whiting. New York: John Wiley. (Reprinted as a separate volume, 1966.)

Lewis, M. 1972. State as an infant-environment interaction: An analysis of mother-infant behavior as a function of sex. *Merrill-Palmer Quarterly* 18:95–121.

Lewis, M., and C. Feiring. 1979. The child's social network: Social objects, social functions, and their relationship. In *The Child and Its Family,* ed. M. Lewis and L. A. Rosenblum. New York: Plenum, pp. 9–27.

Longfellow, C., P. Zelkowitz, and E. Saunders. 1982. The quality of mother-child relationships. In *Lives in Stress: Women and Depression,* ed. D. Belle. Beverly Hills, Calif.: Sage Publications, pp. 163–176.

Lorenz, K. Z. 1943. Die angeborenen Formen moeglicher Erfahrung. *Zeitschrift fuer Tierpsychologie 5.*

—— 1971. *Studies in Human and Animal Behavior,* Vol. 2. Cambridge: Harvard University Press.

Lubin, D., and B. B. Whiting. 1977. Learning techniques of persuasion: An analysis of sequences of interaction. Paper presented at the biennial meeting of the Society for Research in Child Development, New Orleans.

Luria, Z. 1979. Psychosocial determinants of gender identity, role, and orientation. In *Human Sexual Behavior: A Comparative and Developmental Perspective,* ed. H. A. Katchadourian. Berkeley, Calif.: University of California Press.

Luria, Z., S. Friedman, and M. Rose. 1987. *Human Sexuality.* New York: John Wiley.

Maccoby, E. E., ed. 1966. *The Development of Sex Differences.* Stanford, Calif.: Stanford University Press.

—— 1980. *Social Development.* New York: Harcourt Brace Jovanovich.

Maccoby, E. E., and C. Jacklin. 1974. *The Psychology of Sex Differences.* Stanford, Calif.: Stanford University Press.

Maccoby, E. E., and J. C. Masters. 1970. Attachment and dependency. In *Carmichael's Manual of Child Psychology,* Vol. 2, ed. P. H. Mussen. New York: John Wiley, pp. 73–157.

MacCormick, C., and M. Strathern, eds. 1980. *Nature, Culture, and Gender.* New York: Cambridge University Press.

Maretzki, T. W., and H. Maretzki. 1963. *Taira: An Okinawan Village.* In *Six Cultures: Studies of Child Rearing,* ed. B. B. Whiting. New York: John Wiley. (Reprinted as a separate volume, 1966.)

Mariuki, G. 1964. *A History of the Kikuyu: 1500–1900.* Oxford: Oxford University Press.

Martini, M., and J. Kirkpatrick. 1981. Early interactions in the Marquesas Islands. In *Culture and Early Interactions,* ed. T. Field, A. M. Sostek, P. Vietze, and P. H. Leiderman. Hillsdale, N.J.: Lawrence Erlbaum, pp. 189–213.

Mead, M. 1935. *Sex and Temperament in Three Primitive Societies.* New York: William Morrow.

——— 1949. *Male and Female.* New York: William Morrow.

Melson, G. F., and A. Y. Fogel. 1982. Young children's interest in unfamiliar infants. *Child Development* 53(3):693–700.

Miller, B. D. 1981. *The Endangered Sex: Neglect of Female Children in Rural North India.* Ithaca, N.Y.: Cornell University Press.

Miller, T. W. 1971. Communicative dimensions of mother-child interaction as they affect the self-esteem of the child. Paper presented at the annual meeting of the American Psychological Association, Washington, D.C.

Minton, C., J. Kagan, and J. A. Levine. 1971. Maternal control and obedience in the two-year-old. *Child Development* 42:1873–1894.

Minturn, L. 1984. Changes in the differential treatment of Rajput girls in Khalapur: 1955–1975. *Medical Anthropology* 8 (2), Spring special issue: Child survival and sex differentials in the treatment of children, ed. L. McKee.

Minturn, L., D. Boyd, and S. Kapoor. 1978. Increased maternal power status: Changes in socialization in a restudy of Rajput mothers of Khalapur, India. *Journal of Cross-Cultural Psychology* 9 (4):483–497.

Minturn, L., and J. T. Hitchcock. 1963. *The Rajputs of Khalapur, India.* In *Six Cultures: Studies of Child Rearing,* ed. B. B. Whiting. New York: John Wiley. (Reprinted as a separate volume, 1966.)

Minturn, L., and W. W. Lambert. 1964. *Mothers of Six Cultures: Antecedents of Child Rearing.* New York: John Wiley.

Morelli, G. A. 1986. Social development of 1, 2, and 3 year old Efe and Lese children within the Ituri Forest of Northeastern Zaire: The relation amongst culture, setting, and development. Ph.D. diss., Department of Psychology, University of Massachusetts, Amherst.

Moss, H. A. 1967. Sex, age and state as determinants of mother-infant interaction. *Merrill-Palmer Quarterly* 13:19–36.

Munroe, R. H., and R. L. Munroe. 1971. Household density and infant care in an East African society. *Journal of Social Psychology* 83:3–13.

——— 1978. Compliance socialization and short-term memory in an East African society. *Journal of Social Psychology* 104:135–136.

——— 1980a. Household structure and socialization practices. *Journal of Social Psychology* 111:293–294.

——— 1980b. Infant experience and childhood affect among the Logoli: A longitudinal study. *Ethos* 8(4):295–315.

——— 1984. Infant experience and childhood cognition: A longitudinal study among the Logoli of Kenya. *Ethos* 12(4):291–306.

Munroe, R. H., R. L. Munroe, and A. Bresler. 1985. Precursors of spatial ability: A longitudinal study among the Logoli of Kenya. *Journal of Social Psychology* 125:23–33.

Munroe, R. H., R. L. Munroe, C. Michelson, A. Koel, R. Bolton, and C. Bolton. 1983. Time allocation in four societies. *Ethnology* 22:355–370.

Munroe, R. H., R. L. Munroe, and H. S. Shimmin. 1984. Children's work in four cultures: Determinants and consequences. *American Anthropologist* 86:369–379.

Munroe, R. H., H. S. Shimmin, and R. L. Munroe. 1984. Gender understanding and sex role preference in four cultures. *Developmental Psychology* 20:673–682.

Munroe, R. L., and R. H. Munroe. 1971. Effect of environmental experience on spatial ability in an East African society. *Journal of Social Psychology* 83:15–22.

Munroe, R. L., R. H. Munroe, and J. W. M. Whiting. 1981. Male sex-role resolutions. In *Handbook of Cross-Cultural Human Development*, ed. R. H. Munroe, R. L. Munroe, and B. B. Whiting. New York: Garland Press, pp. 611–632.

Nerlove, S. B., R. H. Munroe, and R. L. Munroe. 1971. Effect of environmental experience on spatial ability: A replication. *Journal of Social Psychology* 84:3–10.

Nerlove, S. B., J. M. Roberts, R. E. Klein, C. Yarbrough, and J. P. Habicht. 1974. Natural indicators of cognitive development: An observational study of rural Guatemalan children. *Ethos* 2:265–295.

Nerlove, S. B., and A. S. Snipper. 1981. Cognitive consequences of cultural opportunity. In *Handbook of Cross Cultural Human Development*, ed. R. H. Munroe, R. L. Munroe, and B. Whiting. New York: Garland Press, pp. 423–474.

Nie, N. N., C. H. Hull, J. G. Jenkins, K. Steinbrenner, and D. H. Bent. 1975. *Statistical Package for the Social Sciences*, 2nd ed. New York: McGraw-Hill.

Nugent, J. K., B. M. Lester, and T. B. Brazelton, eds. 1987. *The Cultural Context of Infancy*, Vol. 1. Norwood, New Jersey: Ablex.

Nydegger, W. F., and C. Nydegger. 1963. *Tarong: An Ilocos Barrio in the Philippines*. In *Six Cultures: Studies of Child Rearing*, ed. B. B. Whiting. New York: John Wiley. (Reprinted as a separate volume, 1966.)

Nye, F. I., and L. W. Hoffman, eds. 1963. *The Employed Mother in America*. Chicago: Rand McNally.

Okorodudu, C. 1966. Achievement training and achievement motivation among the Kpelle of Nigeria: A study of household structure antecedents. Ph.D. dissertation, Harvard Graduate School of Education, Harvard University.

Omark, D. R., and M. S. Edelman. 1975. Formation of dominance hierarchies in young children. In *Psychological Anthropology*, ed. T. R. Williams. The Hague: Mouton.

Omark, D. R., M. Omark, and M. S. Edelman. 1973. Formation of dominance hierarchies in young children. Paper presented at the International Congress of Anthropological and Ethological Sciences, Chicago.

Omark, D. R., F. F. Strayer, and D. G. Freedman. 1980. *Dominance Relations*. New York: Garland.

Ortner, S. B., and H. Whitehead, eds. 1981. *Sexual Meanings: The Cultural Construction of Gender and Sexuality*. New York: Cambridge University Press.

Parke, R. O., and S. O'Leary. 1976. Father-mother-infant interaction in the newborn period: Some findings, some observations, and some unresolved issues. In *The Developing Individual in a Changing World*, Vol. 2, *Social and Environmental Issues,* ed. K. Riegel and J. Meacham. The Hague: Mouton.

Parke, R. O., S. E. O'Leary, and S. West. 1972. Mother-father-newborn interaction: Effects of maternal medication, labor, and sex of infant. Proceedings of the Eightieth Annual Convention, American Psychological Association.

Pederson, F. A., and R. Q. Bell. 1970. Sex differences in preschool children without histories of complications of pregnancy and delivery. *Developmental Psychology* 3:10–15.

Pederson, F. A., and K. S. Robson. 1969. Father participation in infancy. *American Journal of Orthopsychiatry* 39:466–472.

Pettigrew, J. 1986. Child neglect in rural Punjabi families. In *Parent-Child Interaction in Transition,* ed. G. Kurian. New York: Greenwood Press, pp. 371–393.

Poffenberger, T. 1981. Child rearing and social structure in rural India: Toward a cross-cultural definition of child abuse and neglect. In *Child Abuse and Neglect: Cross-Cultural Perspectives,* ed. J. E. Korbin. Berkeley, Calif.: University of California Press.

Reiter, R., ed. 1975. *Toward an Anthropology of Women.* New York: Monthly Review Press.

Rogoff, B. 1978. Spot observation: An introduction and examination. *The Quarterly Newsletter of the Institute for Comparative Human Development* 2:21–26.

—— 1981a. Adults and peers as agents of socialization: A Highland Guatemala profile. *Ethos* 9(1):18–36.

—— 1981b. The relation of age and sex to experiences during childhood in a highland community. *Anthropology UCLA* 11(1–2):25–41.

Rogoff, B., M. J. Sellers, S. Pirrotta, N. Fox, and S. H. White. 1975. Age of assignment of roles and responsibilities to children: A cross-cultural survey. *Human Development* 18:353–369.

Romney, K., and R. Romney. 1963. *The Mixtecans of Juxtlahuaca, Mexico.* In *Six Cultures: Studies of Child Rearing,* ed. B. B. Whiting. New York: John Wiley. (Reprinted as a separate volume, 1966.)

Rosaldo, M., and L. Lamphere, eds. 1974. *Women, Culture and Society.* Stanford, Calif.: Stanford University Press.

Ross, M., and T. S. Weisner. 1977. The rural-urban migrant network in Kenya: Some general implications. *American Ethnologist* 4(2):359–375.

Sanday, P. 1973. Toward a theory of the status of women. *American Anthropologist* 75:1682–1700.

—— 1974. Female status in the public domain. In *Women, Culture, and Society,* ed. M. Rosaldo and L. Lamphere. Stanford, Calif.: Stanford University Press.

Sears, R. R. 1972. Attachment, dependency, and frustration. In *Attachment and Dependency,* ed. J. L. Gewirtz. Washington, D.C.: Winston and Sons, pp. 1–27.

Sears, R. R., E. E. Maccoby, and H. Levin. 1957. *Patterns of Child Rearing.* Stanford, Calif.: Stanford University Press.

Seligman, M. E. P. 1970. On the generality of the laws of learning. *Psychological Review* 77(5):406–418.

Selman, R. L. 1980. *The Growth of Interpersonal Understanding*. New York: Academic Press.

Serbin, L. A., K. D. O'Leary, R. N. Kent, and I. J. Tonick. 1973. A comparison of teacher response to the preacademic and problem behavior of boys and girls. *Child Development* 44:796–804.

Seymour, S. 1971. Patterns of child rearing in a changing Indian town: Sources and expressions of dependence and independence. Ph.D. diss., Harvard University.

—— 1974. The active dependence of Indian children. Paper presented at the annual meeting of the American Anthropological Association, Mexico City, November 19–24.

—— 1975. Child-rearing in India: A case study in change and modernization. In *Socialization and Communication in Primary Groups*, ed. T. R. Williams. The Hague: Mouton, pp. 41–58.

—— 1976a. Caste/class and child-rearing in a changing Indian town. *American Ethnologist* 3(4):783–796.

—— 1976b. Household size and infant indulgence in an Indian town. Paper presented at the annual meeting of the American Anthropological Association, Washington, D.C.

—— 1980. Patterns of child-rearing in a changing Indian town. In *The Transformation of a Sacred Town: Bhubaneswar, India*, ed. S. Seymour. Boulder, Colo.: Westview Press, pp. 121–154.

—— 1981. Caste/class and children's workloads in an Indian town. Paper presented at the annual meeting of the American Anthropological Association, Los Angeles.

—— 1983. Household structure and status and expressions of affect in India. *Ethos* 11(4):263–277.

—— 1985. Expressions of responsibility among Indian children: Some precursors of adult sex roles. Paper presented at the annual meeting of the American Anthropological Association, Washington, D.C.

Siegelman, M. 1965. Evaluation of Bronfenbrenner's questionnaire for children concerning parental behavior. *Child Development* 36:163–174.

Sieley, S. J. 1975. Environmental influences on the cognitive development of rural children: A study of a Kipsigis community in Western Kenya. Ph.D. diss., Harvard University.

Slaby, R. G., and K. S. Frey. 1975. Development of gender constancy and selective attention to same-sex models. *Child Development* 46:849–856.

Sostek, A. M., P. Vietze, M. Zaslow, L. Kreiss, F. Van der Waals, and D. Rubenstein. 1981. Social context in caregiver-infant interaction: A film study of Fais and the United States. In *Culture and Early Interactions*, ed. T. Fields, A. M. Sostek, P. Vietze, and P. H. Leiderman. Hillsdale, N.J.: Lawrence Erlbaum, pp. 21–37.

Stayton, D. J., R. Hogan, and M. D. Ainsworth. 1971. Infant obedience and maternal behavior: The origins of socialization reconsidered. *Child Development* 42:1057–1069.

Stern, D. N. 1977. *The First Relationship*. Cambridge, Mass.: Harvard University Press.

Super, C. M. 1981. Behavioral development in infancy. In *Handbook of Cross-Cultural Human Development*, ed. R. H. Munroe, R. L. Munroe, and B. B. Whiting. New York: Garland Press, pp. 181–270.

—— 1983. Cultural variation in the meaning and use of children's "intelligence." In *Expiscations in Cross-Cultural Psychology*, ed. J. B. Deregowski, S. Dziurawiec, and R. C. Annis. Lisse, The Netherlands: Swets and Zeitlinger B.V., pp. 199–212.

—— 1984. Sex differences in infant care and vulnerability. *Journal of Medical Anthropology* 8(2):84–90.

Super, C. M., and S. Harkness. 1982. The infant's niche in rural Kenya and metropolitan America. In *Cross-Cultural Research at Issue*, ed. L. L. Adler. New York: Academic Press, pp. 47–55.

—— 1986. The developmental niche: A conceptualization at the interface of child and culture. *International Journal of Behavioral Development* 9:545–569.

Tronick, E. Z., M. Ricks, and J. F. Cohn. 1982. Maternal and infant affective exchange: Patterns of adaptation. In *Emotion and Early Interaction*, ed. T. Field and A. Fogel. Hillsdale, N.J.: Lawrence Erlbaum, pp. 83–100.

Weisner, T. S. 1973a. Studying rural-urban ties: A matched network sample from Kenya. In *Survey Research in Africa: Its Applications and Limits*, ed. W. M. O'Barr, D. H. Spain, and M. A. Tessler. Evanston, Ill.: Northwestern University Press.

—— 1973b. The primary sampling unit: A non-geographically based rural-urban example. *Ethos* 1:546–559.

—— 1976a. Urban-rural differences in African children's performance on cognitive and memory tasks. *Ethos* 4(2):223–250.

—— 1976b. Kariobangi: The case history of a squatter resettlement scheme in Kenya. In *A Century of Change in Eastern Africa*, ed. W. Arens. The Hague: Mouton, pp. 77–99.

—— 1976c. The structure of sociability: Urban migration and urban-rural ties in Kenya. *Urban Anthropology* 5(2):199–223.

—— 1976d. Consequences of rural-urban migration for families and children in Kenya: Some results and suggested research orientations. *Kenya Education Review* 3:108–115.

—— 1979. Urban-rural differences in sociable and disruptive behavior of Kenya children. *Ethnology* 18(2):153–172.

Weisner, T. S., and S. Abbott. 1977. Women, modernity and stress: Three contrasting contexts for change in East Africa. *Journal of Anthropological Research* 33:421–451.

Weisner, T. S., M. Bausano, and M. Kornfein. 1983. Putting family ideals into practice: Pronaturalism in conventional and nonconventional California families. *Ethos* 11(4):278–304.

Weisner, T. S., and R. Gallimore. 1977. My brother's keeper: Child and sibling caretaking. *Current Anthropology* 18:169–190.

Weisner, T. S., R. Gallimore, and R. G. Tharp. 1982. Concordance between ethnographer and folk perspectives: Observed performance and self-ascription of sibling caretaking roles. *Human Organization* 41(3):237–244.

Weisner, T. S., and J. C. Martin. 1979. Learning environments for infants: Communes and conventionally married families in California. *Alternative Lifestyles* 2:201–242.

Wenger, M. 1975. Child-toddler interaction in an East African community. Unpublished qualifying paper, Harvard Graduate School of Education.

―― 1983. Gender role socialization in an East African community: Social interaction between 2- to 3-year-olds and older children in social ecological perspective. Ph.D. diss., Harvard Graduate School of Education.

Wenger, M., and B. B. Whiting. 1980. Studying the context of children's socialization: Sibling caretakers in a rural community in Kenya. Paper presented at the Second Congress of the Instituto de Psiquiatria y Medicina Psicosomatica, University of Guadalajara, Mexico.

White, D. R., M. L. Burton, and L. A. Brudner. 1977. Entailment theory and method: A cross-cultural analysis of the sexual division of labor. *Behavior Science Research* 12(1):1–24.

White, D. R., and M. M. Dow. 1981. Sexual division of labor in African agriculture: A network autocorrelation analysis. *American Anthropologist* 83(4):824–849.

White, R. W. 1959. Motivation reconsidered: The concept of competence. *Psychological Review* 66:297–333.

White, S. H. 1965. Evidence for a hierarchical arrangement of learning processes. In *Advances in Child Development and Behavior*, Vol. 2, ed. L. P. Lipsitt and C. C. Spiker. New York: Academic Press.

―― 1970. Some general outlines of the matrix of developmental changes between 5 and 7 years. *Bulletin of the Orton Society* 20:41–57.

Whiting, B. B., ed. 1963. *Six Cultures: Studies of Child Rearing.* New York: Wiley.

Whiting, B. B. 1965. Sex identity conflict and personal violence: A comparative study. *American Anthropologist* 67:123–140.

―― 1968. Transcultural code for social interaction. Unpublished manuscript, Harvard Graduate School of Education, Harvard University.

―― 1973. The Kenyan career woman: Traditional and modern. *Annals of the New York Academy of Sciences* 208:71–75.

―― 1974. Folk wisdom and child rearing. *Merrill-Palmer Quarterly of Behavior and Development* 20:9–19.

―― 1977. Changing life styles in Kenya. *Daedalus* 106(2):211–225.

―― 1980. Culture and social behavior: A model for the development of social behavior. *Ethos* 8(2):95–116.

―― 1983. The genesis of prosocial behavior. In *The Nature of Prosocial Development: Interdisciplinary Theories and Strategies*, ed. D. Bridgeman. New York: Academic Press, pp. 221–242.

Whiting, B. B., and C. P. Edwards. 1973. A cross-cultural analysis of sex differences in the behavior of children aged 3–11. *Journal of Social Psychology* 91:171–188.

Whiting, B. B., and N. Marshall. n.d. The effect of social change on maternal behavior in a Kikuyu community. Unpublished manuscript, Harvard Graduate School of Education, Harvard University.

Whiting, B. B., and J. W. M. Whiting. 1975. *Children of Six Cultures: A Psycho-Cultural Analysis.* Cambridge, Mass.: Harvard University Press.

Whiting, J. W. M. 1964. Effects of climate on certain cultural practices. In *Explorations in Cultural Anthropology*, ed. W. Goodenough. New York: McGraw-Hill, pp. 511–544.

—— 1971. Causes and consequences of the amount of body contact between mother and infant. Paper presented at the Annual Meeting of the American Anthropological Association, New York.

—— 1981a. Environmental constraints on infant care practices. In *Handbook of Cross-Cultural Human Development*, ed. R. H. Munroe, R. L. Munroe, and B. B. Whiting. New York: Garland, pp. 155–179.

—— 1981b. Aging and becoming an elder: A cross-cultural comparison. In *Aging*, ed. J. G. March. New York: Academic Press.

Whiting, J. W. M., E. H. Chasdi, H. F. Antonovsky, and B. C. Ayres. 1966. The learning of values. In *People of Rimrock: A Study of Values in Five Cultures*, ed. E. Z. Vogt and E. M. Albert. Cambridge, Mass.: Harvard University Press, pp. 83–125.

Whiting, J. W. M., and I. L. Child. 1953. *Child Training and Personality.* New Haven: Yale University Press.

Whiting, J. W. M., I. L. Child, W. W. Lambert, A. M. Fischer, J. L. Fischer, C. Nydegger, W. Nydegger, H. Maretzki, T. Maretzki, L. Minturn, A. K. Romney, and R. Romney. 1966. *Field Guide for a Study of Socialization.* New York: John Wiley.

Whiting, J. W. M., R. Kluckhohn, and A. Anthony. 1958. The function of male initiation ceremonies at puberty. In *Readings in Social Psychology*, ed. E. E. Maccoby, T. M. Newcomb, and E. L. Hartley. New York: Holt, Rinehart and Winston, pp. 359–370.

Whiting, J. W. M., and B. B. Whiting. 1960. Contributions of anthropology to the methods of studying child rearing. In *Handbook of Research Methods in Childhood Development*, ed. P. H. Mussen. New York: John Wiley, pp. 918–944.

—— 1973. Altruistic and egoistic behavior in six cultures. In *Cultural Illness and Health: Essays in Human Adaptation*, ed. L. Nader and T. W. Maretzki. Washington, D.C.: American Anthropological Association, pp. 56–66.

—— 1975. Aloofness and intimacy of husbands and wives. *Ethos.* 3:183–207.

Worthman, C. M., and J. W. M. Whiting. In Press. Social change and adolescent sexual behavior, mate selection, and premarital pregnancy rate in a Kikuyu community. *Ethos.*

Yarrow, L. J., J. L. Rubenstein, and F. A. Pederson. 1975. *Infant and Environment: Early Cognitive and Motivational Development.* New York: John Wiley.

Zeits, C. R., and R. M. Prince. 1982. Child effects on parents. In *Handbook of Developmental Psychology*, ed. B. B. Wolman and G. Stricker. Englewood Cliffs, N.J.: Prentice-Hall.

Index

Activities, directed and undirected, 55, 57, 83, 235

Age differences: in social behavior, 5–6, 11, 13, 17, 35, 58; in setting, 9; in access to community, 53–57; in task assignment, 70–72; in maternal behavior, 117–118; in maternal nurturance, 118, 119; in maternal training, 122–124; in maternal control, 125–126; in maternal sociability, 128–129; in dependency of children, 137–142; in obedience and cooperation of children, 150–152; in nurturance of child nurses, 171–177; in prosocial dominance, 192–197, 275

Age groups of children. See Knee children; Lap children; School children; Yard children

Aggression, 1, 153–155, 158; insults, 14, 153, 158, 163, 242, 276; playful, 147; toward lap children, 162–163, 173, 175–176, 187; mock, 206; toward yard children, 212–213; in school settings, 241, 253–255, 258; assaults, 253, 259–261, 264; miscellaneous, 242–243, 258; interpersonal, 253; sociable, 254, 264; physical violence, 259–261, 265; male, 261; parental fear of, 261–262

Agricultural communities, 19–20, 63–67, 102, 104. See also Task assignment, agricultural; Workload of women, agricultural chores

Animal care. See Task assignment, animal care

Assaulting behavior, 253, 259–261, 264. See also Dominance; Rough-and-tumble play

"At risk" children, 170–171

Attachment behavior, 7, 167, 170, 271–272

Attention-seeking. See Dependency of children, attention-seeking

Autonomy of children, 266; of yard children (distance from home), 47–51, 82, 198–203, 275; of school children, 52–57; gender differences in, 53, 57, 82; and environmental dangers, 199, 201; and settlement patterns, 199, 201; and mother's workloads, 199, 201; and preschools, 199, 201; and parental beliefs about the nature of children, 199–201; struggle for, 237

Avoidance of females by male children, 235–236

Behavior. See Maternal behavior profiles; Social interaction of children

Bhubaneswar, India, 13, 15; described, 21, 184, 292–293; household structure, 27, 40, 44, 107; sleeping arrangements, 43, 63n; peer interaction, 49; child care assignments, 75; autonomy of children, 83; training of children, 91; maternal